Women on the Run

Gender, Media, and Political Campaigns in a Polarized Era

Claims of bias against female candidates abound in American politics. And although these purported obstacles don't doom women to electoral failure, they raise a formidable series of barriers that complicate women's path to elective office. Or so the conventional wisdom goes. *Women on the Run* challenges that prevailing view and argues that the declining novelty of women in politics, coupled with the polarization of the Republican and Democratic parties, has left little space for the sex of a candidate to influence modern campaigns. The book's in-depth analyses of the 2010 and 2014 congressional elections reveal that male and female House candidates communicate similar messages on the campaign trail, receive similar coverage in the local press, and garner similar evaluations from voters in their districts. When they run for office, male and female candidates don't just perform equally well on Election Day – they also face a very similar electoral landscape.

DANNY HAYES is Associate Professor of Political Science at George Washington University. A former journalist, his research focuses on how information from the media and other political actors influences citizens' attitudes during public policy debates and election campaigns. He is the co-author of *Influence from Abroad: Foreign Voices, the Media, and U.S. Public Opinion* (Cambridge University Press, 2013).

JENNIFER L. LAWLESS is Professor of Government at American University, where she is also the Director of the Women & Politics Institute. She is the author of *Becoming a Candidate: Political Ambition and the Decision to Run for Office* (Cambridge University Press, 2012), and the co-author of *Running from Office: Why Young Americans Are Turned Off to Politics* (Oxford University Press, 2015) and *It Still Takes a Candidate: Why Women Don't Run for Office* (Cambridge University Press, 2010).

Women on the Run

Gender, Media, and Political Campaigns in a Polarized Era

DANNY HAYES
George Washington University

JENNIFER L. LAWLESS
American University

CAMBRIDGE
UNIVERSITY PRESS

CAMBRIDGE
UNIVERSITY PRESS

32 Avenue of the Americas, New York NY 10013

Cambridge University Press is part of the University of Cambridge.

It furthers the University's mission by disseminating knowledge in the pursuit of education, learning, and research at the highest international levels of excellence.

www.cambridge.org
Information on this title: www.cambridge.org/9781107535862

© Danny Hayes and Jennifer L. Lawless 2016

First published 2016

Printed in the United States of America by Sheridan Books, Inc.

A catalogue record for this publication is available from the British Library.

ISBN 978-1-107-11558-3 Hardback
ISBN 978-1-107-53586-2 Paperback

Contents

Figures

Tables

Acknowledgments

So Much Shouting, So Much Laughter is the name of an Ani DiFranco album that came out in 2002. That could also be the title of this book, based on our experience writing it. What began as a series of shouted conversations between our across-the-hallway offices at American University eventually turned into a collaboration that involved almost as much laughing as it did writing. We could never have known that analyzing congressional campaigns with an eye for gender differences – and how those differences might account for women's under-representation – would be so much fun. Most of the time, we even enjoyed engaging the often-skeptical reactions to our findings from politicians, practitioners, and political scientists, exchanges that undoubtedly improved and sharpened our argument, analysis, and presentation.

Of course, as with any book, there were times when it felt like we would never finish. But we were fortunate to receive the generous support and assistance of numerous people who helped us refine our ideas, carry out the research, and turn a mountain of data into a readable (fingers crossed!) book. We should start with Richard Fox, who dutifully – and with only a modest amount of grumbling – read the entire manuscript. He pushed us to provide more evidence for our claims, more context for our conclusions, and more care when challenging others' arguments. He also did it on a moment's notice and when – and he'd be the first to say it – he'd rather be doing anything else.

We also received helpful feedback from others, many of whom read and commented on conference papers and drafts of journal article submissions. We thank Brandon Bartels, Deborah Brooks, Ryan Claassen, Matt Cleary, Pam Conover, Kathy Dolan, Stephanie Ewert, Erica Franklin Fowler, Shana Gadarian, Leonie Huddy, Seth Jolly, Nathan Kalmoe, Jeff Isaac, Eric Lawrence, Cherie Maestas, Tali Mendelberg, Spencer Piston, Markus Prior, John Sides, Sean Theriault, Nick Winter, Chris Wlezien, and Antoine Yoshinaka. We are also grateful to the anonymous reviewers at Cambridge University Press, whose feedback helped improve the final product.

In addition, we benefited from comments we received after presenting components of the project at various professional meetings and research seminars since 2011. We thank participants at the National Capital Area Political Science Association's American Politics Workshop, the roundtable on gender stereotyping at the 2014 meeting of the Midwest Political Science Association, various APSA, MPSA, SPSA, and WPSA panels, and seminars at American University, George Washington University's School of Media and Public Affairs, the University of Maryland, the University of Minnesota, the University of Texas–Austin, the University of Virginia, Syracuse University, Princeton University, the University of California–Berkeley, and the University of North Carolina.

Beyond academic audiences, we are grateful to have had the opportunity to present our results to and receive input from political organizations and practitioners who are devoted to leveling the playing field for female candidates and increasing women's representation. Andrea Dew Steele is at the top of that list. Not only did she facilitate a series of presentations for us, but she also introduced us to many of the people doing the work involved in getting women to run for office. Emily's List, Emerge America, and Emerge Kentucky were welcoming and receptive, and helped to ensure that we had a complete understanding of the electoral playing field in recent elections. We are also grateful to staffers at the Democratic National Committee and the National Republican Congressional Committee, who met with us to discuss the 2010 and 2014 elections, and to Anita McBride, who arranged some of these interviews.

We are grateful to the Women & Politics Institute at American University for generous funding, as well as to the Campbell Public Affairs Institute at Syracuse University. We are probably most indebted to Gail Baitinger, without whose tireless research assistance this book would not exist. No matter what we asked of her, Gail did it, usually in about half the time we expected. Describing her efforts as superhuman is probably unfair – we're not sure even Wonder Woman could have done the work that Gail did (although we're fairly confident that Wonder Woman would have eaten fewer peanut M&Ms while doing it). My-Lien Le also deserves the highest level of praise and thanks. Beyond engaging in countless tasks and logistics involved in writing the book, she also constructed the index. Her patience with us was remarkable, especially given the lack of help, direction, and conviction we provided.

We were fortunate to have benefited from the research assistance of Erica Best, Samantha Guthrie, Diane Hsiung, Clinton Jenkins, Pamela Riis, and Jon Weakley. Dan Chudnov and the staff at George Washington University's Scholarly Technology Group were instrumental in helping us carry out the analysis of Twitter messages in Chapter 3. The dozens of journalists and campaign managers that we quote throughout the book generously gave of their time to answer our questions about the role of gender in contemporary elections. Adam Eck turned our cover idea into a great design. Finally, we appreciate the support of Robert Dreesen, our Cambridge editor, who enthusiastically believed in this project from its inception.

Apart from the professional, we are both lucky to have mind-bogglingly supportive families and friends. Danny's parents, Dan and Charlotte Hayes; his sisters, Janie and Cindy Hayes; and his brother-in-law, Jimmy Bisese, have been enthusiastic cheerleaders over the years. Nikki Raspa is a ceaseless source of support and love and advice and laughter and light – basically, everything a guy could hope for. And the newest member of the family, Scout, is always ready with a spirited tail wag. Especially when there are treats.

Jen's parents, Margie and John Lawless, never stop cheerleading (sometimes literally with pompoms); and Debbie (see!?!), Cory, Shaun, Alec, and Annabella have endured, "liked," and "shared" countless conversations, posts, and articles about women, politics, campaigns, and elections. Richard Fox and Sean Theriault are two of the smartest, funniest, most supportive, and blindly loyal friends anyone could ever have. And Viola, a gorgeous genius of a bulldog with a wiggle in her walk, has ensured that the final stages of writing this book involved tons of laughter, snorting, and love.

Gender, myth, and reality on the campaign trail

To be a woman running for office in the United States is to face bias, sexism, and discrimination at seemingly every turn. That, at least, is the impression that anyone paying attention to American politics in recent years would come away with.

In February 2014, then-U.S. Representative Michele Bachmann told an interviewer that many voters "aren't ready" for a female president.[1] Bachmann's comments were at least in part a thinly veiled attempt to undermine Democrat Hillary Clinton's second bid for the White House. But claims of sexism cross party lines. When Nancy Pelosi was asked in 2008 about Clinton's loss to Barack Obama in that year's presidential primaries, the Democratic Speaker of the House replied that it was partly because Clinton is a woman. "Of course there is sexism," Pelosi said. "We all know that, but it's a given."[2] Allyson Schwartz, who lost the 2014 Democratic primary for governor of Pennsylvania, also blamed her defeat on discrimination: "The political pundits, the media, the Harrisburg establishment couldn't believe a woman could serve as governor – couldn't even imagine it."[3]

Schwartz's swipe at the press is a popular move – even by journalists themselves. Following Clinton's 2008 loss, then-*CBS Evening News* anchor Katie Couric told viewers that "one of the lessons of that campaign is the continued and accepted role of sexism in American life, particularly in the

---

[1] Cal Thomas, "Michele Bachmann: Undeterred and Undiminished," *TownHall.com*, February 18, 2014. Accessed at: http://townhall.com/columnists/calthomas/2014/02/18/michele-bachmann-undeterred-and-undiminished-n1796375 (June 10, 2015).

[2] Austin Bogues, "Pelosi: Clinton Did Face Sexism," *New York Times (The Caucus Blog)*, June 24, 2008. Accessed at: http://thecaucus.blogs.nytimes.com/2008/06/24/pelosi-clinton-did-face-sexism (June 10, 2015).

[3] Larry Mendte, "Is Pennsylvania Not Ready for a Female Governor? Or Just Not Ready for Allyson Schwartz?" *Philadelphia Magazine*, May 21, 2014. Accessed at: www.phillymag.com/news/2014/05/21/allyson-schwartz-pennsylvania-female-governor/ (June 10, 2015).

media."[4] Couric saw the tables turned in May 2015 when she asked Carly Fiorina if her uphill battle for the GOP presidential nomination was really just an attempt to grab the vice presidential spot. "Oh, Katie," Fiorina responded, "would you ask a male candidate that question?"[5] (Couric replied that she would, but more on that later.) Meanwhile, activist Jamia Wilson said in April 2015 that "sexist and misogynist coverage of women candidates is still a sad reality in our media culture."[6] The advocacy group "Name It. Change It." noted in a recent report that "Widespread sexism in the media is one of the top problems facing women."[7]

The root of the problem, according to these arguments, is that portrayals and assessments of female politicians are unfair – starkly and systematically different than what men experience. Julia Louis-Dreyfus, who plays one of the country's most recognizable female politicians – *Veep*'s Selina Meyer – said that her HBO character's new hairdo was a case of art imitating life. "I was fascinated by how people are so judgmental about how women look, and male politicians don't get that shit," she told *Entertainment Weekly*. "A change of hairstyle often gets more attention than legislation they're trying to put forth."[8] Clinton, for her part, has said that because female politicians are held to a "totally different" standard than men,[9] women in public life need to "grow a skin as thick as the hide of a rhinoceros."[10]

It's not just politicians, journalists, and celebrities who take this view. Ordinary Americans believe the same thing. In a 2008 Pew Research Center survey, 79 percent of the public said one reason there aren't more women in political office is that voters aren't ready to elect them. Seventy-five percent said that women active in party politics are held back by men, and 71 percent blamed

[4] Katharine Q. Seelye and Julie Bosman, "Media Charged with Sexism in Clinton Coverage," *New York Times*, June 13, 2008. Accessed at: www.nytimes.com/2008/06/13/us/politics/13women.html?pagewanted=print&_r=0 (June 10, 2015).

[5] Tessa Berenson, "Carly Fiorina Calls Foul on Vice President Question," *Time*, May 4, 2015. Accessed at: http://time.com/3845983/carly-fiorina-vice-president/?xid=emailshare (June 10, 2015).

[6] Tom Watson, "Sexism and the Media: As Election Heats Up, Are We Nearer to Tipping Point for Equality?" *Medium.com*, April 28, 2015. Accessed at: https://medium.com/@tomwatson/sexism-and-the-media-as-election-heats-up-are-we-nearer-to-tipping-point-for-equality-a7d94d9a1280) (June 10, 2015).

[7] "About Name It. Change It." Accessed at: www.nameitchangeit.org/pages/about (June 10, 2015).

[8] Nina Terrero, "Julia Louis-Dreyfus Dishes about Her New *Veep* Hairdo," *Entertainment Weekly*, March 27, 2015. Accessed at: www.ew.com/article/2015/03/27/julia-louis-dreyfus-veep-hair (June 10, 2015).

[9] Ruby Cramer, "Hillary Clinton on the Demands of Campaigning: 'It's Not Easy,'" *Buzzfeed*, October 11, 2015. Accessed at: www.buzzfeed.com/rubycramer/hillary-clinton-on-the-demands-of-campaigning-its-not-easy#.ymNODwqz9 (October 17, 2015).

[10] Francesca Trianni, "Hillary Clinton Advises Women to Grow Skin like a Rhinoceros," *Time*, February 15, 2014. Accessed at: http://swampland.time.com/2014/02/15/hillary-clinton-advises-women-to-grow-skin-like-a-rhinoceros/ (June 10, 2015).

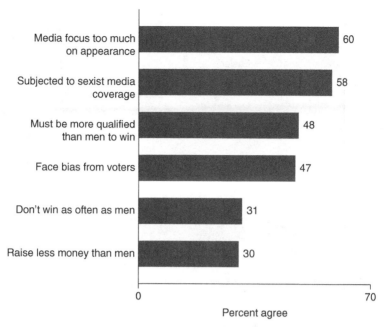

FIGURE 1.1. Public perceptions of female candidates' experiences.
Note: N ranges from 1,973 to 1,982. Bars represent the percentage of respondents who agreed or strongly agreed with each statement. Data come from a module we designed for the 2014 Cooperative Congressional Election Study, a collaborative survey among dozens of academic institutions, conducted by YouGov. Details about the survey design, sampling, and other technical information is available at http://projects.iq.harvard.edu /cces/.

discrimination.[11] By 2014, things hadn't gotten much better. In a national survey conducted just before the midterm elections, six in ten Americans adopted the Louis-Dreyfusian view that the media focus too much on the appearance of female candidates (see Figure 1.1). Nearly the same proportion said that women are subjected to sexist media coverage. Roughly half the country believed that women have to be more qualified than men to win office, and that they face bias from voters. It's no surprise then that nearly one-third said that women who run for office don't win as often as men do, and that they aren't as successful at raising money.

These perceptions don't stem merely from a general view that women in professional life face obstacles that men don't. People view politics as *more* difficult for women than other fields – even industries that have

[11] "Men or Women: Who's the Better Leader? A Paradox in Public Attitudes," Pew Research Center, August 25, 2008. Accessed at: www.pewsocialtrends.org/2008/08/25/men-or-women -whos-the-better-leader/ (June 16, 2015).

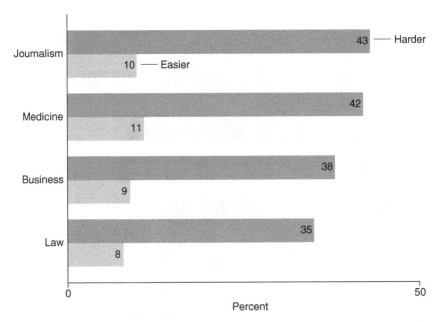

FIGURE I.2. Perceptions of whether politics is harder or easier for women compared to other professions.
Note: N ranges from 1,971 to 1,983. Data come from a module we designed for the 2014 Cooperative Congressional Election Study, a collaborative survey among dozens of academic institutions, conducted by YouGov.

recently been the subject of headline-grabbing allegations of sexism. For instance, just months after Jill Abramson's sudden firing as editor of the *New York Times*, 43 percent of Americans said that women in politics have it harder than women in journalism (see Figure 1.2). Between 35 percent and 42 percent said the same about medicine, business, and law. Just one in ten thought any of these other professions was easier for women than politics.[12] In the public's mind, politics is uniquely inhospitable to women.

The state of women's representation only reinforces these views. After all, the United States is hardly a leader when it comes to the number of women in political office. And it isn't just that all U.S. presidents have been men. As of 2016, women hold only 20 percent of U.S. Senate seats, and just 19 percent of seats in the U.S. House of Representatives (see Figure 1.3). This places the United States ninety-sixth worldwide in the share of women in the national legislature, well behind countries like Rwanda (64 percent), Namibia (41 percent),

---

[12] The remainder said they thought women in politics have it "about the same" as women in the other fields.

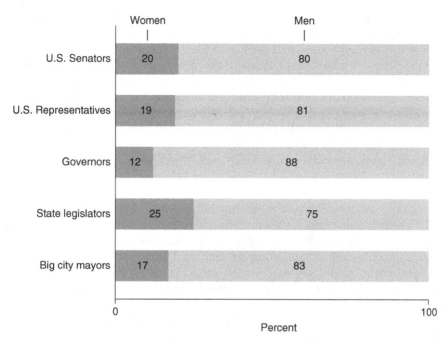

FIGURE 1.3. Women's representation in the United States, 2015.
Source: "Current Numbers," Center for American Women and Politics. Current and historic levels of women's numeric representation are available from the Center for American Women and Politics at Rutgers University. Accessed at: www.cawp.rutgers .edu/current-numbers (October 19, 2015).

Afghanistan (28 percent), and dozens of others.[13] The story is much the same when we go down the ballot to state legislatures, where women occupy one-quarter of the seats. The proportion of female governors and mayors is worse. If you look around, it would seem obvious that women have a tough time getting elected, and that the voters and the media are to blame. But as understandable as that conclusion is, the reality – as we will show throughout this book – is very different.

REVISITING THE CONVENTIONAL WISDOM: WHY FEMALE CANDIDATES DON'T FACE BIAS ON THE CAMPAIGN TRAIL

Women's representation presents a major paradox in American politics. On the one hand, women are numerically under-represented at all levels of elective office. And from election to election, the number of women in office increases

---

[13] "Women in National Parliaments," Inter-Parliamentary Union, September 1, 2015. Accessed at: www.ipu.org/wmn-e/classif.htm (October 27, 2015).

only incrementally. On the other hand, when they do run, female candidates do just as well as men. In federal and state races, they raise just as much money, garner just as many votes, and are just as likely to win (e.g., Cook 1998; Fox 2013; Seltzer, Newman, and Leighton 1997; Smith and Fox 2001). This is true not only in general elections, but also in congressional primaries (Burrell 1992; Lawless and Pearson 2008).[14] The best evidence to resolve this seeming contradiction suggests that women are under-represented in the United States primarily because they are less likely than men to run for political office in the first place, not that they don't win when they do.[15]

But the conventional wisdom – that media coverage and voter attitudes put women at a disadvantage – has proved strikingly sticky. Even if bias and discrimination don't lead to electoral defeat, many political scientists argue that female candidates face a more difficult campaign environment than men do. "There is a growing consensus," Sarah Fulton (2012: 304) writes, "that voters hold preferences for male officeholders and rely on gender stereotypes to infer candidate traits, issue competencies, and ideologies." Because voters expect female candidates to be both feminine and tough, Kelly Dittmar (2015b: 1) concludes that "women confront extra challenges in fulfilling voter expectations about proper feminine behavior at the same time they meet standards for strong election candidates." These challenges are exacerbated by media attention that, for a female candidate, is often "more negative, more focused on her appearance, and more sexist" than the coverage a male candidate receives (Conroy *et al.* 2015: abstract).

We argue in this book that this long-standing conventional wisdom is rooted in an outdated conception of the electoral environment. While female candidates in decades past may have faced stereotypes, skepticism, and bias that impeded their quests for office or presented them with additional challenges, the twenty-first-century political landscape is far more equitable. This is not to suggest that sexism and discrimination are altogether absent from

---

[14] This is not to suggest that election outcomes are as "gender neutral" as commonly described. If the women who run for office are more qualified than the men against whom they compete, then the apparent absence of bias against female candidates might reflect their higher average quality (see Lawless and Fox 2010; Pearson and McGhee 2013). In a similar vein, women may fare as well as men when they run for office because they are more effective legislators. Women in Congress, after all, deliver more federal spending to their districts and sponsor more legislation than their male colleagues (Anzia and Berry 2011). And minority party women in the U.S. House of Representatives are better able than minority party men to keep their sponsored bills alive through later stages of the legislative process (Volden, Wiseman, and Wittmer 2013). What matters for our purposes, though, is that in terms of objective indicators of electoral success – votes and dollars – women and men perform comparably. Further consideration of the influence of candidate quality appears in Chapters 3–5.

[15] In addition to the gender gap in political ambition, other factors, like the incumbency advantage in male-dominated political institutions, as well as women's historical under-representation in the professions that tend to lead to political candidacies, can also slow the ascent of women to high office. For a discussion of the central explanations for women's under-representation, see Lawless (2015).

electoral politics, or that women never face bias on the campaign trail. But our central claim is that two features of contemporary American politics – the declining "novelty" of female politicians and the polarization of the parties – have significantly leveled the electoral playing field. Today, male and female candidates have few reasons to campaign differently, the media have little incentive to cover them differently, and voters have no reason to evaluate them differently. As a result, candidate sex plays a minimal role in the vast majority of U.S. elections.

We develop this argument fully in Chapter 2, but here we can lay out the logic briefly, beginning with the strategies of candidates themselves. In an era in which female politicians have become a common part of American politics, there are few incentives for men and women to conduct substantively different campaigns. All candidates, regardless of sex, want voters to regard them as credible on a wide range of issues and to be perceived as possessing the best personal qualities. These imperatives lead candidates to emphasize the issues and character traits they believe citizens care most about, not themes tailored to their gender. And because the Republican and Democratic parties have staked out divergent positions on most issues, the content of campaigns tends to divide along party, not gender, lines. Only under very unusual circumstances do candidates have a reason to make their sex or the sex of their opponent relevant.

In part because candidates rarely emphasize gender, journalists are unlikely to do so either. News coverage of elections tends to reflect the candidates' messages. And since the issues and traits that male and female candidates talk about in their campaigns don't differ, neither does the resulting media coverage. Moreover, journalistic norms encourage reporters to focus on what is most newsworthy. Partisan conflict between candidates, the horse race, and other features of campaigns are more dramatic and interesting than is the fact that a candidate happens to be a woman. News outlets are also unlikely to portray candidates in plainly gender stereotypical ways, such as focusing on their appearance, because doing so would violate professional norms of balance and fairness. That's why Carly Fiorina was in fact in good company when she got the vice presidency question: Martin O'Malley, Bernie Sanders, and Marco Rubio had all been asked the same thing.[16]

Finally, voters' views of candidates are shaped almost entirely by long-standing party attachments, leaving little room for sex to matter. At a moment in which the divisions between the parties are as large as they

---

[16] Goldie Taylor, "Is Martin O'Malley Running to Be Vice President? *Blue State Review*, April 18, 2015. Accessed at: http://bluenationreview.com/is-martin-omalley-running-to-be-vice-president/ (June 20, 2015); Dylan Stableford, "Bernie Sanders on Hillary Clinton: Would She Be Interested in being my Vice President?" *Yahoo! Politics*, June 1, 2015. Accessed at: www.yahoo.com/politics/bernie-sanders-talks-to-katie-couric-bernie-120458581061.html (June 20, 2015); "Is Rubio Really Running for Vice President?" *The Last Word with Lawrence O'Donnell*, April 13, 2015. Accessed at: www.msnbc.com/the-last-word/watch/is-rubio-really-running-for-vice-president-427567683514 (June 20, 2015).

have been since Reconstruction, partisanship and ideology dominate the way the public evaluates candidates. Combined with the fact that female candidates today only rarely present themselves to voters "as women," candidate sex has little opportunity to shape citizens' assessments.

We test our argument in Chapters 3 through 5 with an in-depth study of hundreds of U.S. House races from the 2010 and 2014 midterm elections. Combined, these contests involve more than 1,500 candidates, nearly 300 of them women. Drawing on an analysis of more than 400,000 campaign ads and 50,000 social media messages, we show that men and women run virtually identical campaigns – from the issues they talk about, to the language they use, to the personal traits they tell voters they possess. The similarities of these campaigns are reflected in the media coverage that candidates receive. Our comprehensive analysis of more than 10,000 local newspaper articles reveals that not only do male and female candidates get the same amount of coverage, but also that the substance of that coverage is similar. Stories about female candidates are no more likely to focus on their appearance, on "feminine" traits, or on "women's" issues than are articles about men. And our analysis of surveys of 3,000 citizens across the country reveals that candidate sex plays virtually no role in shaping the way that voters evaluate candidates' issue competencies or personal traits, nor does it affect who they support on Election Day. These assessments and decisions arise, instead, primarily from partisanship.

The evidence strongly supports our contention that female candidates do not face bias, but we want to be clear about what we are not arguing. We are not suggesting that the entire electoral process is "gender neutral." Structural and institutional conditions make it more difficult for women to enter politics in the first place, as do gender inequities in patterns of candidate recruitment. Nor are we contending that sexism in politics is a thing of days gone by. Women undoubtedly encounter sexism on the campaign trail – whether in the form of a voter yelling "Iron my shirt" at a 2008 Clinton campaign rally or Republican Joni Ernst having to endure comments about being "as good looking as Taylor Swift" during her 2014 U.S. Senate race in Iowa.[17] We probably don't even need to mention Donald Trump's presence in the 2016 Republican presidential race.[18] There is a distinction, however, between examples of sexist behavior and systematic gender bias in campaigns. Structural forces in the contemporary environment – especially party polarization and journalists' adherence to

[17] Sarah Wheaton, "Iron my Shirt," *New York Times*, January 7, 2008. Accessed at: http://thecaucus .blogs.nytimes.com/2008/01/07/iron-my-shirt/?_r=0 (June 19, 2015); and Nia-Malika Henderson, "Tom Harkin Compares Joni Ernst to Taylor Swift, because Sexism. Then He Apologizes," *Washington Post*, November 3, 2014. Accessed at: www.washingtonpost.com/blogs/the-fix/wp/ 2014/11/03/tom-harkin-compares-joni-ernst-to-taylor-swift-because-sexism (June 19, 2015).
[18] Paul Solotaroff, "Trump Seriously: On the Trail with the GOP's Tough Guy," *Rolling Stone*, September 9, 2015. Accessed at: www.rollingstone.com/politics/news/trump-seriously -20150909?page=13 (September 27, 2015).

professional norms – serve to limit gender bias when it comes to media coverage and voters' attitudes. Thus, these two facts of modern political life – sexism sometimes happens *and* women do not face a systematically biased campaign environment – can coexist.

We also do not claim to explain the dynamics of every political campaign for every level of office. We focus on U.S. House races because they are far more similar to the vast majority of American elections than presidential or statewide contests. This makes our results significantly more generalizable to the elections where most women (and men) run than the campaigns that scholars and commentators often emphasize. We are clear, however, that under particular circumstances gender can work its way into a campaign. Our interviews with more than seventy campaign professionals and political reporters, which we detail throughout the book, show that when charges of sexism arise or when campaigns are explicitly gendered, candidate sex can play a more influential role. This occasionally happens when candidates or the press emphasize issues like access to contraception or pay equity, or when electing a woman in a district would break a glass ceiling. In those cases, gender is novel, interesting, strategically relevant, and newsworthy – and thus likely to become part of a campaign storyline. The reality, however, is that in an era in which female candidates are not unusual and polarization has made partisanship the dominant consideration for voters, few contemporary contests reflect the kind of gender dynamics that the conventional wisdom implies.

Our findings, then, pose a puzzle: If female candidates don't routinely experience discrimination, sexism, or unique obstacles on the campaign trail, where do the widespread perceptions of gender bias come from? In the final part of the book (Chapter 6), we rely on original survey data to demonstrate that people's views about women's electoral experiences and fortunes do not arise from the campaigns they observe in their own districts. Instead, their views about gender bias in elections stem from a variety of factors – social identity, national media portrayals of sexism in politics, and exposure to gender bias in the workplace and society. Despite our evidence that bias on the campaign trail is rare indeed, few Americans see it that way. We conclude the book by considering the implications of these perceptions for the prospects of increasing women's representation.

WHY THIS BOOK MATTERS

Debunking the myths about what happens to most female candidates on the campaign trail is critical for women's representation. In the most immediate sense, demonstrating that women do not regularly face electoral bias may help lower a lingering barrier that has been shown to discourage them from running for office. Studies of potential candidates – people who have the professional backgrounds and credentials common among actual candidates – reveal that women are less likely than men to consider themselves qualified to run (see

Lawless and Fox 2012; 2010). These self-doubts are driven in part by the belief that the political arena is rife with sexism and discrimination. Accordingly, many women think that they need, as the saying goes, to be twice as good to get half as far as men. To the extent that this book can begin to undermine the belief that voters and the media are holding women back, it can help close the gender gap in political ambition. Perhaps just as importantly, these findings can educate the party leaders, donors, and activists who play a key role in recruiting candidates. Female candidates will face no more difficulties on the campaign trail than will the men these political networks have traditionally encouraged . to run.

Our findings augur favorably for the likely success of current and future generations of female candidates, and this has substantive and symbolic consequences. Electing more women, for example, is one way to ensure that politicians address a diverse array of policy concerns. Women who replace men in the same district are more likely to focus on "women's" issues, such as child care, reproductive rights, pay equity, and poverty (Gerrity, Osborn, and Mendez 2007). Democratic and moderate Republican women in Congress are more likely than men to use their bill sponsorship and co-sponsorship activity to focus on women's issues (Swers 2002; see also Dodson 1998; Paolino 1995). Women's leadership styles can also affect legislative outcomes (e.g., Kathlene 1994; 1995; Tolleson-Rinehart 1991; Volden, Wiseman, and Wittmer 2013; Weikart *et al.* 2007). After all, it was women on both sides of the aisle who received credit for ultimately ending the federal government shutdown in 2013.[19] To be sure, partisanship is a much more powerful force in shaping policy than is whether a legislator is a man or a woman (Frederick 2009; Osborn 2012; Schwindt-Bayer and Corbetta 2004; Swers 2013), but the policymaking process is no doubt affected by gender diversity among officeholders.

Women's presence in politics can also affect citizens' political attitudes and engagement in positive ways. Women who live in districts with female congressional candidates, for instance, have been shown to be more willing to discuss politics (Hansen 1997; see also Burns, Schlozman, and Verba 2001). As the percentage of female legislators increases, so do female citizens' sense that government is responsive (Atkeson and Carrillo 2007; Wittmer 2011; see also Atkeson 2003). Female voters are more likely to be familiar with the records of their senators when they are represented by women (Fridkin and Kenney 2014; Jones 2014). In a cross-national study, the presence of highly visible female politicians correlated with adolescent girls' expectations of political engagement (Campbell and Wolbrecht 2006).[20] And when women

---

[19] Laura Bassett, "Men Got Us into this Shutdown, Women Got Us Out," *Huffington Post*, October 16, 2013. Accessed at: www.huffingtonpost.com/2013/10/16/shutdown-women_n_4110268.html (June 11, 2015).

[20] As is the case with most research, the findings are not entirely uniform. Dolan (2006) and Lawless (2004a) uncover little empirical evidence – based on American National Elections

win office in places where women's representation is low, more female candidates run in subsequent elections (Gilardi 2015).

For substantive and symbolic reasons, then, women in politics bring to the government a greater sense of political legitimacy (Mansbridge 1999; Phillips 1995; Pitkin 1967). If women do not run for office, at least in part because of a widespread belief that the campaign environment would be biased against them, then that threatens the legitimacy of both public policy and the larger democratic process. This book is an attempt to demonstrate that the key to increasing women's representation lies not in snuffing out sexism in the media or bias on the part of voters. By no means do we think this behavior should be tolerated, and when it happens it must be denounced. But the reality is that media and voter bias are rarely present or consequential in most elections. As a general rule, they do little to keep women out of office. The key to increasing women's representation, therefore, lies in making sure that potential candidates, journalists, political elites, and the public know that when women do run for office, they won't face a unique set of additional barriers.

Studies data – to support the claim that the presence of female candidates translates into any systematic change in women's political attitudes or behaviors. Women represented by women tend to offer more positive evaluations of their members of Congress, but this difference does not consistently translate into political interest, trust, efficacy, or participation (see also Reingold and Harrell 2010).

2

Rethinking and reassessing gender differences on the campaign trail

In the fall of 2010, Connecticut's 4th and California's 47th congressional districts appeared to have little in common. Separated by nearly 3,000 miles, the Connecticut 4th was nestled next to the Long Island Sound, whereas the California 47th was landlocked in Orange County. Demographically, the Connecticut 4th was nearly 80 percent white; California's 47th was majority Latino. And the average high temperature on Election Day in the districts' biggest cities? A crisp 53 degrees in Bridgeport, but a balmy 72 in Santa Ana.

For all of the districts' obvious differences, the midterm campaigns for the U.S. House seat in each turned out to be strikingly similar. Both Democratic incumbents – Jim Himes in Connecticut and Loretta Sanchez in California – faced serious challenges from Republican state legislators. Himes found himself in the crosshairs of State Senator Dan Debicella, and Sanchez was locked in a battle with Assemblyman Van Tran. Although Barack Obama won each district with about 60 percent of the 2008 presidential vote, neither House race was a Democratic slam dunk.

Himes and Sanchez sought to protect their seats in part by outraising their Republican opponents, both by about two to one. This fundraising advantage allowed them to run a stream of ads touting what they characterized as an improving national economy that had been pulled back from the brink of collapse by the actions of a Democratic president. Himes and Sanchez also highlighted and defended their support of the Affordable Care Act, which had passed the House that spring with exclusively Democratic votes. According to data from the Wesleyan Media Project, about 75 percent of the policy discussions in Himes and Sanchez's ads dealt with the economy or social welfare issues, such as health care.

Debicella and Tran, meanwhile, characterized the previous two years as an economic and fiscal disaster owing to the failures of the Democratic Party. They repeatedly told voters to send a more independent voice to Congress. "If you agree that Washington is getting it right, then vote for Jim Himes," Debicella said in an October 24 debate. "He's voted over 94 percent of the time with [Speaker of the House] Nancy Pelosi."[1] Tran, in announcing his bid for Sanchez's seat, told a crowd that "The district needs a real representative and not a rubber stamp for Nancy Pelosi."[2]

During the last month of the campaign, both races also enjoyed frequent and substantive local news coverage. The *Connecticut Post* published thirty-seven stories about the Himes–Debicella race, an average of slightly more than one each day. In those articles, about 40 percent of the issue-related coverage of both candidates focused on the economy, and about one-third on social welfare issues. Things were much the same in the *Orange County Register*, which ran twenty-eight stories about the Sanchez–Tran race. Thirty-six percent of coverage devoted to Sanchez's issue positions focused on the economy, as did about 35 percent of Tran's. While a comparatively small amount of newspaper coverage referred to the candidates' personalities, the most common trait-related mentions in both races were attacks on Himes and Sanchez's competence and leadership, criticisms typically offered by their opponents. Both Debicella and Tran had to contend with questions about their ability to get things done. Virtually none of the coverage in either race referred to the candidates' appearance, spouses, or children.

The parallels between these two races didn't stop at the substance of the campaigns or the media coverage the candidates received. When the votes were finally counted, Himes and Sanchez each managed to win 53 percent, surviving Republican challenges on a night when many of their fellow Democratic House members became former colleagues. In defeat, Debicella and Tran both looked on the bright side. "The Republicans are again in control of the House of Representatives," Debicella reminded supporters gathered at the Norwalk Inn. "We can finally say that sweet phrase, 'House Minority Leader Nancy Pelosi.'"[3] Tran took solace in believing that the new Republican majority in Congress would be the district's "best option to climb out of this recession."[4]

According to the conventional wisdom, the similarities between these two campaigns – one that featured a female candidate and one that did not – would be unexpected. A common portrayal of what happens when women run for office anticipates that Sanchez would have campaigned differently than Himes,

---

[1] Paul Schott, "Debicella, Himes Ratchet up Rhetoric in Latest Debate," *Fairfield Citizen*, October 24, 2010. Accessed at: www.fairfieldcitizenonline.com/news/article/Debicella-Himes-ratchet-up-rhetoric-in-latest-721632.php (October 19, 2015).

[2] Martin Wisckol, "Van Tran Launches Campaign against Representative Loretta Sanchez," *Orange County Register*, May 6, 2009. Accessed at: www.ocregister.com/articles/sanchez-193181-tran-vietnamese.html (October 19, 2015).

[3] Genevieve Reilly and Martin B. Cassidy, "Himes Holds Off Debicella Challenge," *Stamford Advocate*, November 3, 2010. Accessed at: www.stamfordadvocate.com/local/article/Himes-holds-off-Debicella-challenge-791516.php (July 8, 2015).

[4] Chris Prevatt, "Breaking: Van Tran Concedes to Loretta Sanchez," *liberaloc.com*, November 8, 2010. Accessed at: www.theliberaloc.com/2010/11/08/breaking-van-tran-concedes-to-loretta-sanchez/ (July 8, 2015).

would have received more news coverage that focused on "women's" issues, "feminine" traits, her looks or family, and would have had to overcome gender stereotyping by voters. But in this chapter, we argue that the similarities between these campaigns are far from unusual. Building on the existing literature, we suggest that while candidate sex at one time may have significantly influenced campaign strategy, media coverage, and voters' attitudes, the political landscape has changed. In an era when women are no longer electoral novelties, and at a time when polarization has made partisanship the most salient aspect of American elections, campaigns will rarely differ for male and female candidates. In describing the comprehensive data we use to test this argument, we explain why studying U.S. House elections allows us both to expand the empirical scope of the existing work and draw conclusions that can inform our understanding of gender's role in a wide variety of contemporary campaigns.

THE TRADITIONAL CHALLENGES AND TRAVAILS FOR FEMALE CANDIDATES IN AMERICAN POLITICS

The earliest political science research about women's experiences when they run for public office, now some forty years old, uncovered a political arena rife with discrimination (Githens and Prestage 1977; Kirkpatrick 1974). Electoral gatekeepers all but prohibited women from running in the 1970s (Rule 1981; Welch 1978). And those women who did emerge as candidates often faced a hostile environment. "Almost a masochistic experience" is how U.S. Senator Barbara Boxer famously described her first foray into elective office, a 1972 campaign for the Board of Supervisors in Marin County, California.[5] When Patricia Schroeder ran for the U.S. House of Representatives that same year, the National Women's Political Caucus – an organization she helped found, and one whose mission is to elect women – did not endorse her. They said they'd support her candidacy for a lower office, but that "it was too early for a woman to run for Congress."[6] Schroeder's opponent, meanwhile, referred to her as "Little Patsy," despite Schroeder having several inches on him. Two years later, the state of Maryland didn't know what to make of Barbara Mikulski's decision to seek a U.S. Senate seat: "They said no woman could win statewide, they said it just isn't done."[7] It would take little effort to assemble an even longer list of blatantly sexist experiences women faced on the campaign trail in those early days (see Witt, Paget, and Matthews 1994). Not surprisingly, the number of

---

[5] Barbara Boxer, *Politics and the New Revolution of Women in America* (Washington, DC: National Press Books, 1994), p. 73.

[6] Patricia Schroeder, *Twenty-Four Years of Housework ... and the Place Is Still a Mess* (Kansas City: Andrews McMeel, 1998), pp. 14–15.

[7] "Mikulski Remarks on Women in Leadership with Emily's List," May 12, 2011. Accessed at: www.mikulski.senate.gov/newsroom/speeches/mikulski-remarks-on-women-in-leadership-with -emilys-list (June 24, 2015).

female candidates was so scant that systematic data collection and analysis of their experiences was limited.[8]

Throughout the course of the last few decades, though, overt gender bias has become less prevalent. Even as early as 1982, New Jersey Democrat Frank Lautenberg concluded that he was trailing Millicent Fenwick in the polls during his U.S. Senate race because female candidates have an advantage. "Even if we were equivalent candidates," he told a reporter, "she'd have a real leg up on me because she's a woman."[9] Although Lautenberg's assessment might have been a strategic exaggeration, men and women have performed equally well at the ballot box since the 1980s. Female incumbents are reelected at comparable rates to male incumbents. The same is true of challengers. And women seeking open seats have just as good a shot at winning as do the men against whom they compete.[10] Political scientists have gone so far as to conclude that "winning elections has nothing to do with the sex of the candidate" (Seltzer, Newman, and Leighton 1997: 79; see also Burrell 2014; Darcy, Welch, and Clark 1994; Dolan 2004).[11]

Electoral success, however, does not mean that women and men face the same experiences when they run for office. Quite the contrary: the bulk of political science research from the 1990s and 2000s suggests that gender parity on Election Day occurs in spite of gender disparity on the campaign trail. Bias in the electoral process may be less pronounced than it once was, but gender differences in how candidates communicate, the media coverage they receive, and voters' impressions of them remain.[12] The gist of the argument is

---

[8] For a list of female congressional candidates dating back to the 1974 election cycle, see "Women Candidates for Congress, 1974–2014." Center for American Women and Politics. Accessed at: www.cawp.rutgers.edu/fast_facts/elections/documents/canwincong_histsum.pdf (June 23, 2015).

[9] Margot Hornblower, "The 1982 Elections: Women in Politics," *New York Times*, October 22, 1982. Accessed at: www.washingtonpost.com/archive/politics/1982/10/22/the-1982-elections-women-in-politics/703069eb-4103-4a68-a8f0-ee52ec5fb791/ (June 24, 2015).

[10] For a review of the literature about women's electoral fortunes over time, see Lawless and Fox (2010); Palmer and Simon (2008).

[11] These conclusions are based almost exclusively on congressional, statewide, and state legislative candidates. The extent to which they apply to presidential politics is unclear – something we address later in this chapter.

[12] These are not the only ways that gender is relevant in the electoral arena. Women in Congress, for example, still refer to the male culture of the House of Representatives and the Senate. See, for example, Kirsten Gillibrand, *Off the Sidelines: Speak Up, Be Fearless, and Change Your World* (New York: Ballantine Books, 2015); and Marjorie Margolies Mezvinsky, *A Woman's Place: The Freshman Women Who Changed the Face of Congress* (New York: Crown Publishers, 1994). Moreover, female congressional candidates face more primary competition than men do (Lawless and Pearson 2008), and they tend to raise more money to perform as well as men at the polls (Fiber and Fox 2005). In addition, geographical differences facilitate women's election in some congressional districts, but lessen their chances of success in others (Palmer and Simon 2008). Here, we focus on differences in candidate communication, media coverage, and voters' evaluations because they are thought to pose the largest threats to female candidates' success.

that compared to male candidates, female candidates are treated differently – and often worse – in the press and by the public. These patterns raise a formidable series of obstacles that complicate women's path to elective office (see Dolan 2010; Fox 1997; Lawless 2009).

The evidence that scholars have amassed for this argument over the years is substantial. Turning first to the media, many studies find not only that women receive less, and less prominent, campaign coverage than men, but also that several gender differences emerge in the content of the news attention they do get (Conroy *et al.* 2015; Dunaway *et al.* 2013; Heldman, Carroll, and Olson 2005; Kahn 1992, 1994a; Kahn and Goldenberg 1991). First, the news tends to emphasize women's appearance, personality, and family roles, but focuses on men's professional backgrounds, credentials, and office-holding experience. This "hair, husband, and hemline problem," in the words of Georgia Duerst-Lahti (2006: 37), can then undermine female candidates' qualifications (see also Miller and Peake 2013). Second, women are often associated with "feminine" traits – such as compassion and honesty – and advocacy for "women's" issues. Men, on the other hand, are more likely to be described with "masculine" attributes – such as leadership and competence – and strength in the areas of foreign policy, defense, and the economy (Braden 1996; Bystrom *et al.* 2004; Carroll and Schreiber 1997; Kahn 1996; Norris 1997a, 1997b; Weir 1996). Finally, some evidence suggests that news coverage more accurately reflects male candidates' campaign messages than it does women's. "When covering male candidates, reporters emphasize the same personality traits and the same policy areas as the candidates," Kim Fridkin Kahn (1993: 498) writes. "News coverage of female candidates is much less responsive."

These unequal portrayals in the media are consistent with – and are assumed to reinforce – voters' perceptions of politicians. Empirical analyses reveal that women and men in politics are perceived by citizens differently in terms of their ideologies, traits, and policy expertise. Female candidates and officeholders, for example, are generally viewed as more liberal than male candidates of the same party (Alexander and Andersen 1993; King and Matland 2003; Koch 2000). They are also seen as more compassionate and empathetic, but as weaker leaders and less competent than their male opponents (Banwart 2010; Burrell 1994; Huddy and Terkildsen 1993; Lawless 2004b; Leeper 1991; Rosenwasser and Dean 1989). And women are perceived as best suited to deal with gender equity, health care, and other social welfare issues, but less capable than men of handling military crises, crime, and the economy (Alexander and Anderson 1993; Banwart 2010; Burrell 1994; Huddy and Capelos 2002; Huddy and Terkildsen 1993; Lawless 2004b; Sanbonmatsu and Dolan 2009). This can be problematic if the traits and issue expertise accorded to male politicians are viewed as particularly important for politics, which has often been the case (Falk and Kenski 2006; Fox and Oxley 2003; Kahn 1996; Kittilson and Fridkin 2008; Lawless 2004b; Mo 2015).

As a result, women running for office have to be more strategic in portraying themselves to the media and the voters. In some cases, female candidates perceive an advantage when they run "as women," emphasizing gender stereotypic issue competencies on the campaign trail and in their campaign advertising (Bystrom *et al.* 2004; Dabelko and Herrnson 1997; Dittmar 2015a; Herrnson, Lay, and Stokes 2003; Larson 2001; Windett 2014). Female candidates for the U.S. Senate, for instance, are more likely than men to pursue a "gender congruent" trait and issue strategy (Schneider 2014), highlighting the attributes and policy areas on which they have been seen as stereotypically strong. The strategic imperatives can cut the other way as well, with some work suggesting that female candidates may place heavy emphasis on the "masculine" aspects of their platforms, personalities, and backgrounds to overcome gender stereotypes that could work to their disadvantage (Hitchon, Chang, and Harris 1997; Stalsburg and Kleinberg 2015; Wadsworth *et al.* 1987).

In recent years, however, a smattering of research has come to suggest that gender disparities on the campaign trail are now more muted. These studies uncover few gender differences in the content of candidates' campaign communications (Banwart and Winfrey 2013; Dolan 2014; Evans, Cordova, and Sipole 2014; Sapiro *et al.* 2011) and diminished gender disparities in media coverage (Atkeson and Krebs 2008; Hayes 2011; Jalalzai 2006; Smith 1997). Recent observational and experimental studies also suggest that gender stereotypes among voters have declined, and that even when they do surface, they rarely harm female candidates (Brooks 2013; Dolan 2014; Fridkin and Kenney 2009; Hayes 2011; Hayes, Lawless, and Baitinger 2014; Kahn 1994b).

As suggestive as this new body of literature is, it faces significant limitations. Because most studies typically examine the behavior of candidates, the media, or voters (or perhaps two of the three), there has been little effort to develop a unified account of the role that gender plays in the entirety of the electoral process. It has been a full two decades since a large-scale study of gender in elections sought to draw together all three of a campaign's key actors (Fox 1997; Kahn 1996). At the same time, the empirical foundation of much of this newer work is fairly narrow. Many of the findings, for example, are based on just one election cycle or a subset of campaigns. Most draw their conclusions from a very small number of female candidates. Several rely on experimental designs that don't fully capture the conditions of a real election, including the growing influence of partisanship. All of this limits the extent to which this research generalizes to the kind of campaigns where most women actually run for office. Ultimately, though, this new body of work offers an excellent point of departure, and suggests that the prevailing understanding of the campaign environment women navigate in twenty-first-century American politics is outdated and due for a new, comprehensive assessment.

A UNIFIED FRAMEWORK FOR UNDERSTANDING GENDER
ON THE CAMPAIGN TRAIL

This book is an effort to provide that new assessment. We begin with our argument for why the sex of a candidate should exert little influence in most contemporary elections. Put simply, the declining novelty of women in politics, coupled with the growing polarization of the political parties, has reduced the salience of candidate sex and minimized gender differences on the campaign trail. This one broad argument applies to how candidates communicate, how reporters cover them, and how voters evaluate them. We draw from political science research on candidate strategy, journalistic norms, and voter information-processing to explain our logic and elaborate on our expectations.

Candidates

Political scientists often argue that female candidates may have an incentive to campaign differently than men for at least two reasons related to gender stereotypes. First, "feminine" stereotypes could lead voters to believe women are less capable leaders than men, especially when it comes to handling issues like crime or national security. This could force women to campaign heavily on "masculine" traits and issue expertise to prove their credibility. Alternatively, female candidates may have an opportunity to set themselves apart from male opponents by focusing their campaigns on "women's" issues like contraception, pay equity, or child care. But in an era when female candidates are no longer novel and the way that voters think about politicians rests so heavily on partisanship, there are reasons to suspect that these incentives are minimized.

Women are now a common, expected, and highly visible part of the American political landscape. In the last twenty years alone, they have run as general election candidates for the U.S. House of Representatives in every state except Rhode Island.[13] They have served as governor in twenty-two states.[14] They have represented twenty-four states in the U.S. Senate. And they have obtained leadership positions in Congress and within the major political parties.[15] Likely as a result of this "normalization" of women in politics,

---

[13] "Women General Election Candidates for U.S. Senate and U.S. House," Center for American Women and Politics. Accessed at: www.cawp.rutgers.edu/fast_facts/elections/documents/can cong_histst.pdf (July 3, 2015).

[14] The number of states with female governors increases to twenty-three if we count Nancy Hollister's eleven-day term in Ohio in late 1998 and early 1999. She was elected lieutenant governor, but acted as chief executive of the state after George Voinovich was elected to the U.S. Senate and before his successor, Bob Taft, was sworn in.

[15] Since the mid 1990s, women's presence as candidates and elected officials has been lopsided as far as partisanship is concerned. Roughly 70 percent of female congressional candidates in recent election cycles have been Democrats, 73 percent of female members of the U.S. House and Senate are Democrats, and the overwhelming majority of women in congressional and party leadership positions have hailed from the Democratic Party as well. For more on the intersection of gender

social stereotypes of women may not characterize the way that voters think about female politicians (Schneider and Bos 2014). In the current era, the public may view women who run for office first as politicians, and only second as women.

In this context, there may be fewer reasons for female candidates to focus on "women's" issues and less of a need to overcome ostensible deficits on "masculine" issues or traits. Instead, the imperative for candidates – female and male – is to demonstrate they are capable of handling whatever the salient political issues of the day are (Green and Hobolt 2008). Moreover, they need to convey that they possess the personal attributes (competence, leadership, empathy, integrity, and the like) that voters value (Groseclose 2001; Stokes 1963). The upshot is that the content of campaign communication is unlikely to diverge along gender lines.

The polarization of Republican and Democratic party elites suggests another reason that male and female candidates will run similar campaigns. As the parties have grown farther apart in recent decades, they have also become more internally cohesive, with Republicans becoming more reliably conservative and Democrats becoming more consistently liberal (McCarty, Poole, and Rosenthal 2006). The parties' long-term reputations with the public also shape the issues and traits on which Democratic and Republican candidates are viewed as most credible (Hayes 2005; Petrocik 1996). In such an environment, there are fewer opportunities for other candidate characteristics, such as sex, to shape the positions that candidates take, the issues they talk about, or the way they portray themselves to voters.

Relatedly, party polarization means that congressional campaigns are likely to be "nationalized," with candidates within a party adopting a similar set of talking points (Jacobson 2015). For instance, in 2010, Republicans in districts across the country framed the midterm elections as a referendum on how the Obama Administration handled the economy and health care reform (Jacobson 2010). Democrats sought to draw more attention to the president's popular efforts to draw down troop levels in Iraq and Afghanistan. To be sure, all candidates do not run the same campaigns: local constituents' concerns and the candidates' own records and experience no doubt shape electoral strategies. And from time to time, female candidates might find it advantageous to call attention to their status as women. But in a polarized system, party exerts a stronger influence, leaving fewer opportunities for other factors to shape a campaign's content. As a result, we expect to find significant partisan differences in contemporary campaigns, but limited gender differences.

and party in candidate emergence and political recruitment, see Carroll and Sanbonmatsu (2013) and Lawless and Fox (2010).

The media

The declining novelty of female candidates, combined with the fact that campaigns now so heavily feature partisan conflict and ideological division, also leaves fewer opportunities for gender to work its way into campaign news coverage. This argument rests on the importance of journalistic norms – the professional conventions and routines that shape what reporters cover and how they cover it – as drivers of election news.

One of the most basic functions of the press during an election is to tell voters what candidates say on the campaign trail. Despite an antagonistic relationship with politicians, journalists view it as their responsibility to provide voters with a sense of the candidates' positions, ideas, and priorities (Hayes 2010; Weaver *et al.* 2006). As a result, much news coverage reflects the content of candidates' campaigns. If candidates spar over their differences on health care reform and economic policy, for instance, news coverage will convey that disagreement. This is not to suggest that journalists see their job as slavishly repeating politicians' talking points, but there is often a high degree of correspondence between what candidates emphasize on the stump and what appears in the news (Atkeson and Krebs 2008; Dalton *et al.* 1998; Just *et al.* 1996; though see Vavreck 2009). Given these norms and the current electoral landscape, there are at least three reasons we would expect reporters to cover male and female candidates similarly.

First, if the campaigns that men and women run are not substantially different, then that makes it likely that the news coverage they receive will also be fairly similar. Providing comparable coverage to candidates, regardless of sex, is in keeping with the journalistic norm of objectivity, which dictates efforts to cover politics in a balanced and fair way (Bennett 2011; Cook 2005; Graber and Dunaway 2014). Because women who run for office today are no less competitive or more resource-deprived than men (Burrell 2014), there are few reasons for journalists to treat equally qualified male and female candidates differently.

Second, in an era when the presence of a female candidate is not remarkable, covering women "as women" – rather than just as politicians – has less news value than it once did. Even twenty years ago, the fact that a candidate was a woman may have been unusual and thus newsworthy, making journalists more likely to draw attention to female candidates' gender. That coverage tended to emphasize women's personalities over their platforms, highlight their appearance, and focus disproportionately on "women's" issues or traits (e.g., Dunaway *et al.* 2013; Heldman, Carroll, and Olson 2005). "As women have become more common as political actors," though, "the media has become accustomed to reporting on them," explains Farida Jalalzai (2006: 624). Meanwhile, factors like competitiveness and incumbency are far more likely to draw journalists' attention. Compared to uncompetitive elections, competitive contests have more uncertainty, drama, and campaign-trail developments for reporters to cover (Arnold 2004; Hayes and Lawless 2015a; Kahn and Kenney 1999; Westlye 1991). And incumbents often have more resources, long-standing relationships with journalists, and records that make for easy news content. The relative influence of factors like competitiveness and incumbency makes gendered patterns of coverage in contemporary congressional elections unlikely.[16]

Third, the high level of partisan conflict in the current era may diminish the role that candidate sex plays in shaping election news. Polarization is good for the news business because it encourages candidates to stake out starkly divergent positions (Bruni 2002). When this happens, journalists have an easy time constructing narratives around those disputes, which facilitates the conflict-based storytelling that is essential to conventional political reporting (Jamieson and Waldman 2003; Schudson 1996). This does not prevent journalists from framing a contest as a "battle of the sexes" between a male and female candidate. But given the centrality of partisan conflict to the way the media portray modern politics (Iyengar, Sood, and Lelkes 2012; Levendusky and Malhotra 2015), it is far more likely to anchor political news stories than are gender differences.

Voters

Much as the increasing familiarity of female candidates and the growing influence of partisanship may reduce the relevance of candidate sex in campaign strategy and media coverage, these factors likely also diminish candidate sex as a consideration for voters. At the most basic level, the growing number of female candidates and officeholders has helped alter Americans' attitudes to women in politics. Overwhelming majorities of Americans now say they would be willing to vote for a female presidential candidate if she were nominated by the respondent's political party and qualified for the job;[17] disagree that men are "better suited emotionally" for politics than women;[18] and reject the notion that "women aren't tough enough for politics" or that "women don't make as good leaders as men."[19] These opinions are significantly more favorable toward women in politics than they

---

[16] Criticism of the media's coverage of women – from media critics as well as journalists themselves – may also have reduced the kind of gendered news that was widely reported in the 1980s and 1990s. As Kevin Smith (1997: 71) notes, calls for more equitable coverage "have been increasingly loud among media critics, and professional media journals have periodically engaged in self-examinations of gender bias in the press and urged corrective action."

[17] Justin McCarthy, "In U.S. Socialist Presidential Candidates Least Appealing," Gallup, June 22, 2015. Accessed at: www.gallup.com/poll/183713/socialist-presidential-candidates-least-appealing.aspx (July 9, 2015).

[18] "The Changing Role of Women," Roper Center, April 21, 2014. Accessed at: www.ropercenter .uconn.edu/wp/wp-content/uploads/2014/09/The-Changing-Role-of-Women.pdf (July 9, 2015).

[19] "Obstacles to Female Leadership," Pew Research Center, January 14, 2015. Accessed at: www .pewsocialtrends.org/2015/01/14/chapter-3-obstacles-to-female-leadership/ (July 9, 2015).

were even in the last decades of the twentieth century. For most Americans, female candidates are candidates like any other.

Another, perhaps stronger, reason that candidate sex is unlikely to play a major role in shaping voter attitudes is that it must compete with partisanship, which exerts an outsized influence over citizens' political opinions, evaluations of candidates, and voting behavior (e.g., Bartels 2000, 2002; Cohen 2003; Sides and Vavreck 2013). People often make political judgments based on the considerations that are most easily retrieved, those at the "top of the head" (Taylor and Fiske 1978; Zaller 1992; Zaller and Feldman 1992). And attitudes become more accessible the more frequently they are activated (Fazio, Powell, and Herr 1983; Fazio and Williams 1986). As a result, the more chronically accessible a consideration is, the more likely it is to become the foundation for political judgment (Huckfeldt *et al.* 1999; Huckfeldt *et al.* 2005).

The most chronically accessible consideration for voters in American politics is party identification – to the point that some scholars now treat partisanship as a social identity (Green, Palmquist, and Schickler 2002; Iyengar, Sood, and Lelkes 2012). Thus, citizens tend to see the political world through a partisan lens, a view that is encouraged by campaign discourse and news coverage that focuses intently on differences and conflict between Republicans and Democrats. "Candidates," David King and Richard Matland (2003: 67) write, "are partisan creatures, born of party primaries, vying for jobs in intensely partisan institutions. Even more important, voters see candidates first and foremost as partisans."

Consequently, candidate sex, while obviously apparent to most voters, is not likely to be "primed" (Druckman 2004; Iyengar and Kinder 1987; Jacobs and Shapiro 1994) or encouraged as a criterion for judgment. It behooves candidates, instead, to highlight the D or R in front of their names, not the presence or absence of a Y chromosome in their DNA. In a campaign in which candidate sex plays a prominent role in campaign advertising or news coverage – the kind of campaign that was more common in a previous era – voters might be more likely to think about candidates in terms of gender (e.g., Bauer 2015; Paolino 1995). But in the current landscape of American politics, we expect that to be a rare circumstance.

The scope of our argument

Although our logic can shed considerable light on the gender dynamics of contemporary campaigns, we want to be clear about what it can and cannot explain. Most obviously, our argument about partisan polarization applies only to general elections that pit candidates of opposing parties against each other. Because partisan divisions are irrelevant in most primary contests, that part of our argument does not transfer to the earlier stage of the electoral process. And it is possible that gender could play a stronger role in shaping the campaign dynamics of primaries or non-partisan elections, where voters are unable to rely on partisanship as a decision-making shortcut.

Nonetheless, we focus on general elections for several reasons. Foremost, this is where the existing research – and much popular commentary about bias against women in politics – trains most of its attention. Since we argue that the conventional wisdom needs updating, general elections are the appropriate place for us to concentrate our efforts. Moreover, because voters ultimately select their representatives in general elections, these contests are inherently important. Finally – and this is simply a practical consideration – collecting data on the scale we believe is necessary for a comprehensive analysis, and accounting for the political context in which campaigns occur, is much more feasible in general elections than in the decentralized primary election system. Extensions of our framework could undoubtedly be applied to primary or non-partisan contests.

In addition, our analysis of media attention and the information environment voters navigate focuses on mainstream news coverage and the professional norms that have guided the practice of traditional journalism in the United States for roughly a century. The practices that shape the news in non-traditional, newer forms of media, like partisan cable news outlets or ideologically driven blogs, are different and may not uniformly lead to the patterns of coverage we expect to find in mainstream outlets (e.g., Belt, Just, and Crigler 2012; Bradley and Wicks 2011; Ritchie 2013; Shor *et al.* 2014). But for reasons we elaborate on below, mainstream news is the venue most appropriate for studying gender dynamics in most American political campaigns, including congressional races.

Finally, we do not claim to explain the contours of every single American political campaign. We are not trying to predict, for instance, the role gender will play in a presidential campaign involving the first female major-party nominee. As was the case with Hillary Clinton's first bid for the presidency, her sex has figured in the campaign's strategy and the media coverage she has received in 2016. Indeed, research suggests that during the 2008 Democratic primary, Clinton was treated poorly by the media, the voters, and some political gatekeepers (Carroll 2009; Lawless 2009). Other work chronicles the ways in which references to Clinton's appearance and family background sought to undermine her credibility (Carlin and Winfrey 2009). And in a book-length treatment of the 2008 race, Regina Lawrence and Melody Rose (2009) argue that gender stereotypes, journalistic norms, and Clinton and her competitors shaped – and will continue to affect – female presidential candidates' prospects for the foreseeable future. This work makes clear that presidential campaigns, or very high-profile statewide contests, may provide opportunities for gender biases and stereotyping to play a part that is often missing from other electoral environments.[20]

---

[20] Of course, analyzing Hillary Clinton's campaign and extrapolating from her experiences to those of other women who might run for president is likely an endeavor with limited generalizability. After all, Clinton was not a "typical" female candidate in 2008 or 2016. Not only did she begin the races with levels of name recognition that many candidates never achieve, but she also entered the electoral arena with nearly two decades of public accomplishments and access to

Our argument, however, is that the vast majority of contests are not meaningfully "gendered," and that in those elections candidate sex is likely to play virtually no role in the campaign's content, coverage, or outcome. This is not to say that gender can't matter or that sexism never occurs. It can and does. But in modern American politics, the argument we make suggests that campaigns in which candidate sex plays a prominent role are few and unrepresentative. Of course, like any claim, whether it is to be believed depends on the persuasiveness of the empirical evidence we offer for it.

A NEW EMPIRICAL APPROACH TO STUDYING GENDER DIFFERENCES ON THE CAMPAIGN TRAIL

In order to put our unified framework to the test, we rely on a new empirical approach – one that allows us to test our expectations about how candidate sex shapes (or doesn't shape) the behavior of three central campaign actors: candidates, journalists, and voters. Our method involves systematically analyzing candidate communication, news coverage, and public opinion during two cycles of actual U.S. House elections. This approach allows us to expand the empirical foundation of previous research and cast an unusually wide net over the political terrain where gender differences could emerge.

The benefits of studying House elections

The vast majority of research on gender and elections has focused on presidential, vice presidential, or statewide candidates' campaigns. As a consequence, most inferences about gender dynamics on the campaign trail have been drawn from studies of relatively few female politicians running in the highest-profile elections.[21] While such studies speak to what happens when women run in the most prominent contests, these elections – and the

---

political operatives and donor networks that most presidential candidates – male or female – spend years attempting to cultivate. Clinton also brought with her nearly two decades of well-publicized baggage, much of which emerged once again as fodder for commentary. See Lawless (2009) for a discussion of what we can learn about women and politics from Hillary Clinton's 2008 bid for the White House.

[21] Johanna Dunaway and her colleagues (2013), for example, conducted a content analysis of nearly 10,000 newspaper articles covering thirty Senate and gubernatorial elections in 2006 and 2008. These races, however, included just eight female candidates, only two of whom were Republican. Danny Hayes' (2011) investigation of gender stereotyping in the 2006 U.S. Senate elections is based on the twelve women who ran for Senate that year. Kim Fridkin Kahn's (1996) pioneering work on media coverage of U.S. Senate and gubernatorial campaigns – among the most comprehensive in the field – analyzes just twenty-two female candidates. The challenge of drawing generalizable conclusions is exacerbated in studies of presidential or vice-presidential campaigns, whose subjects are an even smaller and more elite group of women (Aday and Devitt 2001; Conway *et al.* 2015; Heith 2003; Heldman, Carroll, and Olson 2005; Miller and Peake 2013; Miller, Peake, and Boulton 2010).

candidates who compete in them – are hardly representative of the environment faced by the vast majority of female politicians.

Studying U.S. House elections, on the other hand, provides an opportunity to examine gender dynamics in a venue that makes it easier to generalize about what happens when women run for office. One reason is that we are able to examine races involving a large number of female candidates. The 2010 and 2014 general elections saw a combined total of 1,350 male and 297 female candidates. Because of the number of candidates, we can leverage variation in competitiveness, partisanship, incumbency, and other politically relevant factors. In studies with smaller numbers of women running for office, accounting for these potential confounds is often impossible. Yet it is vital if we want to isolate the independent effect of sex.

Beyond overcoming the "small-N problem," a focus on House races allows us to test our argument in a venue where gender dynamics are particularly likely, making for a hard test. House elections tend to be low-information affairs (McDermott 1997; Sanbonmatsu and Dolan 2009), so voters may be more likely to rely on information shortcuts, such as sex, than in elections where they have more substantive knowledge about candidates. The fact that many congressional races are relatively low-profile – they tend not to have the multi-million-dollar advertising budgets or non-stop news coverage typical of many statewide and all presidential campaigns – also makes them more comparable to other electoral contexts. Accordingly, the extent to which we find that the sex of a candidate affects campaign communication, media coverage, or voter evaluations in U.S. House races likely applies to lower-level races that garner even less attention. This gives us confidence when extrapolating from our findings to campaigns for many of the more than 500,000 elective offices in the United States (Lawless 2012). This ability to "generalize downward" is difficult in studies of high-salience statewide contests and national campaigns.

The benefits of casting a wider net

Although most research about gender dynamics in political campaigns does not focus on House races, we are not the first to recognize the benefits of doing so. Our empirical approach, however, goes beyond the relatively small body of existing literature in several ways. Whereas most research relies on one election cycle or a subset of districts (e.g., Dolan 2014; Fox 1997; Gershon 2012), we analyze all House races in multiple elections. In addition, we systematically examine candidate communication, news coverage, and voter attitudes in a single study. Most research – whether it focuses on House races or statewide contests – examines one set of actors. Studies of candidate communication, for example, tend to address strategies that campaigns pursue to mitigate or exploit the gender stereotyping expected to make its way into news coverage and voter evaluations (e.g., Banwart and Winfrey 2013; Dittmar 2015a; Dolan 2005; Fox 1997; Sapiro *et al.* 2011; Schneider 2014; Windett 2014). But with a few exceptions (e.g., Kahn 1993), this research typically stops short of examining how these strategies actually shape journalists' portrayals of the campaign. Similarly, few studies of gender and media coverage assess the way that voters respond to candidates amid the campaign information environment (Devitt 2002; Fowler and Lawless 2009; Gidengil and Everitt 2003; Kahn 1994b; Kahn and Goldenberg 1991; Kittilson and Fridkin 2008; Miller 2001; Smith 1997).

A comprehensive analysis is critical, however, because all three of these campaign elements are linked. Campaign ads, even if their effects are more limited than commentators often suggest, can be crucial for election outcomes (e.g., Brader 2006; Hillygus and Shields 2009; Holbrook 1996; Ridout and Franz 2011; Thurber, Nelson, and Dulio 2001; West 2013). News coverage is a vital source of information for voters in the vast majority of American elections (Druckman 2005; McCombs and Shaw 1972; Weaver 1996). And much of what journalists cover during an election can be traced back to candidates' television advertising, direct mail, and communications strategies (Atkeson and Krebs 2008; Dalton *et al.* 1998; Popkin 1994). Gaining a full understanding of gender's role throughout a campaign, therefore, demands an expansive assessment of the campaign environment – one that examines candidate, journalist, and voter.

Our more holistic approach also allows us to consider the interplay of party and gender cues amid the hurly-burly of real-world elections (see Fridkin and Kenney 2009; Hayes 2011). Because candidates and journalists transmit multiple cues and voters rely on multiple cues during any campaign, we do not expect sex to be a particularly salient one. Many research designs are ill-equipped to test this expectation, though. In some experimental work, a typical approach involves asking respondents to consider the capability of "a Democrat [or Republican] who is a man" or "a Democrat [or Republican] who is a woman" to handle various issues (e.g., Sanbonmatsu and Dolan 2009), or not even mentioning a candidate's party at all (Brooks 2013, 2011). For example, Kira Sanbonmatsu and Kathleen Dolan (2009) find that voters of both parties give an advantage to women when the issue at hand is education, a domain in which women are ostensibly perceived as capable. But because such questions hold party constant, they presumably encourage subjects to base their responses on candidate sex, perhaps inflating its effects (see also Gordon, Shafie, and Crigler 2003). Indeed, when party and sex operate as competing cues in an experimental design, gendered findings are more limited. Leonie Huddy and Theresa Capelos (2002), for example, find that whether a candidate is a man or a woman influences voters' perceptions of how well that candidate would address "women's" issues. On most other issues, however, a candidate's party trumps sex as a predictor of vote choice. This suggests that when gender is not cued, party predominates. If we want to understand whether and how sex matters in contemporary campaigns, then it is critical to examine its effects when many pieces of information about candidates, including both sex and party, are available to voters during real elections.

THE DATA WE USE IN THIS BOOK

We base our analysis on the 2010 and 2014 midterm elections. Focusing on midterms in general offers the most appropriate test of our argument. Without a presidential candidate at the top of the ticket, we can be confident that the results we uncover are not driven by statewide presidential campaigns that have little to do with House race candidates. The 2010 and 2014 cycles, in particular, serve as difficult cases for us. As we will demonstrate, "men's" issues were more prominent than "women's" issues in both years. In addition, the economy, often considered the domain of male candidates, was a top issue in House campaigns in both 2010 and 2014. The overall environment, then, appears to have carried ample opportunities for gender stereotyping and significant potential for women to find themselves at a disadvantage.

Putting our improved empirical approach into practice requires more than identifying election cycles to study. It also demands a wide-ranging set of data – candidate communications, news coverage, and public opinion from these election cycles. We describe here the four original data sources we draw on to paint a comprehensive picture of the landscape in contemporary congressional elections.

Candidate communication

We focus on two types of candidate communication: (1) television advertisements aired during the 2010 U.S. House campaigns and (2) Twitter feeds of U.S. House candidates during the 2014 midterms. As we explain in Chapter 3, these media serve different purposes and are used to reach different audiences, but both hold significant strategic value for campaigns. To the extent that men and women campaign differently, we should be able to detect those patterns in either or both types of communication.

The campaign ad data were collected by the Wesleyan Media Project (WMP), which contracts with a private firm, Kantar Media/CMAG, to gather information on political advertisements run in the United States. A team of coders watches each spot and codes it for a number of attributes, including the issues mentioned and the language the candidate uses. The data from WMP (and its earlier incarnation, the Wisconsin Advertising Project) have become the gold standard for work on election communication in the United States. Unlike many other compilations of campaign ads, the data set provides information not only on all of the ads produced by a campaign, but also on how many times each ad aired. Because some ads run frequently and others only rarely, knowing how often each aired is far more informative than simply knowing that an ad was produced. We focus on advertisements aired during the last month of the election (October 2 – November 2, 2010), the period when campaign activity is most intense and voters are most likely to pay attention.[22] During this period, campaign ads aired in 220 districts, from a total of 367 major-party candidates. Our analysis is based on a total of 478,495 individual spots.

For the 2014 elections, we use Twitter to examine campaign agendas. This allows us to conduct a full assessment of gender differences in campaign communication, comparing not just the traditional advertising strategies of men and women, but also the way they use social media. This is essential at a time when social media has become a standard tool of modern campaigns. Just as with our ad analysis from 2010, we focus on tweets from the last month of the 2014 campaigns (October 4 – November 4, 2014). We scraped each major party candidate's tweets and classified them with the same broad issue categories used in the 2010 campaign ad analysis. We also coded mentions of candidates' traits. Of the 744 candidates with a Twitter handle, 657 tweeted at least once, producing a total of 54,083 individual tweets for us to analyze.[23]

Media coverage

Our examination of campaign news coverage during the 2010 and 2014 midterms focuses on the attention the candidates received in their local newspapers. In an ever-expanding information environment, it might seem surprising, even anachronistic, that we rely on local papers to analyze gender dynamics. Despite the changing media world, though, the vast majority of information available to voters during congressional campaigns comes from local print media (Graber 2010; Vinson 2003). Competing outlets like television stations and national newspapers provide little political reporting on individual congressional campaigns. And according to a 2015 Pew Research Center report, fewer than one in ten media consumers relies on non-traditional outlets for local news.[24] In fact, blog readers constitute just a fraction of the public (Lawrence, Sides, and Farrell 2010), fewer than one in four Americans are on Twitter,[25] and only one out of every 300 outbound clicks from Facebook links to substantive news.[26] Social media sites are growing in importance for

---

[22] See Charles Franklin, "Pres08: Is Anyone Paying Attention? You Bet!" *Pollster*, July 31, 2007. Accessed at: www.pollster.com/blogs/pres08_is_anyone_paying_attent.php?nr=1 (August 5, 2014).

[23] The tweets were collected using the Social Feed Manager application developed by staff at the George Washington University Libraries.

[24] "Local News in a Digital Age." Pew Research Center: Journalism and Media Staff, March 5, 2015. Accessed at: www.journalism.org/2015/03/05/local-news-in-a-digital-age (July 8, 2015).

[25] "Social Networking Fact Sheet." Pew Research Center, Internet, Science, & Tech, September 2014. Accessed at: www.pewinternet.org/fact-sheets/social-networking-fact-sheet/ (July 6, 2015).

[26] Seth R. Flaxman, Sharad Goel, and Justin M. Rao, "Ideological Segregation and the Effects of Social Media on News Consumption," Social Science Research Network, December 4, 2013. Accessed at: http://papers.ssrn.com/sol3/papers.cfm?abstract_id=2363701 (July 7, 2015). See also Drew DeSilver, "Facebook Is a News Source for Many, but Only Incidentally," Pew

both candidates and news consumers, but local newspaper coverage remains the most thorough and influential political news source during House campaigns.

In both 2010 and 2014, we identified in every congressional district the largest circulation local newspaper we could access through one of several electronic databases or the paper's online archives. In each paper, we then identified every news story during the thirty days leading up to the election that mentioned at least one of the two major-party candidates. (Note that the time period maps onto the dates for which we collected campaign ad data in 2010 and Twitter data in 2014.) We collected straight news reports, news analyses, editorials, and op-ed columns. Overall, our data set contains 5,851 news stories involving the 787 major-party candidates in 2010 who received at least some coverage, and 4,524 stories about the 763 candidates who received coverage in 2014.

Coders read the full text of each article and manually recorded a number of pieces of information. First, they coded every reference that would draw a reader's attention to a candidate's sex or gender. References included explicit mentions of a candidate being a man or woman, material that clearly identified a candidate as one gender or another ("mother," "father," etc.), as well as mentions of a candidate's physical appearance. Second, they recorded every explicit reference to a candidate's traits, both positive and negative (e.g., "honest" and "dishonest"). These references could come from candidates themselves, their opponents, or reporters. Overall, they coded mentions of more than 200 individual traits. Finally, they tracked every time an issue was mentioned in association with a candidate, beginning with a list of issues commonly included in previous studies and then recording references to additional issues as they emerged in the coverage (for a total of more than 230 separate issues). This in-depth coding allows us to conduct dozens of comparisons of the way the media cover male and female candidates.

Voter attitudes

To assess voter attitudes toward male and female House candidates, we designed modules as part of the 2010 and 2014 Cooperative Congressional Election Study (CCES), a nationally representative survey conducted by YouGov and in collaboration with dozens of academic institutions. Conducted in two stages – respondents complete one survey in the days leading up to the midterm elections and another shortly after Election Day – the CCES is an excellent source of data about public opinion during congressional elections. All CCES respondents answer basic demographic and political questions, including who they plan to vote for in their House elections. Respondents are then randomly assigned to various modules and complete an

Research Center, February 4, 2014. Accessed at: www.pewresearch.org/fact-tank/2014/02/04/facebook-is-a-news-source-for-many-but-only-incidentally/ (July 6, 2015).

additional set of questions. In our case, we designed modules that could detect evidence of gender stereotyping.

Across the two election cycles, we collected public opinion data about House candidates and their campaigns from 3,000 citizens. In 2010, we asked 1,000 CCES respondents a series of questions to gauge the extent to which they evaluated congressional candidates' traits in ways that reflect traditional gender stereotypes, as well as about their support for the candidates. In 2014, we expanded our module to 2,000 citizens and supplemented the trait questions with a battery that allowed us to examine issue stereotypes. Moreover, we included in the 2014 survey a series of open-ended questions to get at respondents' general impressions of the candidates running in their districts. We also asked about citizens' experiences with sexism and discrimination and their general perceptions of how women are treated in politics. These questions allow us to match respondents' general perceptions of gender bias to the actual electoral environment in their districts.

Interviews with journalists and campaign professionals

These large quantitative data sets are the centerpiece of our analysis. But we also draw on more than seventy in-depth interviews with journalists and campaign professionals involved in the 2010 and 2014 congressional races. These interviews provide a valuable addition to our main empirical approach, allowing us to get "under the hood" of our findings and gain a more complete sense of gender dynamics in contemporary campaigns. We also use the interviews to identify the circumstances under which candidate sex can be salient and the conditions that may facilitate the use of gender stereotyping. Although we have reasons to believe that these instances are rare, the interview evidence adds nuance to our argument and demonstrates when and how gender differences can still emerge in congressional elections.

We compiled the sample of journalists and campaign managers from two types of House races. Competitive races tend to have larger advertising budgets, more media coverage, and bigger staffs, so we included in the sample the forty-six races in 2010 and the seventeen contests in 2014 that the *Cook Political Report* rated as "toss-up" one month before the election.[27] Because we were particularly interested in gaining a firmer handle on when gender can matter in campaigns, we augmented the sixty-three toss-ups with twenty-one non-toss-up races that we defined as "high gender" contests. We classified these races based on our newspaper content analysis. High gender races received at least ten mentions of candidate sex or gender in the combined coverage the two candidates received. These races did not necessarily have to feature a female

---

[27] For the 2010 elections, we relied on the Cook Report's rankings from October 5. The list of the forty-six races is available at: http://cookpolitical.com/archive/chart/house/race-ratings/2010-10-05_10-33-50 (July 6, 2015). For 2014, we used the October 3 rankings, available here: http://cookpolitical.com/house/charts/race-ratings/7889 (July 6, 2015).

candidate, and many did not. In 2010, eleven races met the high gender threshold. In 2014, ten races fell into this category. All told, this method of selection generated eighty-four contests from which to draw a sample of journalists and campaign managers.

In each of those races, we relied on our newspaper coverage data set to identify the reporter who wrote the most stories about the campaign. When two reporters seemed to share responsibility, we included both of them in the sample. This resulted in ninety-one potential reporters to interview. We then located email addresses for each and sent requests asking if we could interview them for a book about congressional elections. Two weeks later, we sent follow-up emails. We heard from forty-one journalists; taking into account undeliverable emails, this represents a 49 percent response rate.[28] From January through May 2015, we conducted semi-structured interviews with thirty-three of them (twenty-six spoke for attribution and seven asked to remain anonymous).[29] The interviews ranged from ten to thirty minutes in length. We also conducted three pilot interviews with journalists who covered a variety of races in New England in 2010 and 2014, giving us a total of thirty-six interviews.

Our approach for interviewing campaign managers was similar. We conducted internet searches to identify the Democratic and Republican candidates' campaign managers in these eighty-four races, and then we searched for current contact information for them. Through exhaustive (and sometimes ridiculous) efforts, we tracked down email addresses for 98 of the 168 individuals who ran the campaigns in which we were interested (forty-six Democrats and fifty-two Republicans). As with the journalists, we sent a letter requesting a phone interview and followed up two weeks later. Forty-one campaign managers responded.[30] We conducted interviews, ranging from ten to forty-five minutes in length, with thirty-one of them in February and March 2015. Seventeen spoke to us on the record, and fourteen requested anonymity.[31] In addition to those, we interviewed four Washington, DC-based campaign operatives involved in multiple congressional races for the

---

[28] After sending the initial email, we received bounce-backs for seven reporters for whom we were unable to locate an alternative email address that didn't also bounce back. From the remaining eighty-four journalists, thirty-seven told us they were willing to be interviewed, and four declined to participate.

[29] Of the thirty-three journalists we interviewed, twenty-three covered races in the 2010 cycle, and ten reported on contests from 2014. This ratio is what we would expect given that there were almost three times as many toss-up races in 2010 as in 2014.

[30] Fifteen emails bounced back. From the remaining eighty-three campaign managers, thirty-seven agreed to an interview and four refused.

[31] Of the thirty-one, twenty-five ran campaigns in 2010 (fourteen managed Democratic candidates and eleven managed Republicans). The remaining six ran campaigns in 2014 (four for Democrats and two for Republicans). The response rate within each group is similar, as our sample included many more 2010 contests than it did 2014 races.

Democratic and Republican parties in 2014. All told, we rely on interviews from thirty-five campaign professionals.

In the chapters that follow, we put these quantitative data sets and interviews to use, scrutinizing a variety of expectations from the existing literature and the conventional wisdom about what happens when women run for office in the United States. In doing so, we test our argument that in an era in which female candidates are not novel and party polarization is the defining feature of politics, the campaigns of men and women – including their campaign messages, media coverage, and assessments by voters – will differ little.

3

That's what she said, and so did he

Carol Shea-Porter hoped she had found an opening. Locked in a tough 2014 reelection battle for her U.S. House seat, the New Hampshire Democrat aired an ad accusing her opponent, Republican Frank Guinta, of setting back decades of progress for women. Against a backdrop of vintage cars, telephone operators, and black-and-white TVs, Shea-Porter told voters that "Back in the fifties, women's rights were restricted. Equal pay? Forget about it." My opponent, she said, "has never once stood up for equal pay … Letting Frank Guinta take us back to the fifties is the wrong direction."[1]

Two states over, central New York Democrat Dan Maffei was reading from the same playbook. His ad featured an eight-year-old boy named Fred, an aspiring entrepreneur in a business suit who operates a lemonade stand where two of his friends just finished a shift. "Great work," Fred tells Jason, handing him $10. "And Sally, since you did the same work, here's $8 for you." Across the street, Maffei turns to the camera and says, "You don't have to be a grown up to know that isn't fair. We've got to make sure that women get equal pay for equal work."[2] Further west, California Democrat Scott Peters ran an ad informing voters that Republican Carl DeMaio pledged to support the agenda of "Tea Party extremists who oppose pay fairness for women."[3]

While Democrats tried to draw voters' attention to issues of pay equity, Republican candidates sounded alarm bells about the consequences of leaving national security in Democratic hands. Amid images of first responders, undocumented workers, and Arabic text, a narrator in U.S. House candidate

---

[1] "Fifties," Carol Shea-Porter for Congress. Accessed at: www.youtube.com/watch?v=tzXZG8PMiWs (April 4, 2015).

[2] "Lemonade Stand," Friends of Dan Maffei. Accessed at: www.youtube.com/watch?v=Ok_tJO2OwWU (July 14, 2015).

[3] "Fair," Scott Peters for Congress. Accessed at: www.youtube.com/watch?v=YisGeUbvQL4 (July 15, 2015).

David Trott's ad warned Michigan voters, "Open borders. Less funding for security . . . It's a dangerous world alright. And if [Democrat] Bobby McKenzie had his way, it would be worse."[4] Florida Republican Steve Southerland juxtaposed his commitment to national security with what he considered his Democratic opponent's dangerously cavalier approach. "The first obligation of government is to keep us safe. But look around: open borders, threats of terrorism, Ebola. Obama has no plan. Pelosi just points fingers," the ad alleged. "Can you trust Obama, Pelosi, and Gwen Graham to protect us?"[5] In Arizona, Martha McSally issued the same indictment against Democratic incumbent Ron Barber. The ad, which included shots of Nancy Pelosi with Barber, stated: "We're losing. No border security . . . Is Congress helping? We can choose different."[6]

While Democrats and Republicans clearly adopted different strategies during the 2014 midterms, there were few gender differences in campaign communication. Regardless of whether candidates were men or women, or whether they faced male or female opponents, co-partisans' issue emphases looked similar. In this chapter, we go beyond these few examples to explore systematically the campaign communication of male and female candidates. Despite the prevailing view that women often have to portray themselves in ways designed to attenuate the damage that gender stereotypes could do to their bids for office, we report little evidence that candidate sex shapes the issues candidates talk about, the words they use in their communications, or the personal traits they emphasize. Female candidates do not campaign in ways that attempt to take advantage of, or inoculate themselves from, gender stereotypes. Nor do male candidates' substantive campaign communications differ when their opponent is a woman. Instead, the main divergence in candidate messages stems from party affiliation, with Republicans and Democrats placing slightly more emphasis on different issues. Gender dynamics are not irrelevant on the campaign trail, however. When men face female candidates, they must take a measured approach to avoid being cast as overly aggressive or engaging in inappropriate attacks. Although not inconsequential, the difference is fairly subtle, playing its strongest role in shaping candidates' interpersonal interactions and tone, not the substantive focus of their campaigns. Taken as a whole, our findings suggest that, in the current era, candidate sex exerts only a minimal influence on the content of campaign communication.

---

[4] "Borders," Trott for Congress. Accessed at: www.youtube.com/watch?v=KkXvzhA568I (July 14, 2015).
[5] "Southerland Campaign Releases New TV Ad: Keep Us Safe," *Capital Soup*, October 27, 2014. Accessed at: http://capitalsoup.com/2014/10/27/southerland-campaign-releases-new-tv-ad-keep-us-safe/ (July 14, 2015).
[6] "Time," McSally for Congress. Accessed at: www.youtube.com/watch?v=hGnFfHjM9wE (July 15, 2015).

WOMEN, MEN, AND TWO MODES OF CAMPAIGN
COMMUNICATION

In an earlier era, women and men might have had an incentive to campaign differently, emphasizing divergent issues, themes, or personal characteristics. But as women have become commonplace in the political arena, there are fewer reasons for candidates to call attention to their (or their opponents') sex, or to campaign in ways that reflect or deflect gender stereotypes. Instead, as we argued in Chapter 2, men and women's campaigns should look very similar. Differences in campaign communication will be driven not by sex, but by party affiliation, the dominant feature of modern campaigns.

In testing our argument, we bring to bear comprehensive data on two types of candidate communications from the last two midterm election cycles: television advertising and social media. While candidates use a variety of methods to communicate, TV spots and Twitter have become indispensable. There is also substantial evidence that these media serve different purposes and are used to reach different audiences, which allows us to cast a wide net in the search for potential gender differences. We begin by providing an overview of the role ads and social media play in contemporary campaigns.

The preeminence of campaign ads

Candidates communicate with voters in myriad ways – from news coverage to direct mail to grassroots engagement – but campaign ads are clearly the most important to congressional campaigns. One piece of evidence is the amount of money campaigns spend on them. The average winning bid for the U.S. House of Representatives now costs roughly $1.6 million,[7] and more than 50 percent of spending by Democratic and Republican candidates alike goes toward paid media.[8] Rare is the successful campaign that doesn't have a well-articulated and well-funded media strategy.

Our interviews with nearly three dozen people who managed House races in 2010 and 2014 shed light on the underlying reasons why campaigns devote such a large portion of their budgets to the airwaves. From the perspective of campaign professionals, ads are essential for achieving legitimacy and communicating with voters. A campaign manager in a 2010 competitive open

---

[7] Paul Steinhauser and Robert Yoon, "Cost to Win Congressional Election Skyrockets," *CNN.com*, July 11, 2013. Accessed at: www.cnn.com/2013/07/11/politics/congress-election-costs/ (March 23, 2015).

[8] In 2013, the Center for Responsive Politics analyzed the $10 billion spent by federal candidates in the 2002 through 2012 election cycles. They broke campaign expenditures into six categories: administrative, campaign expenses, fundraising, media, strategy and research, and wages and salaries. Whereas media consumed more than 50 percent of Democratic and Republican candidates' expenditures, no other category constituted more than 15 percent of the budget. See Andrew Mayersohn, "Campaign Spending Habits: Democrats versus Republicans," *OpenSecrets.org*, October 22, 2013. Accessed at: www.opensecrets.org/news/2013/10/campaign-spending-habits-democrats-v-republicans/ (March 23, 2015).

seat race explained that they "made it a priority to get up on TV early, and to stay up." In terms of getting out a message and building name recognition, he said, "there's nothing as legitimizing as being on TV."

The goal of raising enough money to pay for advertising can define a campaign's strategy from the outset. Consider one example from 2010, when a Republican challenger faced a Democratic incumbent in a Midwestern congressional district. The Republican's campaign manager told us that he knew they would be outraised and that the incumbent would be viewed as invincible. So their strategy was to portray him as vulnerable: "If we could convince the media and the voters that he was, then we could raise more money and have a real campaign." When they caught the incumbent at a health care town hall suggesting that he had little regard for the Constitution, the GOP manager thought, "Jackpot, brother. This will let us get on TV ... That comment let us raise money and attack him on other issues. We seemed like a credible alternative."

TV ads are vital even for candidates who aren't attempting to establish name recognition or legitimacy. West Virginia's 3rd Congressional District, where in 2014 Republican Evan Jenkins defeated long-time Democratic incumbent Nick Rahall, serves as an example. According to Rahall's campaign manager, Samuel Raymond, the entire campaign was about "buffing up paid media." He estimated that 95 percent of their $3 million budget went into campaign ads. MaryAnne Pintar, who managed Scott Peters' 2014 successful reelection bid against Carl DeMaio, agreed. "Campaigns really have two tracks," she explained. "Paid media and earned media. Earned media is important, and it does help define your candidate. It drives what a lot of voters see ... But it's not as effective as what you put in a commercial."

Communicating in the Twitterverse

Whereas TV ads have been central to campaigns for decades, the use of social media is still in its infancy. The extent to which social media – and Twitter in particular – is changing the nature of political campaigns has attracted substantial attention from campaign practitioners and political scientists (e.g., Druckman, Kifer, and Parkman 2014; Graber and Dunaway 2014; Herrnson 2011; LaMarre and Suzuki-Lambrecht 2013; West 2013). On one hand, it is clear that social media use by congressional candidates has become the norm (Gulati and Williams 2013). On the other hand, just 9 percent of Americans report that they use Twitter to access political news and information, which means social media is not the primary way that candidates reach voters.[9]

---

[9] Amy Mitchell, Jeffrey Gottfried, Jocelyn Kiley, and Katerina Eva Matsa, "Social Media, Political News, and Ideology," Pew Research Center for Journalism and Media, October 21, 2014. Accessed at: www.journalism.org/2014/10/21/section-2-social-media-political-news-and-ideology/ (March 23, 2015).

Even if voters tend not to rely heavily on Twitter, it still serves as an important vehicle for candidate communication. Most congressional candidates maintain active Twitter accounts. Ninety-two percent of the 805 major-party general election House candidates in 2014 had a Twitter handle; 82 percent tweeted at least once. Moreover, the content of the tweets they transmit is well integrated into their overall campaign strategy. Our interviews with campaign managers from the 2010 and 2014 cycles revealed three reasons why.

First, Twitter has become a standard way to communicate with the media. "Twitter is aimed at reporters," noted a campaign manager for a Democrat in California. "It was almost like a press release type deal. If there was a day that was dedicated to a particular bill or something that was happening, we would focus on that." Bryan Holladay, who ran Republican Harold Johnson's 2010 winning campaign against Larry Kissell, told us, "We did a lot of Twitter, that's where you communicate with reporters." This is true even in rural, economically disadvantaged districts, where social media will reach hardly any voters. Andy Sere, Evan Jenkins' campaign manager, recognized that in his West Virginia district most voters would never read anything the campaign sent via Twitter. Instead, the Twitter account was "a mechanism to keep reporters engaged." This kind of engagement, incidentally, has the potential to disseminate more than a candidate's message. It can also pay dividends when a campaign would prefer not to go negative. In 2014, for instance, Scott Peters' campaign team uncovered evidence that his opponent had plagiarized a report. Peters' campaign manager explained that the incident "was not something that was in our ads. But we did push it out on Twitter, because we wanted reporters to look at it."

Second, Twitter provides an opportunity for candidates to, in the words of one campaign manager, "hit influencers" – potential donors and activists engaged in elections. "Social media can be helpful for stakeholders," explained a Democratic campaign manager. "If you're doing something and Democracy for America retweets it, that's great. You want your story to stay in front of your donors and the political class. It's not about the voters. You're trying to expand the network for donations, to keep the stakeholders happy." Andy Yates, the campaign manager for North Carolina Republican Ilario Gregory Pantano, also pointed out the distinction between who is reachable on Twitter and who is not: "Twitter was all about fundraising and keeping our supporters engaged. We used social media to recruit volunteers too. It wasn't a way to advertise or reach swing voters."

Finally, Twitter can be used to convey a campaign's energy and momentum. "We did as much as we could with social media," recalled a campaign manager who defeated an incumbent in 2010. "It was good for keeping our supporters and followers informed." Another highlighted the virtues of Twitter as "a tool to show folks that [our candidate] was out and about in

the district ... You want to show that you're engaging with the community."
Beyond signaling enthusiasm, Twitter affords easy opportunities to highlight
a candidate's likeability. "A lot of folks use Twitter to show how hard
a candidate is working and to humanize a candidate. I'm thinking of Claire
McCaskill showing how she got stuck in the elevator," said a campaign
manager from an upstate New York district. "People use Twitter to make
candidates seem like regular people." For Democrat John Yarmuth in 2010,
social media was a way to develop his "cult, hip, cool status. We did this whole
'Keep Louisville Yarmuth' branding, like Keep Austin Weird," explained
a strategist connected to the campaign. "TV ads wouldn't have been able to
incorporate branding like that."

These accounts make clear that both television ads and Twitter hold
significant strategic value for campaigns. As a result, messages in both venues
are carefully developed to highlight a candidate's preferred agenda and reflect
the campaign themes that a candidate believes will give her or him the best
chance to win. Studying both ads and social media allows us to examine
campaign communication when candidates are appealing directly to voters, as
well as when they are targeting the media, activists, and other groups active on
Twitter. To the extent that gender differences emerge in either venue, we should
be able to detect them.

TRACKING ADS AND TWEETS IN U.S. HOUSE ELECTIONS: THE DATA SETS

Our comparison of male and female candidates' campaign communication is
anchored by two data sets: (1) television advertisements aired during the 2010
U.S. House campaigns and (2) Twitter feeds of U.S. House candidates during
the 2014 midterms.

The campaign ad data were collected by the Wesleyan Media Project (WMP),
which gathers information on political advertisements run in the United States.
A team of coders at WMP then watches each spot and codes it for a number of
attributes, including the issues mentioned and the language the candidate uses.
Because the data set includes information on every time an ad aired, rather than
just a list of all of the ads produced by a campaign, it provides a comprehensive
account of a campaign's messages.

This is particularly consequential for capturing the amount of attention
a campaign devotes to various issues, and ultimately for assessing gender
differences in candidates' ads. Imagine a campaign where a candidate produced
two ads, one about unemployment and one about equal pay for women. If we
simply coded the content of those two ads, we would conclude that the candidate's
campaign was equally focused on those two issues. But if the WMP data reveal that
the unemployment ad ran ninety times and the pay equity ad ran only ten times, we
would know that the campaign was far more concerned about unemployment.

This would yield a more accurate picture of the campaign's substantive focus than relying on a list of ads produced.

We focus on advertisements aired during the last month of the election (October 2 – November 2, 2010), the most intense period of campaigning.[10] In analyzing the ads, we train our attention primarily on candidates' issue agendas, because this has been the focus of much previous work. To compare the issue content of male and female candidates' ads, we draw on the coding done by the WMP team. Following previous scholars' coding schemes (Hayes 2010; Hayes and Lawless 2015a; Petrocik 1996), we then collapse the fifty-eight specific issues coded by WMP into eight broad categories: (1) Civil and social order, (2) Defense and security, (3) Social welfare, (4) Taxes and spending, (5) Foreign affairs, (6) Race and social groups, (7) Government functioning, and (8) Economy.[11] This aggregation provides a larger number of observations within each category than if we were to analyze each specific issue separately. The list of issues within each category appears in Appendix 1.

For each candidate, we created an issue profile. To do this, we summed up every issue mention contained in that candidate's ads. This sum accounts for the total number of times each spot aired. We then calculated the share of issue mentions that fell into each of our eight categories. If a candidate's ads mentioned issues a hundred times over the course of a campaign, and twenty-five of those mentions were economic issues, we would know that 25 percent of his attention was devoted to the economy. The issue profile for each candidate facilitates comparisons of "men's" and "women's" issue agendas.

Our analysis for 2014 is similar, but rather than rely on ad data to develop a measure of campaign agendas, we use Twitter, as other scholars have begun to do (e.g., Evans, Ovalle, and Green 2016).[12] Just as with our campaign ad analysis, we focus on the last month of the campaign (October 4 – November 4, 2014). During this period, we scraped each major party candidate's tweets, giving us a comprehensive account of each campaign's Twitter feed. To analyze the tweets' content, we developed dictionaries to capture the attention that candidates devoted to various topics. We compiled a list of more than 200 specific issues and sorted them into the same eight issue categories we used for the 2010 campaign ad analysis (see Appendix 2 for the complete list of issues).[13]

---

[10] The decision to focus on the last month of the campaign is inconsequential for our findings; when we analyze the entire universe of ads, including those aired before October, we draw the same conclusions. Our analysis includes ads sponsored by candidates, political parties, and outside groups because they all contribute to a candidate's public image. When we restrict the analysis to ads sponsored only by candidates themselves, the results are also unchanged.

[11] In addition to the fifty-eight issues we assign to our eight categories, WMP also codes for "local issues" and "other." We don't classify these because their content is ambiguous.

[12] Ideally, we would be able to analyze advertising from 2014 as well. But the WMP 2014 campaign data will not be publicly available until 2018. Any campaign ad data set we would assemble would lack the nuance and scope of the 2010 data set and serve as a poor comparison.

[13] To build a dictionary that could plausibly capture the wide range of issues candidates might discuss in their tweets, we drew on our large-scale content analysis of U.S. House race coverage in

Using the automated text analysis software Lexicoder (Daku, Soroka, and Young 2011; Young and Soroka 2012), we then identified tweets that mentioned any of the issues included in our eight categories. Our calculation of each candidate's issue profile was at that point identical to the measure we used for the ad analysis. We first counted the total number of issue mentions that appeared in a candidate's tweets throughout the thirty-day time period. Then, we calculated the share of those mentions that fell into each of the eight various issue categories. Like the campaign ad issue profiles, these allow for a straightforward comparison of the content contained in male and female candidates' tweets.

HIS AND HER ISSUE PROFILES: VOLUME AND CONTENT
OF CAMPAIGN ADS AND TWEETS

Our argument predicts that candidate sex will play little role in shaping candidate communication. And, put simply, the data bear out our expectations: male and female candidates' campaigns look remarkably similar, in terms of both volume and substance.

Consider first the campaign ads from 2010. In the 220 races involving 367 candidates with television spots, a total of 478,495 ads aired. Democratic

local newspapers from the 2010 and 2014 midterm elections. As we summarized in Chapter 2, and describe in detail in Chapter 4 (see also Hayes and Lawless 2015a, 2015b), we conducted an analysis of campaign news coverage in the largest-circulating newspaper in every House district during the last month of the 2010 and 2014 campaigns. This yielded a total of more than 10,000 individual newspaper articles, which we coded for a variety of attributes, including any policy issue that was mentioned. In all, we identified more than 200 different issues that received coverage. This list of issues, shown in Appendix 2, constituted the starting point for developing the dictionaries that we used to analyze the Twitter data. Using Lexicoder, we then built a dictionary for each of our issue categories based on words and phrases associated with the issues that fell into each category. For instance, candidates referring to unemployment might talk about "unemployment," "jobs," or people being "out of work." Lexicoder then searched the tweets and identified instances in which particular words and phrases were used, allowing us to determine which tweets mentioned which issues. Unemployment mentions, to stick with the example, would of course fall into the economy category.

One potential concern is that our issue list is made up only of those topics that appeared in local news coverage. If a candidate regularly tweeted about an issue that never received coverage in 2010 or 2014, our technique might very well miss it. But two factors suggest this is not a threat to our analysis. First, because our content analysis was so exhaustive, it is very unlikely that any issue a candidate tweeted about did not come up at least once in one of the more than 10,000 news articles from 2010 and 2014. Even if the candidate's own local outlet did not cover the issue, it would appear in our dictionary as long as it appeared in news coverage at least once in any of the articles in our database. Second, we conducted a supplementary analysis using a dictionary built by the Lexicoder developers from the issue list developed by the Policy Agendas Project (see www.policyagendas.org). Because the Policy Agendas Project uses a different, yet similarly comprehensive, issue categorization scheme, this serves as an effective robustness check of our results. When we analyzed our data using this alternative measure, we replicated our basic findings. All of this suggests that our results are not simply a product of our particular measurement approach.

candidates ran an average of 1,402 ads. For Democratic men, that number was 1,444, and for women it was 1,190, a difference that is not statistically significant. On the Republican side, candidates aired an average of 1,167 ads. GOP men aired an average of 1,149 ads, slightly fewer than the 1,306 aired by women. This difference, too, does not reach statistical significance. The volume of advertising by male and female candidates, in other words, was virtually identical.[14]

As with the ads, we find negligible gender differences in the likelihood of candidates using social media. Of the 805 major-party candidates who competed in the 2014 general election, 80 percent were men and 20 percent were women. These ratios were basically mirrored on Twitter. We found Twitter accounts for 744 candidates, of which 79 percent were men and 21 percent were women. And we found that of the 657 candidates who tweeted at least once during the campaign, 78 percent were men, and 22 percent were women. Of those, female candidates tweeted ninety-three times on average, while men tweeted seventy-nine times (this difference is not statistically significant).

The bulk of our analysis focuses on the issue content of advertisements and tweets. We find in general that neither a candidate's sex, nor the sex of a candidate's opponent, has much to do with how much attention any issue received during the campaign. Turning first to TV advertising, Figure 3.1 presents summaries of the issue profiles we constructed for House candidates based on their 2010 ads. The bars represent the average amount of attention candidates devoted to each issue category, broken down by candidate sex.[15] Because Democratic and Republican candidates may focus on different issues (Bergbower, McClurg, and Holbrook 2015; Petrocik 1996), we control for this potential confound by separating the data by party. For both parties, the economy, social welfare, and taxes and spending comprised the lion's share of the issue agendas. Importantly, this was the case for both women (dark bars) and men (light bars). Among Democrats, male and female candidates' overall agendas across our issue categories correlate at 0.99; among Republicans, the correlation is 0.97. In none of the eight issue categories does a statistically significant gender difference emerge.

At the bottom of the figure, we break down the data by candidates' attention to "men's" and "women's" issues.[16] These categories are a subset of, and their components come from, the eight issue areas described above. Men's issues, for instance, include terrorism, which falls within the defense and security category,

[14] The candidates who can afford television advertising tend to be of higher "quality" – that is, they have previous electoral experience – than those who can't. But our results are not driven by a small group of quality female candidates. Among quality candidates, 47 percent of women and 53 percent of men ran TV spots. Among non-quality candidates, 33 percent of women and 39 percent of men produced ads. Neither of these gender differences is statistically significant.

[15] The issue categories are shown in descending order of the overall share of attention they received. For both Democrats and Republicans, less than 1 percent of issue attention was devoted to race and social group issues, which is why bars are absent for that category.

[16] We assigned "women's" and "men's" status only to issues for which the literature has reached a consensus and the classification is intuitive (see Appendix 1).

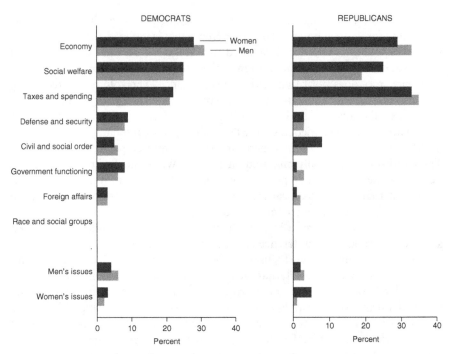

FIGURE 3.1. Issue content in 2010 campaign ads, by candidate sex.
Note: Bars represent the percentage of issue mentions in campaign ads devoted to each category. Democratic women, N = 31; Democratic men, N = 156; Republican women, N = 22; Republican men, N = 158. The difference between men and women is significant (p < 0.05) on "women's" issues for Republicans.

and crime, which is classified as part of civil and social order. Women's issues include abortion (civil and social order) and child care (social welfare). One important finding to emerge from this exercise is that relatively little advertising is devoted to these topics. Most of the issues that candidates talk about in their ads are not unambiguously connected to gender, and even among the handful that are, men and women are, in most cases, equally likely to emphasize them. For Democrats, the proportion of attention men and women devoted to these topics is statistically indistinguishable. Among Republicans, there are no differences on men's issues. Female GOP candidates are statistically more likely than their male counterparts to talk about women's issues (p < 0.05), but the amount of attention given to these topics (5 percent of Republican women's ad content) is very small.

Even if candidate sex doesn't dictate issue emphases, it could be that candidates adopt different strategies when running against women. But for the same reasons we hypothesized that issue agendas would not vary by candidate sex, we also expect that opponent sex will not matter. Indeed, the data displayed in Figure 3.2 show that men running against other men (light bars) included in

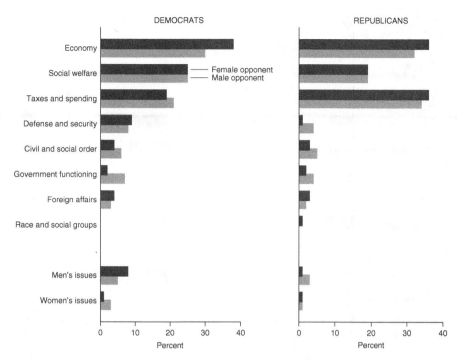

FIGURE 3.2. Issue content in male candidates' 2010 campaign ads, by opponent sex. *Note*: Bars represent the percentage of issue mentions in campaign ads devoted to each category. Democratic men with female opponents, N = 20; Democratic men with male opponents, N = 136; Republican men with female opponents, N = 29; Republican men with male opponents, N = 128. None of the comparisons between men running against women and men running against men is significant at $p < 0.05$.

their ads the same amount of attention to each issue category as did men running against women (dark bars). Across all twenty issue category comparisons – ten each for Republicans and Democrats – there are no significant gender differences, and the correlations between the pairs always exceed 0.90.

We also find no difference when we compare women running against men to women competing with other women (results not shown). Certainly, the number of races featuring two female candidates in which campaign ads were aired is small (just three), but there is nothing to suggest that women or men calibrated their issue agendas based on the sex of their opponent. For instance, if women who were running against men were disproportionately concerned with establishing their credentials on issues traditionally viewed as "masculine," then we should be able to show that those races involved a focus on different issues than when the opponent was a woman. But the data do not indicate such a pattern.

Candidates' Twitter feeds in 2014 tell a similar story. For both Democrats and Republicans, the economy and social welfare – a category

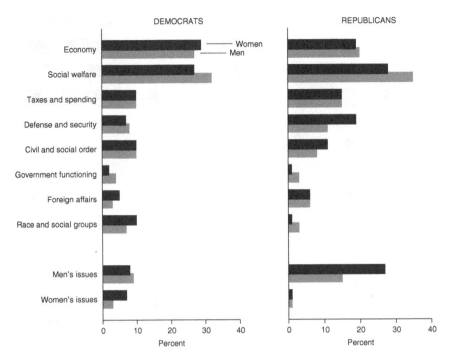

FIGURE 3.3. Issue content in 2014 tweets, by candidate sex.
Note: Bars represent the percentage of issue mentions in tweets devoted to each category. Democratic women, N = 90; Democratic men, N = 202; Republican women, N = 30; Republican men, N = 228. The difference between men and women is significant (p < 0.05) on "women's" issues for Democrats and "men's" issues for Republicans.

that includes health care – represent the most tweeted issues, and women and men's issue profiles are almost entirely indistinguishable from each other (see Figure 3.3).[17] "More Americans say #Obamacare has hurt families than helped," tweeted GOP Congresswoman Diane Black (TN-11) on October 8, linking to a story in *The Hill* newspaper. The next day, Congressman Randy Neugebauer, the Republican who represents Texas' 19th Congressional District, asked his followers to retweet "if you agree #Obamacare will make healthcare worse." Numerous examples just like this emerged every day in the month leading up to the election. Overall, among Republicans, male and female candidates' issue agendas correlate at 0.92. For Democrats, the correlation is 0.97.

When we consider "men's" and "women's" issues, we again find small differences – but ones that are inconsistent with what we found in 2010.[18] Democratic women in 2014 were slightly more likely than men to tweet about

[17] Figures reflect the agendas of the 550 candidates who tweeted about at least one issue.
[18] See Appendix 2 for the list of "women's" and "men's" issues included in the analysis.

"women's" issues (7 percent compared to 3 percent; $p < 0.05$), a pattern we did not see in the ad data. Female Republicans, meanwhile, were more likely than GOP men to discuss "men's" issues (27 percent versus 15 percent; $p < 0.05$). It is not entirely clear, however, what this tells us about the role of candidate sex in systematically structuring campaign communication. After all, it is at odds with the finding from 2010, when Republican women were more focused than male GOP candidates on "women's" issues, not "men's" issues. In one year, Republican women seem to be playing to their "stereotypical" strengths; in another, they are adopting a "counter-stereotypical" strategy.

One possibility, consistent with the conventional wisdom, is that the strategic demands of the campaign trail might vary from year to year. In some cycles, women might gain from emphasizing "women's" issues. In other years, they might benefit from focusing on "men's" issues. It's unclear, however, that such an interpretation is justified. After all, we do not see an analogous pattern among Democrats. Moreover, the overall issue terrain of the 2010 and 2014 campaigns is quite similar. If women were systematically reflecting or deflecting gender stereotypes in their campaign messages, then it is likely that women from both parties – across election cycles – would adopt such behavior. Instead, it seems just as plausible that these patterns are driven by the relatively small number of Republican women and the specific circumstances of a handful of contests. Nonetheless, it is worth noting that the only three gender differences we find emerge on the small subset of issues coded as corresponding most directly to gender stereotypes.

When we turn to the sex of the opponent, we find, as we did with campaign ads in 2010, that it is unrelated to a candidate's issue profile. The left-hand panel of Figure 3.4 presents the Twitter issue profiles for Democratic men, with the bars representing whether they are competing against a male or female Republican. The right-hand panel presents similar data for Republican men, again separated by the sex of their Democratic opponent. For both parties, the issue profiles of men running against men correlate with the issue profiles of men running against women at 0.97. We find no statistically significant differences.

When we compare the small number of contests in which women ran against other women to those where they ran against men, we also find no differences in their issue agendas (results not shown). "We must raise the federal minimum wage in order to help stimulate our local economy," tweeted Democratic Congresswoman Ann Kuster, who faced Republican Marilinda Garcia in New Hampshire's 2nd Congressional District. Voters heard virtually the same message from dozens of Democratic women who ran against Republican men. Take, for instance, Marihelen Wheeler, who challenged incumbent Ted Yoho in Florida's 3rd Congressional District. "We need to raise the minimum wage," read one of Wheeler's tweets, "and we need to make sure everyone has a chance to get a good job – even those who don't go to college."

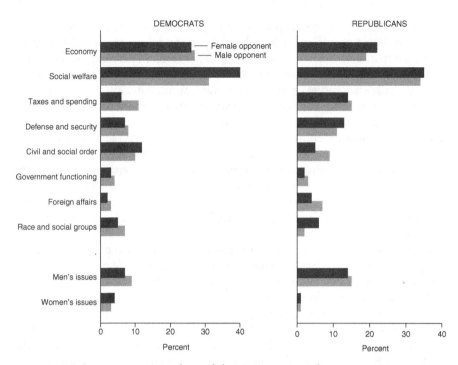

FIGURE 3.4. Issue content in male candidates' 2014 tweets, by opponent sex.
Note: Bars represent the percentage of the issue mentions in tweets devoted to each category. Democratic men with female opponents, N = 30; Democratic men with male opponents, N = 172; Republican men with female opponents, N = 59; Republican men with male opponents, N = 169. None of the comparisons between men running against women and men running against men is significant at p < 0.05.

This is admittedly a lot of data to digest. So let us recap what we've found thus far. Across the issue categories for both 2010 and 2014, we offered eighty comparisons of male and female candidates' agendas. In seventy-seven cases, we found no statistically significant gender difference. In the three cases that did reach conventional levels of statistical significance, the substantive differences were generally small and gave way to no particular pattern. Taken as a whole, the data suggest that candidate sex explains little about the content of campaign communications.

THE POWER OF PARTY: WHY CANDIDATE SEX DOES NOT SHAPE CAMPAIGN COMMUNICATION

Why doesn't candidate sex play a more prominent role in shaping campaign messages? A central reason is party affiliation. Time and again, the campaign managers we interviewed recounted strategies that were determined almost entirely by their party's response to national conditions and the district's partisan makeup, leaving precious few opportunities for gender to play a role. Consider Jason Fitzgerald's experience managing Republican Thomas Marino's 2010 winning campaign against Democratic incumbent Christopher Carney in Pennsylvania. At the beginning of the race, the campaign learned from its polling that Carney's vote for Obamacare, coupled with his Democratic record in a Republican district, were serious problems for the incumbent – liabilities that Fitzgerald said influenced Marino's communication strategy:

We didn't want anything to be about anyone other than Pelosi and Obama. Any attacks they leveled at us, we responded with, "Congressman Carney votes with Nancy Pelosi 95 percent of the time." We told our candidate, if you're at the grocery store and someone asks how you're doing, you say, "Fine, thanks. Do you know that Congressman Carney votes with Nancy Pelosi 95 percent of the time?"

Max Cummings, who ran Carney's campaign, was caught off guard. "The problem for all sixty-three of us [Democratic incumbents] who lost in 2010 was that individuality didn't matter," he reflected. "It was about Democrats and Republicans more broadly. That wasn't the kind of campaign we were used to."

Indeed, most campaign managers spoke about strategies that were far less about individual candidates than they were about the substantive distinctions between the two parties:

We were inundated with negative stuff about Obama, Pelosi, Obamacare, you name it ... All of their communications were great. It was just too much for us to overcome. (Michael Stratton, 2010 Campaign Manager for Democrat John Salazar, CO-3)

We ran the same issue campaign that most Republicans did around the country. It was Obamacare. It was the stimulus. It was Dodd-Frank. It was just running against Obama ... The single most effective image was [Democrat] Chet Edwards endorsing Obama on the steps in Waco. (Matt Mackowiak, 2010 Campaign Manager for Republican Bill Flores, TX-17)

We live in a world now where, when you're door knocking, they won't open the door if you're wearing the other party's shirt. It's all about whether the candidate supports the president or not. (Jennifer Koch, 2010 Campaign Manager for Democrat Glenn Nye, VA-2)

[Republican David] McKinley's strategy was to attack Oliverio on the same issues that Democrats across the country were being attacked on. It didn't matter that he had just defeated a Democratic incumbent in the primary. It was all about associating him with Pelosi and Obama. (Curtis Wilkerson, 2010 Campaign Manager for Democrat Michael Oliverio, WV-1)

These remarks suggest that because party is so powerful, the sex of the messenger is usually not relevant. This appears to be the case even when it comes to "women's" issues. "If you know that 60 percent of the voters will be female and women's health is an issue, then you want to make sure that your candidate can speak with authority on women's health issues," said one campaign manager for a male Democrat in 2010. "On this particular issue, Democrats have an advantage. It doesn't matter if the Democrat is a man or a woman." A political consultant for dozens of female Democratic candidates in 2014 sounded a similar chord, noting that Democrats – men and women alike – have found a strategic advantage by focusing on issues that disproportionately affect women, families, and children. "Things like women's economic security, paid sick leave, the minimum wage," the consultant said.

To test the argument that party should play a far stronger role than candidate sex in shaping campaign agendas, we first took the WMP advertising data from 2010 and ran ten logistic regression models. The dependent variable in each model is whether an advertisement mentioned an issue in one of our issue categories (the eight broad categories, plus our subset of "women's" and "men's" issues). As covariates, we include whether the candidate is a woman and whether the candidate is a Democrat. This allows us to determine how much influence candidate sex and party have on the likelihood of a candidate running an ad on a given issue.[19]

In Figure 3.5, we present the results. Throughout the book, we display regression results like this many times. So let us take just a moment to explain how to read and interpret the figure. The dots represent the coefficients (or point estimates) for the sex and party variables in each regression equation. The horizontal lines represent the 95 percent confidence intervals for each coefficient. If the confidence interval crosses the vertical dotted line, that means that the variable is not statistically significant; its effect is essentially zero (at $p < 0.05$). Positive point estimates with confidence intervals entirely to the right of the zero line mean that women (left panel) or Democrats (right panel) are more likely to air an ad about the issue. Negative coefficients with confidence intervals entirely to the left of the zero line mean that men or Republicans are more likely to run an ad about the topic.

Turning first to the left-hand panel, we see that not once is there a statistically significant effect for the female candidate coefficient. In all ten cases, the confidence intervals cross the zero line. The variable approaches statistical significance ($p < 0.07$) in the model for government functioning – women were slightly less likely than men to run such ads – but that is the only case

---

[19] We are of course not suggesting that this simple model offers a comprehensive account of campaign agendas. That would require considering a candidate's background, political experience, district characteristics, and other factors. But this simple model allows us to determine whether a relationship exists between sex and campaign messages, once we account for party. If we cannot find gender differences here, it is highly unlikely they would emerge in a model with more covariates. More complicated models (e.g., Sides 2006) fail to find independent gender effects.

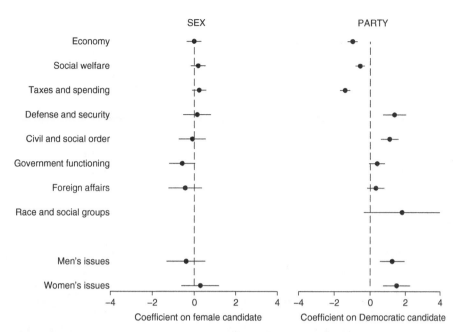

FIGURE 3.5. The effects of sex and party on issue content in 2010 campaign ads.
Note: Dependent variable is whether a campaign ad mentioned a particular issue. Dots represent logistic regression coefficients, with 95 percent confidence intervals. See Table A3.1 for the full regression equations. Because all of the very few race and social groups ads were aired by men, we do not present a coefficient for sex.

that suggests any difference. With nearly 480,000 observations in the model, that is hardly evidence of a strong gender effect.

Notice, however, that in the right-hand panel the party coefficient achieves statistical significance in seven of ten models. Democrats were less likely than Republicans to run ads on the economy, social welfare, and taxes and spending. Meanwhile, they were more likely than Republicans to run ads on defense and security and civil and social order. They also had a higher likelihood of producing ads that included mentions of "men's" and "women's" issues. Candidates' partisanship plays a substantial role in shaping their issue agendas. Sex does not.

Although our focus is primarily on issues, we can take advantage of the extensive coding in the WMP data to run a similar analysis on word usage in 2010 campaign ads. In addition to issues, coders identified whether particular words were mentioned in an ad. We include in the analysis the seven words that appeared in at least 2.5 percent of all ad airings.[20] Just as before, the graphs in

---

[20] That eliminated nine words coded in the WMP data. We set these aside because they were mentioned in just a tiny fraction of ads, which makes it impossible to generalize about gender differences. For instance, while "experience" was used only in men's ads, those ads comprise just 0.36 percent of all spots (and aired only in a handful of districts). Thus, we restrict the analysis to

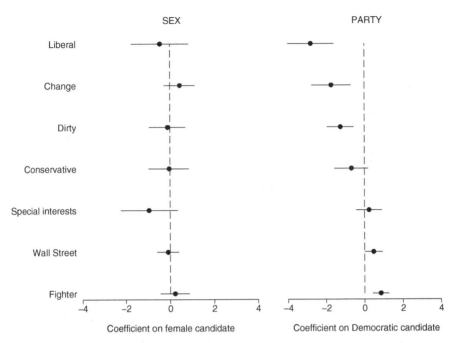

FIGURE 3.6. The effects of sex and party on word usage in 2010 campaign ads.
Note: Dependent variable is whether a campaign ad mentioned a particular word. Dots represent logistic regression coefficients, with 95 percent confidence intervals. See Table A3.2 for the full regression equations.

Figure 3.6 plot the coefficients for candidate sex and party from a series of regression models. As shown by the confidence intervals around every coefficient for female candidate, sex offers no explanatory power. A word that has traditionally been associated with women in the political realm (Change) is no more likely to be used by female candidates. Likewise, a word typically associated with men (Fighter) is no less likely to be used by women.

Party, however, relates to word usage in five cases. In three (Liberal, Change, and Dirty), Democrats were less likely than Republicans to use the word in an ad. Change, in particular, is not surprising. With Democrats having controlled Congress and the White House for two years, Republicans across the country in 2010 argued in their campaign ads for an overhaul in Washington. Democrats, meanwhile, were more likely to run ads mentioning Wall Street and Fighter, suggesting a focus on protecting consumers and the middle class. In a contest between party and sex, party is the clear winner.

The data from the 2014 Twitter analysis tell much the same story. In Figure 3.7, we plot the results of the logistic regression analyses we ran for the issue

cases where the number of observations is sufficiently large for us to make meaningful comparisons.

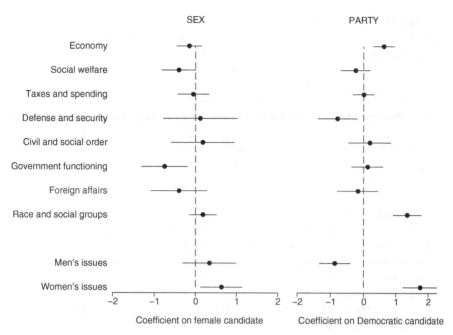

FIGURE 3.7. The effects of sex and party on issue content in 2014 tweets.
Note: Dependent variable is whether a tweet mentioned a particular issue. Dots represent logistic regression coefficients, with 95 percent confidence intervals. See Table A3.3 for the full regression equations.

content of the tweets. Here, the unit of analysis is an individual tweet, and the dependent variable is whether it mentioned one of the ten categories of issues we coded. In the left-hand panel, we see that sex plays a limited role in explaining issue mentions. In eight categories, including the economy and social welfare, which are the most prominent topics mentioned in tweets, candidate sex is not statistically significant. We do find, however, that similar to the nearly significant result in the ad data, women were less likely to tweet about government functioning. But this difference is not consistent with what the conventional wisdom might predict: if anything, we would expect women to focus more heavily than men on scandals or campaign finance, the kind of reform issues often argued to be advantageous for female candidates. Women were also more likely than men to tweet about "women's" issues. The effect is limited, though, because so little attention is devoted to "women's" issues. The predicted effect of a candidate being a woman rather than a man means that her odds of tweeting about a "women's" issue move from 2 percent to 5 percent.

When we turn to party, we find more consistent effects. Democrats were more likely than Republicans to tweet about the economy, race and social groups, and women's issues. For instance, in Ohio's 6th District, Jennifer Garrison tweeted on October 11 that "women deserve equal pay for equal work." Eight days later,

Pat Murphy, the Democratic nominee in Iowa's 1st District, tweeted that he would "sign Paycheck Fairness Act in Congress and keep working for women and equal pay." (Notably, the size of the party effect for women's issues is nearly three times the size of the effect for sex.) Republicans were more likely to tweet about defense and security and (consequently) men's issues. "National security requires strong convictions to defend America," tweeted Wendy Rogers in Arizona's 9th District. "@BarackObama puts White House and political concerns above the national security of our country," read a tweet from the GOP's nominee in Florida's 18th District, Carl Domino.

Although our analysis focuses on issue content, we also combed the Twitter data for mentions of personal qualities, or traits. Trait emphases are another place where scholars have looked for gender differences in campaign trail communication because traits can be connected to gender stereotypes and voters' perceptions of candidates' issue competencies (Huddy and Terkildsen 1993). Following previous work (Hayes and Lawless 2015b; Kinder 1986), we focus on four broad categories of attributes relevant to politics: leadership, competence, empathy, and integrity. Leadership and competence are ostensibly "masculine" attributes, while empathy and integrity are considered "feminine" traits. We separate the data in Figure 3.8 by whether the trait references were positive or negative.[21]

Again, we find that candidate sex does not predict the likelihood that a tweet mentioned a particular trait. In all eight models, women were no more or less likely than men to make positive or negative references to any of the traits. And although party explains less about trait mentions than it does issue emphases, we do find that Democrats were more likely to tweet positive competence references, and Republicans were nearly more likely to discuss positive leadership.

In all, the evidence from these analyses is clear: sex provides little explanation for the issue, language, or trait emphases in candidate communications. Party, however, is consistently related to issue discussions, and somewhat useful in explaining word and trait usage. These findings lend solid support to our argument that at a time of sharper conflict and wider divisions between the parties, few gender differences emerge in candidates' campaign messages.

DO THE RACES FEATURING "WOMEN'S" ISSUES
DISPROPORTIONATELY INVOLVE WOMEN?

Our analyses reveal few differences in the campaign communications of male and female candidates and that only a small fraction of campaign discourse is

---

[21] Just as with the issue analysis, we created dictionaries in Lexicoder based on words associated with each of the four major trait groups. These were again derived from our analysis of local news coverage during the 2010 and 2014 midterms. The list of words associated with each trait appears in Appendix 3, and is discussed in detail in Chapter 4. Figure 3.8 is restricted to the 459 candidates whose tweets included at least one trait mention.

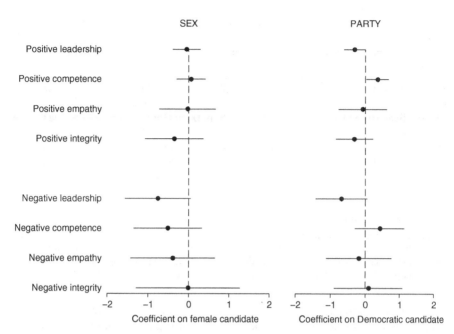

FIGURE 3.8. The effects of sex and party on trait content in 2014 tweets.
Note: Dependent variable is whether a tweet mentioned a particular trait. Dots represent logistic regression coefficients, with 95 percent confidence intervals. See Table A3.4 for the full regression equations.

devoted to "women's" or "men's" issues. It is possible, however, that our approach, by aggregating hundreds of contests and candidates together, could miss important gender dynamics that occur in a small subset of races. In particular, if the races with the most attention to "women's" issues disproportionately involve female candidates, then that would suggest that candidate sex structures campaign communications at least in a fraction of contests. Yet here, too, we find very limited evidence that candidate sex is important.

For 2010, we return to the candidates' television advertising. Table 3.1 lists the ten candidates from each party who devoted the most attention to "women's" issues in their ads. These data are taken from the issue profiles we calculated for each candidate, so the percentages represent the share of issue mentions (out of 100 percent) that were devoted to "women's" issues. Again, Democrats have a tendency to talk about these issues more frequently than Republicans, so we separate the data by party (Winter 2010). "Women's" issues comprised anywhere from 20 to 58 percent of the issue profiles of the Democratic candidates who devoted the most attention to them, but only 12–30 percent of the GOP candidates who did so.

TABLE 3.1. *House candidates who devoted the most attention to "women's" issues in campaign ads, 2010 (%)*

Democrats		Republicans	
William Van Haaften (IN-8)	58	Bill Huizenga (MI-2)	30
Ravi Sangisetty (LA-3)	50	Todd Rokita (IN-4)	25
Melissa Bean (IL-17)	44	Billy Long (MO-7)	23
Daniel Seals (IL-10)	35	Eddie Zamora (TX-15)	22
David Price (NC-4)	31	Greg Harper (MS-3)	19
Ted Deutch (FL-19)	25	David Reichert (WA-8)	15
Russ Carnahan (MO-1)	24	Mike Pompeo (KS-4)	15
Bob Etheridge (NC-2)	21	James Lankford (OK-5)	14
Travis Childers (MS-1)	20	Jeff Landry (LA-3)	13
Scott Eckersley (MO-7)	20	Dan Debicella (CT-4)	12

Note: Each column lists the ten candidates in each party who devoted the most attention to "women's" issues in their 2010 campaign ads. Entries indicate the percentage that "women's" issues comprised in each candidate's issue profile. See Appendix 1 for issue coding.

The most striking finding to emerge from the table is that nineteen of the twenty candidates who spent the most time in their campaign ads addressing women's issues were men. Only one woman (in bold) makes the Democrats' top-ten list; no women appear on the Republican list. And because women constituted nearly four in twenty of all candidates who ran in 2010, they are actually *under-represented* in this list. Moreover, the men who most emphasized women's issues in their campaign ads were not trying to compensate for the perception that female candidates are better suited than men to address women's issues: there were no female candidates in the overwhelming majority of these races. Only Bob Etheridge and David Reichert faced female opponents (Renee Ellmers and Suzanne Delbene, respectively).

In Table 3.2, we present for 2014 the ten candidates in each party with the highest percentage of tweets devoted to "women's" issues.[22] Once again, we notice significant party differences, with the top ten Democrats emphasizing "women's" issues as a much greater share of their Twitter content than the top ten Republicans. As for gender differences, among the most prolific "women's" issues tweeters, women were slightly more likely than men to make the list relative to their proportions as candidates in each party.[23] Of course, the two women who made the GOP list tweeted about "women's" issues just 5 percent of the time. As with the ads, the men on the list were not especially likely to face female opponents. Among the Democrats, none of the men ran against

---

[22] Because some candidates tweeted just a handful of times, we restrict the analysis to those with at least thirty tweets. This ensures that our analysis is not skewed by candidates who tweeted only once or twice about a particular issue.

[23] Among Democrats, women comprised 28 percent of the general election candidates in 2014. Women constituted 13 percent of the GOP's general election candidates.

TABLE 3.2. *House candidates who devoted the most attention to "women's" issues in tweets, 2014 (%)*

Democrats		Republicans	
Lenda Sherrell (TN-4)	60	Pete Olson (TX-22)	17
David Cox (FL-6)	50	Mark Walker (NC-6)	17
Nita Lowey (NY-17)	50	Mike Coffman (CO-6)	14
Mark Pocan (WI-2)	50	George Leing (CO-2)	10
Frederica Wilson (FL-24)	39	Michael MacFarlane (KY-3)	9
April Freeman (FL-19)	33	Tom MacArthur (NJ-3)	8
Donna Edwards (MD-4)	30	Martha McSally (AZ-2)	5
Mark Lester (AL-6)	29	Marilinda Garcia (NH-2)	5
Patrick Murphy (FL-18)	25	Rick Allen (GA-12)	4
Tim Ryan (OH-13)	25	Jeff Byrd (NM-3)	3

Note: Each column lists the ten candidates in each party who devoted the most attention to "women's" issues in their tweets, and who also tweeted at least thirty times during the last month of the campaign. Entries indicate the percentage that "women's" issues comprised in each candidate's issue profile. See Appendix 2 for issue coding.

a woman (only Donna Edwards did). Among the Republicans, Mark Walker and Michael MacFarlane competed against female Democrats (as did Marilinda Garcia). In no case is there evidence of "women's" issues "conversations" between two candidates in the same district.

Overall, the campaign ad and Twitter data make it difficult to conclude that the presence of a female candidate is required for a race to see heightened attention to "women's" issues. "Women's" issues, of course, are not the only way that a candidate might draw attention to sex. But issues provide a vehicle for candidates to make gender identity salient. Thus, detectable gender dynamics, when they do emerge, are likely to do so through the issue content of the candidates' campaigns. And we find little evidence of such a pattern.

THE "RICK LAZIO PROBLEM" AND THE RELEVANCE OF GENDER IN CANDIDATE COMMUNICATION

Although our data fail to turn up systematic gender differences in the content of campaign communication, the campaign managers we interviewed did repeatedly mention one way that gender matters in campaign strategy: interpersonal dynamics between the candidates. This aspect of communication is difficult to measure, and we lack quantitative evidence for this point. But time and again, political professionals argued that men who run against women must be particularly cognizant of their tone and the substance of their "attacks" – much more so than when they compete against other men. In a nutshell, male candidates want to avoid what several campaign managers referred to as the "Rick Lazio problem." In a debate against Hillary Clinton during the 2000 U.S. Senate campaign in New York, then-Congressman Lazio famously approached Clinton's podium, waved a sheet of paper directly in her face, and aggressively asked her to sign a pledge to stop spending soft money.[24] The *Washington Post* includes the incident in its list of "Worst Debate Moments Ever," and characterized Lazio's behavior as "bullying and inappropriate."[25]

Fifteen years later, the episode remained salient in campaign managers' minds. "You know the famous Rick Lazio problem? When he waved that petition in Hillary's face? We can't have that," explained the manager of a male Democratic candidate's 2010 House race. "It's an overused trope, but it really encapsulates the danger ... You want to avoid the icky feeling, especially among female voters, that a man treating a woman poorly can invoke." She went on to note that, had her candidate faced a woman in the general election, "We would have instructed him to talk differently. It wouldn't have affected what he talked about – that part of our strategy would have been the same. But we'd want to make sure that there was no air of condescension." Lazio was also on Bill Cortese's mind when he readied Republican Andy Tobin for debates against Democrat Ann Kirkpatrick in 2014: "In debate prep, we said, 'Look, Andy, you need to use caution when you go on the attack. You can't be Rick Lazio' ... We were aware of that. When you have a female candidate, you're aware of it. Everyone is. You just have to understand that there are certain things you don't do." Even Jason Fitzgerald, who did not face a female opponent when he led Thomas Marino to victory, remarked on the important lesson he learned watching Lazio debate Clinton: "You can't encroach on a woman's space. If it's a man, no one cares."

It is not only in debates, of course, where "men worry about beating up on a woman," as one campaign manager put it. Several others noted that these concerns can affect an entire campaign's tone. Vance Phillips, who ran Republican Glen Urquhart's 2010 race in Delaware, drew a contrast between his experience running against a woman (Michelle Rollins) in the GOP primary and a man (John Carney) in the general election: "We had to treat her with the highest degree of respect and courtesy, and that wouldn't have been the case running against a man." Others mentioned that "men can't attack women as vociferously," that "they have to be a little bit softer and take a kinder approach," and that "men just aren't as mean to women as they might be to each other." Jennifer Koch's experience running a male candidate's campaign in Colorado against another man epitomizes this point. She recalled that one of the candidates

[24] Joyce Purnick, "Clinton vs. Lazio in 2000, a Portent of Debates to Come," *New York Times*, January 10, 2008. Accessed at: http://cityroom.blogs.nytimes.com/2008/01/10/clinton-vs-lazio-in-2000-a-portent-of-debates-to-come/?_r=0 (April 8, 2015).

[25] Rachel Weiner, "The Worst Debate Moments Ever," *Washington Post*, November 10, 2011. Accessed at: www.washingtonpost.com/blogs/the-fix/post/the-worst-debate-moments-ever/2011/11/10/gIQATweo8M_blog.html (April 8, 2015).

kept using the word "sleazy" to refer to the other: "I don't think that kind of attack can be directed at a female candidate," she said. "When you attack your opponent, I think you have to use a little more caution when a man is running against a woman. And this is true for both parties. It doesn't mean you can't attack. But the words that are acceptable are different." The same is true in the rare contests that feature two female candidates. "We could attack her and no one would say that we were attacking a woman," a GOP campaign manager told us. "So perhaps she was able to be harsher and draw more contrasts without having to worry about it the way that a male candidate would."

Andy Sere, who managed Evan Jenkins' successful 2014 race in West Virginia, summarized the concern that he thinks is "out there among political professionals." He explained that "tone is more important when there's a woman in the race. You need to be more judicious in the way you talk about your opponent. It can't be a brawl. As long as it's respectful, you can attack. But you need to watch it a little more than if it's two men in the fight." Indeed, a failure to do so can be problematic. Consider the Monday-morning quarterbacking of a campaign manager who sent a male candidate to Congress when he ran against a man in 2010, but then back home when he ran against a woman in 2012:

We employed the same strategy both times. Plain and simple, it was wrong. We went full on negative. We weren't mean spirited or anything like that. We strictly hit her on spending and taxes. As a city councilwoman, she made some bad spending decisions. But we were not well-received. We should have waited for her to go negative first and then it would have been fine ... It's ridiculous, by the way, because she's really tough. That's why we went all out. But the public just doesn't like it when you attack a girl.

Others made similar points. One campaign manager found a picture of their female opponent dressed as a clown. He thought it was "a great visual," so they used it. He was stunned when the opponent held a press conference and criticized them for launching personal attacks. "And it worked for her!" he recalled in disbelief. "We wouldn't have had the same response if it was a male candidate."

Although male and female candidates might run very similar campaigns in terms of substance, these anecdotes suggest that the presence of a female candidate can affect the tone of a race or, at the very least, factor into the way that candidates communicate directly with each other. And this may be important for shaping the "feel" of a campaign or the style that characterizes the candidates' discourse. But for the most part – and even in congressional campaigns with the heaviest emphasis on "women's" issues – this appears to be the exception to the larger rule: gender differences in candidate communications are rarely detectable.

CONCLUSION

Having established that little of the content of contemporary House campaign communication is shaped by candidate sex, we turn in Chapter 4 to a consideration of the media. More specifically, we focus on what local newspaper coverage of these campaigns looks like, whether it reflects the candidates' messages, and whether the media cover men and women differently. Even if candidates do not seem to be campaigning "as women" or "as men," or highlighting different issues in their ads and social media communications, some prior work has found that news coverage disproportionately reflects aspects of candidates' campaigns that are consistent with gendered expectations. On the other hand, if – as we expect – other features of campaigns, such as partisan conflict and competitiveness, largely determine election coverage, then candidate sex should have little to do with the media attention candidates receive. Not only will these analyses shed light on gender differences in media coverage, but they will also help complete our depiction of the information environment voters navigate during election season.

4

Sex is no story

At first glance, it would seem like a campaign manager's dream. In the midst of a U.S. House race in the fall of 2014, Samuel Raymond found himself fielding interview requests from the most prominent political news outlets in the country. With his boss, West Virginia Democrat Nick Rahall, locked in a fierce reelection fight, *Politico*, the *New York Times*, and other major media organizations were clamoring for a story. Given this national platform, Raymond tried to cast the congressman as independent-minded, unafraid of sticking to his principles in the face of party pressure. "I truly believe he has reinforced his brand by standing up to President Obama," Raymond told *Politico* in September.[1] The next month, *The Hill* newspaper in Washington, DC, reported on Rahall's efforts to help one of his constituents get the veteran's benefits she was owed. "Nick Rahall does make sure that the little people and his state are covered," Terri Fullerton-Clark told a reporter. "He stood up for me and I'm a nobody."[2] Although the stories typically framed Rahall's prospects as dim, this was the kind of high-profile exposure that you'd think even political veterans would kill for.

But to the campaign, all that national attention was irrelevant. "We didn't care," Raymond said. It wasn't that the campaign wasn't concerned about the media. They were. But it was the local news that mattered. "The two Charleston papers, plus these local outlets that are even smaller – those are the ones we tried to push the local issues on," Raymond explained. "We wanted to portray him as the congressman delivering local results. And working closely with local papers is the best way to do that."

---

[1] Tarini Parti, "Red-Seat Dems Fight for Survival," *Politico*, September 28, 2014. Accessed at: www.politico.com/story/2014/09/red-seat-dems-keep-swimming-against-the-tide-111375.html (July 29, 2015).

[2] Scott Wang, "Can Manchin Save Coal Country Dems?" *The Hill*, October 23, 2014. Accessed at: http://thehill.com/blogs/ballot-box/house-races/221611-can-manchin-save-coal-country-dems (July 29, 2015).

The Rahall campaign's perspective was hardly unique. For all the attention to the rapid transformation of the news environment in the first decades of the twenty-first century, traditional news outlets remain essential to U.S. House campaigns, for male and female candidates alike. A 2010 senior campaign advisor to New Hampshire Democrat Ann Kuster told us that despite "a lot of personal relationships with the national political media," he relied most heavily on the local paper "to reach the voters." Survey data from October 2014 reveal that citizens were more than four times as likely to get information about the House race in their district from a local newspaper than a national one.[3] Voters were also at least 40 percent more likely to consult local print media for information about their House race than they were national news broadcasts, cable news, blogs, or talk radio, and they relied more heavily on local newspapers than on the candidates' ads or websites.[4] It's no surprise that campaigns spend much of their time courting local reporters, "identifying them, meeting with them for background, sending press releases," as one campaign manager told us. In short, mainstream venues like local newspapers are, in the words of Michael Stratton, the 2010 campaign manager for Colorado Democrat John Salazar "where voters get their news."

But local papers are important for more than their large audiences. Favorable coverage can boost a candidate's fortunes, while negative news can threaten them (Druckman and Parkin 2005; Kahn and Kenney 2002). Coverage that reflects a candidate's issue agenda can encourage voters to make their choices based on factors that are advantageous to the candidate (Hayes 2008; Iyengar and Kinder 1987). And stories in local news outlets can help campaigns demonstrate the candidate's commitment to the community. "People want to see that you understand their particular town," said one campaign manager from an East Coast state. Cesar Blanco, the 2010 campaign manager for Democrat Ciro Rodriguez, considered the local press in Rodriguez's South Texas district indispensable to the campaign's strategy. "We wanted the member of Congress – from a messaging standpoint – to show he understood what the voters in TX-23 needed," Blanco said. "The best way to localize an election is to rely really heavily on the local media." According to one victorious 2010 Republican campaign manager, "It's all about local press. What's the value of national press in a House race? There is none."[5]

---

[3] These data come from our module of the 2014 Cooperative Congressional Election Study (CCES). We asked, "In the last month, where did you get information about the U.S. House race in your district?" Respondents could indicate that they accessed news from as many as ten sources. They could also respond that they had not followed the House race in their district, which was the case for 29 percent of the people we surveyed. Chapter 2 describes the CCES survey, and Chapter 5 presents many of its results.

[4] The other leading source of campaign news was local television. We focus on newspapers, however, because the reality is that coverage of local politics on local TV is rare (Stevens *et al.* 2006) and has weaker effects on voter attitudes than print news does (Schaffner 2006).

[5] Some campaign managers suggested that national news exposure can help raise money from outside the district. But that has little to do with the way that voters perceive a candidate. And that

Because local news is so important in U.S. House races – potentially shaping voters' impressions of candidates and their decisions on Election Day – examining the way the press cover male and female candidates is essential to understanding gender dynamics on the campaign trail. If the conventional wisdom is right, then news outlets will pay less attention to female candidates, portray them in ways that reflect gender stereotypes, and undermine their credibility. This coverage, which is a critical component of the campaign landscape, may then affect voters' evaluations and pose additional obstacles to women running for office.

But, as we show in this chapter, our analysis of thousands of local news stories from hundreds of congressional campaigns during the 2010 and 2014 midterms uncovers no such thing. In contrast to much of the existing literature and popular commentary, we detect almost no gender differences in the volume or substance of news coverage. Women are no more likely than men to receive coverage of their appearance, family, or gender roles – in fact, this kind of media attention is exceedingly rare for any candidate. Female candidates are no more likely than men to be described as possessing "feminine" traits or less likely to be described as possessing "masculine" ones. And the issue coverage for male and female candidates does not differ. These patterns, we demonstrate, emerge in part because men and women run virtually identical campaigns. Journalistic norms encourage the media to reflect candidates' campaign messages, resulting in very similar coverage for female and male candidates. In addition, reporters regard electoral competitiveness and incumbency as far more newsworthy features of a congressional race than the presence of a female candidate. We do find that journalists may be slightly more attentive to discussions of "women's" issues in campaigns that involve at least one female candidate. This finding emerges from a small fraction of contests and a small number of stories, but it suggests at least one way that the presence of a woman in a race can shape news coverage. Combined with our findings from Chapter 3, however, our news analysis in its entirety reveals that only rarely does gender become a salient feature of the information environment in U.S. House campaigns.

TRACKING LOCAL NEWS COVERAGE: THE DATA SET

From the perspective of campaign professionals and voters, local newspaper coverage remains the most important news source during House campaigns.

national exposure still pales in comparison to the importance of local news. Andy Yates, who managed North Carolina GOP candidate Ilario Gregory Pantano's race, explained the distinction well: "We wanted some national attention for fundraising purposes ... And because of that, we were able to have a national plan to raise money. But the Wilmington media market – the local news – that was the most important thing in the district ... where we placed most of our focus." This sentiment crosses party lines. Jennifer Koch prioritized local over national media for similar reasons in Virginia Democrat Glenn Nye's 2010 race: "The more exposure you have, the better chances you have to increase your donor base ... But for getting our message out, it was more important to have the local papers pick up our press releases."

Yet despite the importance of local print media, very little political science research has sought to analyze coverage of House elections from more than a handful of districts. Thus, there is no accepted method of identifying or analyzing the local news outlets that serve a particular House contest. The approach we developed allows for a comprehensive assessment of whether and how gender affects the volume and substance of coverage candidates receive during congressional campaigns.

We began by selecting the appropriate newspaper for each House race in 2010 and 2014. We consulted maps of every congressional district, identified the largest city in each, and then determined whether that city had a daily newspaper we could access through one of several electronic databases or the newspaper's online archives.[6] In the vast majority of cases, this was a straightforward, though time-consuming, task. In the few cases for which we could not gain access to newspaper coverage from the district's largest-circulation daily paper, we relied on coverage from the next-largest paper. The daily circulation of the newspapers in our sample varies quite a bit, which is to be expected given differences in district composition. Our smallest paper, the *Suffolk News Herald* in Virginia's 4th Congressional District, has a daily circulation of only 5,012. Compare that to the *New York Times*, which is the local paper of record for several New York City congressional districts, and whose daily circulation exceeds 1.8 million. The average newspaper circulation size in our congressional districts is roughly 178,000.

Once we chose a newspaper for each district, we identified every news story during the thirty days leading up to the election that mentioned at least one of the two major-party candidates. We did not limit the analysis strictly to "campaign" stories because we assume that any information about the House candidates is potentially relevant for voters. Accordingly, we collected any straight news report, news analysis, editorial, or op-ed column that mentioned either the Democrat or the Republican seeking the House seat in the district.[7] Our data set thus includes a wide variety of articles. Some stories were very short, providing brief mentions of campaign events or fundraising totals. Others reported the highlights of candidate forums or debates. And some – often profile pieces or endorsements – were lengthy. An October 12, 2010 *Daily Herald* "Q&A" with the candidates in Illinois' 9th Congressional District, for instance, ran to 3,400 words, covering Democrat Jan Schakowsky's jobs plan, Republican Joel Pollack's proposal to rehabilitate the region's transportation infrastructure, and more. The average article length in the data set is just less than 700 words.

Our data collection efforts produced 10,375 stories about 1,550 candidates who received at least some local news coverage in either the 2010 or 2014 midterms. Across the two election cycles, in the 815 districts for which we

---

[6] Because of redistricting, we did this for every district in 2010 and then again for every district in 2014.

[7] We did not code letters to the editor.

located at least one story about the congressional race, 275 candidates were women, and 1,275 were men. Districts with coverage were more likely than those without it to feature open seat contests and more competitive races, but they were no more or less likely to include a female candidate.

Coders read the full text of each article and recorded several pieces of information.[8] First, they tracked the number of times a candidate's sex or gender was mentioned. Gender references included explicit mentions of a candidate being a man or a woman (e.g., "As a woman running for political office ... "), as well as gender-specific roles. For example, if a candidate was referred to as juggling her role as campaigner and mother, then that was coded as a gender mention. We also coded material that clearly drew a reader's attention to the sex of the candidate, such as physical appearance, clothing, or hairstyle. (We did not count use of feminine and masculine pronouns, such as "she" and "he.") In 2014, we expanded our content analysis to record whether the "War on Women" was associated with the candidate's campaign and whether the article mentioned any electoral implications of female voters' support ("As a Republican, Smith could be hurt by the longstanding gender gap ... ").

Second, we recorded the number of explicit references to candidate traits, both positive and negative (e.g., "capable" and "ineffective"). These references could come from candidates themselves ("I have shown the leadership abilities to represent this district effectively"), their opponents ("My opponent does not care about the people of this district"), or reporters ("Questions about Thompson's trustworthiness have been a problem for her campaign"). Although we began the coding with a list of traits commonly included in previous studies, we recorded references to every additional trait we encountered in the coverage. In all, we coded for 207 separate specific traits, all of which are listed in Appendix 3.[9] We then collapsed those traits into one of the four dimensions that previous research has identified as salient for voters: competence, leadership, integrity, and empathy (see Hayes 2005; Kinder 1986).[10] We divided each category into positive and negative mentions.

Third, we tracked every time an issue was mentioned in connection with a candidate. Once again, we began with a list of issues commonly included in previous studies and supplemented it with every additional issue that emerged in the coverage. (Appendix 2 presents the complete list of the 218 issues we recorded.) We then classified issues in two ways: (1) We assigned each issue to one of the eight broad categories we used to develop issue profiles for

---

[8] Before undertaking the content analysis, two coders participated in several hours of practice coding, using news stories from House elections in previous years. This allowed us to refine the coding scheme and to minimize confusion and maximize consistency between the coders.

[9] We did not code "latent" or implied references to character traits.

[10] In addition to these 207 traits, we identified 23 traits that did not fall into one of these four categories (e.g., "loyal"). We do not focus on this small subset of traits, but we found no differences in coverage on this "general character" dimension for male and female candidates.

candidates' campaign ads and tweets in Chapter 3 (Civil and social order, Defense and security, Social welfare, Taxes and spending, Foreign affairs, Race and social groups, Government functioning, and Economy); and (2) we classified a subset of the topics as "women's" or "men's" issues.

In contrast to many studies of campaign media coverage, which tend to conduct the analysis at the story or paragraph level, we carried out our coding at the level of the individual reference. In other words, we account for *every* time a particular attribute or issue was mentioned. This method allows us to capture multiple references to gender, traits, and issues when they appear in the same paragraph, or even the same sentence. In an October 29, 2014 *Greensboro News and Record* story about the race in North Carolina's 6th District, for example, a reporter wrote that Republican Mark Walker's gaffes in early debates "could be used to paint him as the less thoughtful and careful candidate."[11] Our coding scheme allows us to capture both references to Walker's lack of competence: thoughtlessness and carelessness. If we coded the article at the story or paragraph level, we would only capture one, as we'd simply be recording whether a paragraph included at least one mention of competence. Compared to previous work, the detail and depth of our coding and the large number of female candidates in our data set significantly increase the validity and generalizability of our analysis.[12]

MALE AND FEMALE CANDIDATES IN THE NEWS: THE VOLUME AND CONTENT OF CAMPAIGN COVERAGE

From the outset, it is important to note that newspaper coverage of congressional campaigns is fairly common. The average number of stories per race in the 2010 cycle was 14.4 (about one article every other day in the month leading up to the election.) In 2014, the average number of stories in a district was 11.9. There is of course a great deal of variation, with more competitive races receiving significant amounts of coverage and less competitive races seeing less (see Hayes and Lawless 2015a).[13] And many of the articles we coded did not include lengthy discussions of the candidates' issue positions or personal

---

[11] Susan Ladd, "No Big Surprises Expected in Debate," *Greensboro News and Record*, October 29, 2014. Accessed at: www.greensboro.com/news/no-big-surprises-expected-in-debate/arti cle_a76913ec-5f09-11e4-9120-0017a43b2370.html (July 31, 2015).

[12] We did not measure the "tone" of coverage toward candidates. This is partly because there is no agreement in the literature about how to assess the overall tenor of media attention (e.g., Dalton *et al.* 1998; Smith 1997). In addition, subjective indicators of tone or favorability can be difficult to code reliably). We chose to focus instead on the aspects of coverage of male and female candidates where previous research has reported the most consistent differences – discussions of gender or appearance, portrayals of candidate traits, and attention to issues.

[13] In 2010, competitive races – which we define as races deemed by the Cook Report as "toss-up," "leaning," or "likely" for one party – received on average twenty-three stories. Safe races received eleven. In 2014, competitive races averaged twenty-three stories and safe races received ten.

characteristics (though some did). Our contention is not that every voter was exposed to a dozen or more substantive stories about a district's House race (though some were). But these numbers make clear that the amount of attention to House races in local newspapers is conceivably high enough to shape voters' evaluations of candidates, making the local press a central part of the electoral landscape. Accordingly, we can begin our investigation of the media's treatment of male and female candidates by examining how much news coverage they received.

Turning first to the 2010 midterms, women and men were equally likely to make it into the news. During the last thirty days of the campaign season, races between two male candidates averaged 14.7 stories in the local newspaper. If there was one female candidate in the race, the average contest saw 14.3 stories. Campaigns between two female candidates received 15.0 stories on average. Regardless of the sex of the candidates running, the amount of media attention in a typical race varied by less than a single story. None of these differences is statistically significant.

In 2014, there was more variation. Campaigns with two male candidates saw 11.0 stories on average. Contests in which one of the candidates was a woman averaged an additional 2.4 stories. And races involving two female candidates received another 2.4 stories beyond that. In both cases, that is significantly more coverage than in races with two male candidates ($p < 0.05$). The substantive difference is meaningful too. With an average of 15.8 stories, same-sex races with female candidates garnered roughly one more story per week than same-sex contests featuring two men. This is one of the few instances in which we find a measurable gender difference in news coverage. And one possible explanation is that the presence of two female candidates in many congressional districts in itself is unusual – relatively few House races have seen a Democratic woman face a Republican woman. This novelty may make journalists more likely to devote attention to the contest. The difference does not, however, suggest bias against female candidates, nor is it consistent with the assumption that women have a harder time than men garnering news coverage when they run for office.

The volume of coverage candidates receive is important, since it affects their ability to get messages to voters. But the primary focus of the existing literature, as well as popular discussions about women in politics, is the content of that coverage – more specifically, whether male and female candidates are treated differently when their campaigns are discussed in the news. We address this question by examining coverage of candidates' gender, personality traits, and the issues with which they are associated.[14]

[14] In 2014, we also examined whether women and men received different amounts of horse race coverage, or attention to their standing in the polls. They did not. Female candidates received an average of 1.43 mentions and male candidates received 1.29. Thirty-eight percent of women and 35 percent of men received at least one horse race mention. Neither difference is statistically significant.

Coverage of candidate gender and appearance

One prominent claim about campaign news coverage is that journalists devote more attention to gender – including mentions of candidate sex, family roles, or appearance – when they write about women than when they cover men. Disparities of this kind, so the argument goes, can be problematic, undermining women's credentials and encouraging voters to evaluate candidates on the basis of sex. Despite this argument's intuitive appeal, our 2014 data lend no support to it.

Figure 4.1 presents the average number of gender mentions candidates received in the final month of campaign coverage, broken down by the sex of the candidate. The scale of the graph, which goes from just 0 to 1.5 mentions, is one of its most important features – there are very few references to candidates' gender. The top two bars ("All gender") show that, on average, one month's worth of coverage contained only 1.33 gender references for women and 1.31 mentions for men, a trivial and statistically insignificant difference.[15] Fifty-nine percent of candidates saw no gender mentions at all in their coverage; the numbers are statistically indistinguishable for women (55 percent) and men (61 percent).[16] Not only does gender receive virtually no attention in news coverage of House campaigns, but women are no more likely than men to be discussed in those terms.

The bottom portion of the graph breaks down the "All gender" category into its various components. References to the candidates' families – their children, spouses, or roles as mothers or fathers, for instance – are the most common way that gender made its way into coverage. But the (in)frequency with which those references appeared was the same for men and women, both of whom received on average less than one family mention during the last month of the campaign. The days when women running for office were regularly described as mothers first and politicians second appear to be long gone.[17]

---

[15] "All gender" comprises references to family, appearance, and other gender mentions, such as explicit references to a candidate's sex. It does not include references to the "War on Women" or female voters, because those discussions are typically about political strategy rather than the candidates themselves. Even if we include the latter two elements as part of "All gender," however, the results are the same.

[16] The same is true in 2010. On average, female candidates received 1.02 gender mentions in the last month of the campaign, while men received 1.06. Sixty-one percent of women and 66 percent of men saw no mentions of their gender. Neither difference is statistically significant. Figure 4.1 presents only the 2014 data because our 2010 coding did not break out family, appearance, and other gender mentions.

[17] It is possible, of course, that references to family structures and roles – even if they use the same language – could convey different things when describing male and female candidates. A reference to a female candidate's children, for example, could ostensibly cue voters to evaluate her based on how well she has handled her dual roles. Referring to a male candidate as a father, on the other hand, may not prime voters to assess him according to how well he has balanced his family responsibilities with his political ambition. If this is the case, then the fact that men and women receive a similar number of family mentions would not tell the whole story. Because

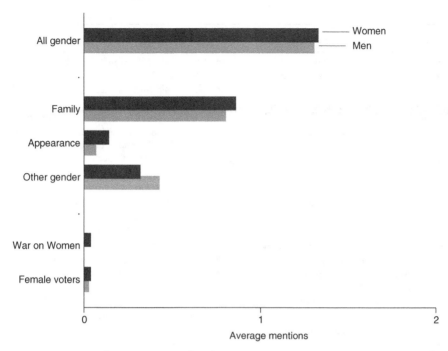

FIGURE 4.1. Gender mentions in local newspaper campaign coverage in 2014, by candidate sex.
Note: Bars represent the average number of mentions in local newspaper coverage devoted to each category during the last thirty days of the campaigns. "All gender" comprises references to family, appearance, and other gender mentions, such as explicit references to a candidate's sex. Women, N = 152; men, N = 611. None of the comparisons between women and men is significant at $p < 0.05$.

The claim that the media devote considerable and disproportionate attention to female candidates' appearance also does not hold up to empirical scrutiny. When we examine references to appearance – discussion of candidates' clothes, hairstyles, physical features, and the like – we find that they are even less frequent than the sporadic mentions of candidates' families. On average, women received 0.15 of a mention across thirty days' worth of coverage, while men received 0.07 (a non-significant difference). Perhaps the more telling statistic is that 95 percent of women and 96 percent of men received no coverage of their appearance at all.

There was so little coverage of the way that candidates look that we can array in Table 4.1 every single reference to a candidate's appearance from the more than 4,000 stories we coded in 2014. On the left-hand side, we present the

family mentions are so rare, however, it is unlikely that, even if these differential effects exist, they would be consequential.

TABLE 4.1. *Every appearance-related mention in local newspaper coverage of the 2014 House elections*

Men (23 candidates, 20 districts)	Women (8 candidates, 7 districts)
• a curmudgeonly figure given to bolo ties • from Aguilar's blue tie to Chabot's red one • a youthful 40 • who has gained attention for dressing as a woman • who prefers to dress in women's clothing • arguably known more for his "six-pack abs" • singled him out this year in the categories of "gym rat," "hottest male," and "best dressed" • their neckties were about all that clashed • won't have any NASCAR-styled decals on his suits • strolled through downtown in khaki pants and a navy blue tennis polo • a casual change from his usual suit-and-tie combo • admitted to swimming nude in the Sea of Galilee • a suit that doesn't have holes in it • in a dark suit • sporting a plaid shirt • silver-haired representative • a prominent gap between two front teeth • I'd love to talk about the issues, not about my hair • appear fascinated with Stewart Mills' hair • nearly shoulder-length locks • smoothing his hair behind his ears • his Navy SEAL uniform • age over beauty • I do try to work out and eat right • shed his suit coat and tie • there's a reason I wear pants in my ads • I did not go skinny-dipping in the Sea of Galilee • wiping his brow • brownish hair flying every which way in the breeze • wearing blue pajamas covered with yellow ducks • towered over his opponent in both height and volume • donned an unforgiving yellow jumpsuit	• She is "Most Partisan" in the House. She is also "Best Dressed." • power-suit success lies in her gumball-inspired necklaces • a fondness for neutral palettes and prints • dons an apron Thursday to cook up some yogurt-based ranch dressing with TV's "Top Chef" Tom Colicchio • voted "best dressed" and "most partisan" House member • named by a magazine as the second "hottest" member of Congress • pregnant with her first child • who lost both legs • lost both legs and partial use of her right arm • who lost both legs when her helicopter took fire in Iraq • I have thick skin • whom [a blogger] called "ugly as sin." • frequently wears dark sober colors • wears her dark-rimmed eyeglasses • two immaculately manicured hands, with 10 long hot-pink fingernails • known for her hundreds of colorful hats • the stitches have started coming out of a pair of black patent leather shoes she's worn campaigning

Note: The table displays every appearance mention in the 4,524 newspaper articles we coded from 2014.

thirty-two references to twenty-three male candidates' appearance we identified. Several called attention to the candidates' clothes. An October 29 story in the *Alaska Dispatch News* described Republican Representative Don Young as "a curmudgeonly figure given to bolo ties." Democratic incumbent Jim McDermott "donned an unforgiving yellow jumpsuit" at a museum exhibit, according to an October 18 piece in the *Seattle Times*. An October 14 article in the *Corpus Christi Caller-Times* described a photo of Republican Representative Blake Farenthold "wearing blue pajamas covered with yellow ducks." And a November 1 *San Diego Union-Tribune* story noted, without comment, that Republican challenger Stephen Meade had "gained attention for dressing as a woman." Other stories mentioned a candidate's physical features – he was "silver-haired" or had a "prominent gap between two front teeth" or "towered over his opponent in both height and volume." There were two references to whether Republican Congressmen Michael Grimm and Kevin Yoder had gone skinny-dipping in the Sea of Galilee during a 2011 trip.

Other than the absence of nude bathing stories, the references we found to the appearance of a total of eight female candidates were similar to those for men. Displayed on the right-hand side of the table, some mentioned candidates' clothes or fashion choices. A *Charlotte Observer* article on October 27 said that North Carolina Democrat Alma Adams was "known for her hundreds of colorful hats." The *San Francisco Chronicle* reported that *Washingtonian* magazine's survey of congressional staffers identified Nancy Pelosi as the "Most Partisan" member of Congress, as well as the "Best Dressed," noting that her "power-suit success lies in her gumball-inspired necklaces" and her "fondness for neutral palettes and prints." An October 28 dispatch in the *Buffalo News* described Republican Kathy Weppner laying her "two immaculately manicured hands, with 10 long hot-pink fingernails" across a pile of documents. (Balance being the grail of journalism, the story also described her opponent, Democratic Congressman Brian Higgins, giving an outdoor speech with "his brownish hair flying every which way in the breeze.")

But other references to women's appearance had nothing to do with fashion, attractiveness, or the kind of coverage assumed to trivialize or harm female candidates. In fact, three of the seventeen appearance mentions – 18 percent – referred to Illinois Democrat Tammy Duckworth, who lost both legs and sustained other injuries during the war in Iraq. While discussions of Duckworth's combat wounds clearly drew attention to her appearance, they are hardly evidence of sexist or inappropriate coverage. If we remove them from consideration, that leaves us with a mere fourteen mentions of female candidates' appearance in hundreds of campaign stories. Evidently, few things are less newsworthy in U.S. House campaigns than what candidates wear or how they look.[18]

---

[18] Visual images can also be important to voters' assessments (e.g., Todorov *et al.* 2005), and news organizations do occasionally publish photographs of candidates alongside a story. But much of what voters learn about congressional candidates' appearance comes from the way reporters describe them (see Hayes, Lawless, and Baitinger 2014).

To round out our assessment of coverage of gender, toward the bottom of Figure 4.1 we show that there is no difference between women and men in the "Other gender" mentions category (which includes explicit references to the sex of a candidate). There is also little coverage of the "War on Women" or references to female voters. In fact, just four candidates received any reference to the "War on Women" in their coverage, and just fifteen received coverage that referred to their standing with female voters.

Coverage of traits and issues

Of course, even if news stories about U.S. House races contain few references to candidate gender, that does not rule out the possibility that coverage of male and female candidates could differ in other ways. As we discussed in Chapter 2, one consistent finding in the literature is that women are more likely to be described as representative of "feminine" traits like empathy and integrity, while men are more likely to be described in terms of "masculine" traits like competence and leadership. Because competence and leadership are highly valued in politicians, this kind of coverage could create distinct challenges for female candidates. In addition, some work has found that women receive more trait coverage and less issue coverage than men, the implication being that this makes it harder for female candidates to be seen as effective policymakers.

Our analysis of news coverage in 2010 and 2014 uncovers nothing of the sort. The top of Figure 4.2 presents the average number of trait mentions for female (dark bars) and male (light bars) candidates in both election cycles. Just as with gender mentions, the figure represents the average number of times traits were mentioned in the thirty days of coverage leading up to the election. We find relatively little coverage of candidates' personal attributes and, most importantly, that the volume of trait coverage does not differ for men and women. In 2010, men received on average 2.7 trait mentions in the last month of coverage in their local newspaper. For women, the figure was 2.4. In 2014, men received 2.3 trait mentions compared to female candidates' 2.2. Neither of these gender differences is statistically significant. The likelihood of a candidate receiving any trait coverage also does not differ significantly by sex. In 2010, 56 percent of women and 55 percent of men saw at least one mention of their personal traits. In 2014, the numbers were 54 percent for women and 48 percent for men.

The rest of the figure breaks down the overall trait mentions into their component parts. First, we home in on positive references to the candidates' competence, leadership, empathy, and integrity. If candidates are covered in terms that reflect gender stereotypes, we would expect men to receive more positive references to competence and leadership than women. Women, on the other hand, should receive more favorable coverage of their empathy and integrity. But they don't. In both years, competence and leadership receive the most attention, but men were not more likely than women to receive coverage of

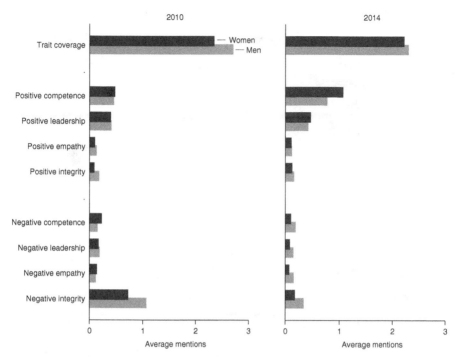

FIGURE 4.2. Trait mentions in local newspaper campaign coverage, by candidate sex. *Note*: Bars represent the average number of mentions in local newspaper coverage devoted to each category during the last thirty days of the campaigns. In 2010, women, N = 124; men, N = 663. In 2014, women, N = 152; men, N = 611. The difference between men and women is significant (p < 0.05) for positive competence in 2014.

these attributes. In fact, the only statistically significant gender difference in the entire graph emerges on the positive competence dimension in 2014, where women received more attention than men did (1.07 mentions for women vs. 0.77 mentions for men; p < 0.05). The gap is not substantively meaningful, but it is notable that the only measurable difference we report runs contrary to what the conventional wisdom would predict. When we consider in the bottom part of the figure negative references to the candidates' traits – for instance, mentions that suggest a candidate's lack of integrity – we find no statistically significant gender differences.

The story is much the same when we consider coverage of candidates' issue positions. Eighty-seven percent of female candidates and 82 percent of male candidates in 2010 received some issue coverage. In 2014, 88 percent of women and 83 percent of men did. Neither difference is statistically significant. And just as with candidate traits, women and men received statistically indistinguishable amounts of issue coverage. In the top row of Figure 4.3, we present the average number of issue references male and female candidates saw in their newspaper

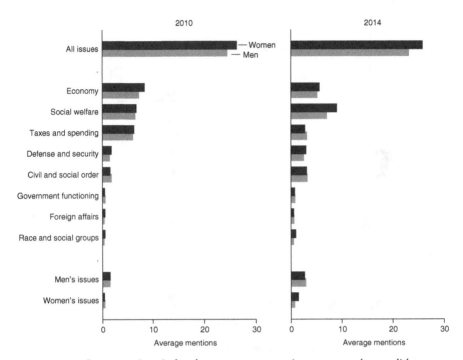

FIGURE 4.3. Issue mentions in local newspaper campaign coverage, by candidate sex.
Note: Bars represent the average number of mentions in local newspaper coverage devoted to each category during the last thirty days of the campaigns. In 2010, women, N = 124; men, N = 663. In 2014, women, N = 152; men, N = 611. The difference between men and women is significant (p < 0.05) for social welfare and "women's" issues in 2014.

coverage. In 2010, women received 26.3 issue mentions, compared to 24.5 for men. In 2014, local papers published 25.9 issue mentions on average about women, and 23.2 about men.

As we have noted, however, previous research suggests that even if the volume of coverage is the same, there may be differences in the particular issues associated with candidates. Women may get more attention in the context of debates over reproductive rights, gender equity, and policies related to families and children. At the same time, they may receive less coverage on crime, defense, or economic issues than men. To the extent that coverage reflects gender stereotypes by pigeonholing women into particular policy areas, it could make it more difficult for them to convince voters that they can handle a wide range of issues.

But Figure 4.3 reveals no evidence of such a dynamic. In 2010, the issue profiles for male and female candidates were almost identical. The economy, social welfare, and taxes and spending topped the list for both men and women. The remaining issue areas received just a smattering of attention. Most importantly, we find no significant gender differences in the number of issue mentions within any issue category. The same is true when we consider our categorization of "men's" and "women's" issues at the bottom of the graph. In 2014, issue coverage followed a similar pattern. Both male and female candidates received the most coverage on the same top issues – social welfare and the economy. Unlike in 2010, however, social welfare coverage was more common for women (9.1 mentions) than men (7.1 mentions). Partly as a consequence, women received more attention than men on "women's" issues as well (1.5 mentions for women versus 0.74 for men). Both of these gender differences are statistically significant (p < 0.05).

This result suggests that there may be circumstances under which journalists devote more attention to women's issues when there is a female candidate in a race – a point we return to later in the chapter. But this additional coverage of women's issues for female candidates does not come at the expense of coverage of other topics. For instance, the amount of attention journalists gave to women on the economy and defense and security in 2014 was no less than the attention they gave to male candidates. The media are not diminishing female candidates' ability to get their policy messages – on a wide range of issues – out to voters.[19]

WHY DOESN'T COVERAGE DIFFER FOR WOMEN AND MEN?

The data make two things clear: women and men receive virtually identical coverage of their campaigns, and only the tiniest fraction of that coverage calls attention to the sex of the candidate. Of course, demonstrating that candidate sex rarely influences news coverage is one thing. Understanding why men and women get similar coverage is another. Our interviews with local newspaper reporters suggest that two major factors play a role in equalizing coverage for men and women. Journalistic norms that encourage relatively faithful reporting of candidates' messages, coupled with electoral conditions that draw reporters' attention, crowd out candidate sex as a storyline in most campaign coverage.

Reporting it straight from the horse's mouth

Perhaps the best explanation for why there are few differences in media coverage of male and female candidates is that they run very similar campaigns. As we showed in Chapter 3, the issues men and women talk about and the traits they emphasize are virtually identical. And because much of what journalists do in congressional elections is report what the candidates say on the

---

[19] It is possible that even if the issues men and women are associated with are largely the same, they could be described in different ideological terms consistent with gender stereotyping. As part of our 2014 content analysis, we examined whether the candidate was described as liberal, conservative, or moderate. We restricted the coding to terms that clearly indicate placement on the left–right continuum. This includes words like left-wing, moderate, and far-right, but not references to a candidate simply making difficulties for his or her party, being unorthodox, a maverick, and so forth. We found no gender differences.

campaign trail, media outlets often reflect those messages, resulting in similar news coverage for men and women.

This dynamic occurs not because journalists see it as their jobs to parrot the candidates' talking points. Instead, reporting the candidates' messages allows journalists to adhere to three prominent norms that guide the practice of contemporary journalism. First, it helps the media put candidates on the record. Not only does this give voters the opportunity to hear it "straight from the horse's mouth," but it also allows journalists to hold candidates accountable if they later deviate from statements they made on the stump. Second, by reporting what candidates say, journalists can demonstrate their objectivity, or fairness and balance in political reporting. For both of these reasons, covering the positions that candidates take is "what you're supposed to do," said Kelley Allen, who covered politics for several years at the *Star-Democrat* on Maryland's Eastern Shore.

Journalists do occasionally try to force candidates to talk about issues they'd prefer to avoid. But reporters told us that candidates, in many cases, set the campaign agenda. "The bulk of my coverage is reactive," remarked Timm Herdt, a reporter at the *Ventura County Star*. "I use my role as a reporter to analyze and assess what the campaigns throw out there." Jack Torry, who has covered Ohio House races for the *Columbus Dispatch* for more than twenty-five years, said much the same thing:

I decide what to write about based usually on what the candidates are talking about . . . Don't get me wrong. Sometimes, there are things we want to cover that the candidates just don't care about. Like the deficit, or foreign policy. In those cases, we do ask those questions and write those stories . . . But we rely on the candidates to set a lot of the agenda.

Several other journalists described their roles as "adding context, not deciding what is news," "not spending much time setting the agenda," and serving as "an arbiter of the facts" the campaigns lay claim to in their ads and other communications. One implication, then, is that what candidates say should correspond strongly to the content of the media coverage they receive.

The third norm that encourages journalists to be responsive to candidates' messages is the desire to build storylines around conflict, the sine qua non of political reporting. This encourages reporters to highlight differences between candidates, often reflecting the strategies of the campaigns themselves. "In any campaign, it's always about figuring out what issues create substantive divides between the candidates," explained Curtis Wilkerson, 2010 campaign manager for West Virginia Republican Michael Oliverio. "You don't want to compare two brands of cornflakes." In practice, this means that campaigns consistently appeal to the media to draw distinctions between one candidate and the other. "There are lots of attacks, and lots of campaign proxies making attacks," noted James Nash, who reported on House races for the *Columbus Dispatch* from 2005 to 2011. "It never lets up," said Jim Morrill, who has been at the *Charlotte*

Observer since 1981. "They call us with preemptive attacks, with post-emptive attacks, with emails. We just get bombarded." Campaigns do this because they know that controversy is catnip to most political reporters. "When I'm covering a race, I care about the issues the candidates emphasize and how they contrast themselves with their opponent," said Ed Fitzpatrick, now a political columnist at the *Providence Journal*. "Any conflict or disagreement is great; it makes it that much easier to write the story."

Conflict can manifest itself in many ways. In the 2014 race in Colorado's 6th District, for example, Mike Coffman questioned Andrew Romanoff's character. For *Denver Post* reporter Jon Murray, that meant writing about whether Romanoff "acted less than honorably" in his previous campaigns. Meanwhile, *Omaha World Herald* reporter Henry Cordes concentrated on the barbs between Democrat Brad Ashford and Republican incumbent Lee Terry in Nebraska's 2nd District. Cordes avoided what he considered "silly" allegations: "I mean, really? You're having a press conference to blame the Republicans for Ebola?" he laughed. But others deserved ink. Take, for instance, Ashford's attempts to cast Terry as out of touch. When then-Congressman Terry was asked if he would continue to collect a paycheck while thousands of government workers were furloughed during the 2013 government shutdown, he replied, "Dang straight ... I've got a nice house and a kid in college."[20] Ashford seized on these comments. And Cordes covered the dust-up, as well as Terry's counter-charges. "When Ashford was in the state legislature, he chaired the Judiciary Committee," Cordes told us. "Terry painted him as responsible for every crime that was committed in the state, including a pretty sensational murder the previous year." Ashford and Terry's campaign trail allegations made it into the paper.

In most cases, it is partisan conflict that shapes journalists' stories, largely because partisan conflict is the prevailing theme of most campaigns. For *Times Herald Record* reporter Chris McKenna, his coverage of the 2010 race in New York's 19th District was "dominated by the candidates' positions on three White House actions: the stimulus, Obamacare, and Dodd–Frank ... I didn't have to do a lot of soul searching to figure out what would be relevant." Gilbert Garcia focused his *San Antonio Express-News* coverage of Republican Francisco Canseco and Democrat Ciro Rodriguez on partisan differences, "which were pretty clear that year. Canseco had adopted the Tea Party world view, so he was pretty negative about the Obama agenda." Others mentioned "hammering away at the differences" in candidates' immigration positions, views on privatizing Social Security, or their attitudes to the Department of Education. "The most important part of any campaign story is what sets the candidates

---

[20] Joseph Morton, "Lee Terry Says He 'Cannot Handle' Giving Up Own Paycheck During Government Shutdown," *Omaha.com*, October 4, 2013. Accessed at: www.omaha.com/news/lee-terry-says-he-cannot-handle-giving-up-own-paycheck/article_06c17b2b-84ac-54f9-ad38-248b4ffb d423.html (July 30, 2015).

apart from each other," said one former reporter for a New England newspaper. "Where's the conflict? Nowadays, it almost always all comes down to party."[21]

These accounts suggest that our data should show significant (though not complete) convergence between candidate messages and the media coverage candidates receive. And although some previous work has found that news coverage less accurately reflects female candidates' agendas than men's (Kahn 1993), our interviews suggest no reason that this should be the case in contemporary congressional elections.

We test this expectation by comparing candidates' issue emphases in their campaign communications to the news coverage they received.[22] To do so, we appropriate a measure created by Lee Sigelman and Emmett Buell (2004) and use it to gauge the similarity between a candidate's issue agenda and the issue content of his or her coverage (Hayes 2010; Ridout and Mellen 2007). This measure of "agenda convergence" has two components. First, we use the issue profiles we created for each candidate in Chapter 3. Those profiles tell us what share of a candidate's issue emphases was devoted to each of our eight issue categories.[23] Second, we rely on our 2010 and 2014 news content analysis to determine for each candidate the percentage of coverage devoted to the same eight issue categories. Our measure simply compares these two distributions and creates a "convergence score" that indicates how similar a candidate's agenda was to the news coverage he or she received. Convergence scores can range from 0 to 1, with higher values indicating more overlap between candidate and media agendas.[24]

[21] Even when the candidates hold similar policy positions, partisan conflict can still dominate the coverage. A reporter who covered a close race in 2010 saw few differences between the candidates' actual issue stands. But because the GOP candidate made the race "a referendum on Obama," the journalist said that "partisanship made its way into how we wrote about the campaigns."

[22] Because we do not have data on candidates' trait emphases in the 2010 ad data, we focus on issue agendas, which we have measures of for both 2010 and 2014.

[23] In 2010, we used campaign ads to create the issue profiles. In 2014, we relied on candidate tweets (see Chapter 3).

[24] Calculating a convergence score involves a simple formula. Imagine a campaign in which only three issues received attention: taxes and spending, social welfare, and foreign affairs. Suppose that Candidate A devoted 40 percent of her campaign to taxes and spending, 30 percent to social welfare, and the remaining 30 percent to foreign affairs. News coverage of Candidate A's campaign, meanwhile, devoted 60 percent to taxes and spending, 10 percent to social welfare, and 30 percent to foreign affairs. To obtain our convergence score, we first sum up the absolute values of the differences between the percentage Candidate A and the media devoted to each issue area, like this:

$$|0.40 - 0.60| + |0.30 - 0.10| + |0.30 - 0.30| = 0.40.$$

The sum will range from 0 to 2, with higher scores representing more dissimilarity. Then, we divide by 2 (to take into account the double counting that occurs in the above equation), and subtract from 1 (to convert the score from a measure of dissimilarity into one of similarity). The resulting convergence score will always be on a scale from 0 (complete divergence) to 1 (complete convergence). In our example, it is 0.80, which indicates an 80 percent overlap between Candidate A's issue agenda and the media's coverage of her campaign.

TABLE 4.2. *Candidate–media agenda convergence*

	2010		2014	
	Female candidates	Male candidates	Female candidates	Male candidates
Democrats	0.62	0.57	0.44	0.47
	(0.20)	(0.19)	(0.25)	(0.22)
Republicans	0.64	0.65	0.47	0.45
	(0.20)	(0.23)	(0.27)	(0.24)

Notes: Cell entries are average convergence scores. Standard deviations in parentheses. Convergence ranges from 0 to 1, with higher scores indicating more similarity between the issues the candidates mentioned in their campaign ads (2010) or tweets (2014) and attention those issues received in the news coverage the candidates received. None of the gender differences is statistically significant.

In 2010, we calculated convergence scores for the 328 candidates who ran issue ads and who received at least some issue coverage. And in 2014, we did the same for the 459 candidates who tweeted about issues and who also received issue coverage. We then averaged together the convergence scores for men and women, broken down by election cycle and political party. Table 4.2 presents the results.

The top left-hand portion of the table shows that the convergence score for female Democrats in 2010 was 0.62. In other words, there was on average a 62 percent overlap between candidates' issue agendas and the media's issue coverage. This was statistically indistinguishable from the convergence score of 0.57 for male Democrats. The bottom row shows the same data, and the same finding, for female and male Republicans. With convergence scores of 0.64 and 0.65, there is no gender difference in how responsive media coverage was to candidates' agendas. We find the same pattern in 2014 (on the right-hand side of the table). While news coverage was less responsive to candidate agendas than in 2010, convergence did not vary by candidate sex.[25] These results confirm what our discussions with news reporters suggested: much of what candidates emphasize on the campaign trail makes its way into the news, and that dynamic does not vary by candidate sex. For reasons closely tied to journalistic norms, the news gives candidates a forum to tell the voters what their ideas (and differences) are, regardless of whether they are women or men, Democrats or Republicans. And because male and female candidates tend to run campaigns that look very similar, the media coverage they receive ends up looking very similar as well.

[25] The lower level of convergence in 2014 could stem from the fact that news outlets are less responsive to candidates' tweets than they are to ads. Given that we do not have ad data from 2014, we can't compare the two. The difference across the years, however, has no bearing on the finding that candidate sex plays no role.

The prevailing newsworthiness of competitiveness and incumbency

Journalists' responsiveness to campaign agendas helps explain why male and female candidates' coverage does not differ. But it is not the only reason. Journalists also told us that candidate sex, in most circumstances, is simply not very newsworthy, so it rarely shapes the way reporters frame their coverage. In part because female candidates are no longer viewed as a novelty in congressional elections, their presence does little to alter the way that journalists approach a campaign. This came through as soon as we asked about how gender might be relevant for coverage – a question that didn't get us very far.

"Gender's just not an issue at all," said Chris McKenna, the *Times Herald Record* reporter who has covered New York politics since the mid 1990s. In 2010, he reported on the state's 19th District race, where Republican Nan Hayworth defeated Democratic incumbent John Hall. "The fact that there was a Republican woman challenging a male incumbent never entered into the equation," he said. Other reporters' reactions were much the same: the sex of the candidate just doesn't make its way into the stories they write. Ronald Hansen, who covered the 2010 Arizona 1st District race in which Republican Paul Gosar defeated Democrat Ann Kirkpatrick, told us that Kirkpatrick's presence was no different than any other incumbent's. "We had a female figure, but there wasn't gender-specific coverage, because there just wasn't any place where it was obviously important to the race," Hansen said. One veteran reporter in the Midwest who has covered politics since the early 1990s remarked, "I don't think I've ever thought about [candidate] sex. I try to anticipate the issues that we know the voters will care about and face on Election Day and then we use those topics as the initial way to talk to candidates about where they stand . . . It's hard to imagine when or how being a man or a woman would play into that." Other reporters told us unequivocally that "gender doesn't matter here" or that from the perspective of newsworthiness, "the idea of a woman running for office is just a 'nothing.'"

We realize that reporters' responses to our questions could be subject to social desirability or professional pressures, leading them to minimize the role that gender plays in shaping the news. Moreover, gender differences could work their way into coverage unconsciously. But these statements about the lack of newsworthiness of candidate sex become more credible when we consider other features of the electoral environment – especially competitiveness and incumbency – that may draw journalists' attention. The importance that reporters ascribed to these factors suggests that candidate sex must compete with other considerations that often play a stronger role in shaping both the volume and substance of campaign coverage.

When it comes to competitiveness, Jon Murray's experiences covering the House race in CO-6 is a case in point. Murray ordinarily covers City Hall, but in 2014, he was brought in to supplement the *Denver Post*'s coverage of the

Coffman–Romanoff contest because it was expected to be a nail-biter. "We knew going in that the race was going to get tons of coverage," Murray said. "It was one of the most competitive nationally and the district was really split. Also, Coffman had eked out a really tight win in 2012, so we were going to cover the hell out of it this time." The uncertainty and drama of a close race, combined with aggressive campaigning by two well-funded candidates, would give reporters numerous attractive storylines. The race was "an embarrassment of riches as far as political reporting goes," Murray said. "Competitiveness determines everything about volume, and this was as competitive as it gets going in."

The *Arizona Daily Star* made a similar decision about its coverage of Republican Martha McSally's bid to unseat Democrat Ron Barber. Reporter Joe Ferguson said that they knew as early as January 2014 – more than ten months before Election Day – that the contest was "shaping up to be the most competitive race in the state." Both candidates announced early and had campaign teams in place. From the outset, Ferguson was able to "work with the staff of each campaign to provide as much and as thorough coverage" as he could. Eventually, the competitiveness of the race became a story in itself: "The sheer volume of money spent, the ad buys ... We couldn't pass up the opportunity to talk about how this contest was one of the most important and competitive in the country."

In fact, virtually every reporter offered the same answer when we asked what matters most for determining how much coverage a race receives:

The volume of coverage a race gets is driven by how competitive it is ... We're not going to cover unqualified candidates who will lose in landslides. (Henry Cordes, *Omaha World Herald*)

Is it a really competitive race, or is it a blow out? I'm going to spend more time on the campaign trail if I don't know going in that this is going to be a 65/35 deal. (Scott Powers, *Orlando Sentinel*)

Most obviously, is it competitive? Is there real potential for either candidate to win? Usually, the answer is no, and that means that I just don't spend that much time on it. (Timm Herdt, *Ventura County Star*)

What drives the amount of coverage more than anything else is how competitive of a race it is. (Maury Thompson, *Post-Star*)

In addition to competitiveness as a driver of coverage, our interviews also suggested that sitting members of Congress may get more attention than non-incumbents. In part, this is because current representatives often generate news more easily than challengers do. One reason is that incumbents, by virtue of having been in office for some time, have preexisting relationships with reporters, which works to their benefit during the campaign season. Max Cummings, the 2010 campaign manager for Democrat Christopher Carney, for example, said the campaign had an easy time getting attention in local papers because of their long-standing ties with small-town journalists: "As a two-term incumbent, we could take advantage of pre-built relationships," Cummings said. "And then having an official office helped as well." Cesar Blanco's experience managing Ciro Rodriguez's campaign in TX-23 was similar: "As an incumbent, he had no trouble getting covered."

Incumbents make news for reasons beyond the fact that they are better known to local reporters. Journalists also frequently frame House elections as contests between the status quo (the incumbent) and an alternative vision for the district (the challenger). In doing so, the incumbent's record becomes the pivot point for a campaign. "Campaigns are often a referendum on the incumbent, and challengers talk about the record of the incumbent," *Salt Lake Tribune* reporter Matt Canham told us. "If the challenger is talking about the record, and the incumbent is defending the record, that is the issue" that drives the coverage.

Moreover, with the overwhelming majority of incumbents seeking and winning reelection, credible attempts to unseat them, or national tides that work against them, are newsworthy.[26] According to a reporter who covered a 2010 race in the South, the contest was "particularly interesting" because in 2008 the sitting incumbent had unseated the previous incumbent. "There were lots of questions as to whether he'd be able to hold the seat." David Scharfenberg, now at the *Boston Globe*, recounted a similar storyline for an article he wrote in 2006 about Sue Kelly's House race in upstate New York. "She was already in office, but was a Republican," he said. "It was a Democratic year, so the question was whether she'd be able to hold onto her seat. Could she withstand the wave?"

The upshot is that because competitiveness and incumbency strongly influence how reporters approach campaigns and the candidates running, there are simply fewer opportunities for candidate sex to do the same. We put this expectation to the test with a series of regression models in which we examine the relative power of candidate sex, competitiveness, and incumbency to explain variation in the coverage that candidates received in 2010 and 2014. We explore the extent to which each of these factors explains the number of stories a candidate received, as well as the number of gender, trait, and issue mentions in a candidate's coverage. In doing so, we can systematically test the accounts that emerged from our interviews.[27]

---

[26] In 2010, only thirty-seven members of the U.S. House of Representatives chose not to seek reelection (sixteen of whom stepped down to pursue a bid for higher office); and only fifty-eight incumbents were defeated (four in primaries and fifty-four in general elections). In other words, 85 percent of incumbents seeking reelection won their races. The 2014 cycle was similar; just forty-one incumbents chose not to seek reelection (seventeen sought another office). Of those who did run, five lost their primaries and thirteen were defeated in the general election. Overall, then, 95 percent of incumbents who wanted to keep their jobs were sent back to the House of Representatives.

[27] Table A4.1 presents the full regression models, which also control for candidate party and the presence of a female opponent. In the models for gender, trait, and issue mentions, the dependent

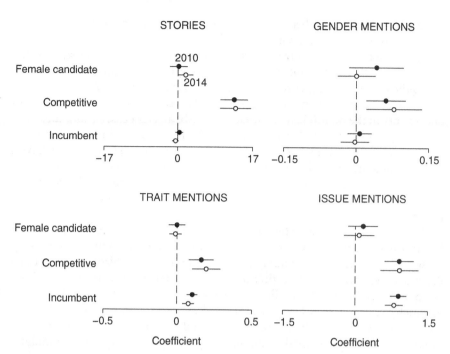

FIGURE 4.4. The effects of sex, competitiveness, and incumbency on news coverage. *Notes*: Dots represent unstandardized OLS regression coefficients, with 95 percent confidence intervals. See Table A4.1 for the full regression equations.

The upper left-hand panel of Figure 4.4 presents the results for the number of stories. Consider first the "Female candidate" row. Here, we present the regression coefficient for a variable indicating whether the candidate was a woman. The dot labeled "2010" represents the effect that being a woman had on the number of stories written. The coefficient is effectively zero, and the confidence interval – which measures statistical uncertainty – overlaps the zero line. That indicates that candidate sex had no effect on the volume of coverage in a race. The dot labeled "2014" presents the result from that election cycle. As we found in the descriptive data, races involving a female candidate received more coverage in 2014 than races involving two men. But a key take-away from the entire graph is that in no other case is the coefficient for female candidate statistically different than zero; the confidence interval always crosses the zero line. Confirming the descriptive results, the regressions reveal that women

variables are scaled; that is, the number of mentions is divided by the total number of stories about the race. This allows us to control for the total volume of coverage and ensures that our models are not simply picking up the effect of more coverage overall. When we run the analysis using Poisson count models, the results are the same.

received the same number of gender mentions, trait mentions, and issue mentions as did male candidates.

At the same time, the figure suggests that one reason sex doesn't matter is that competitiveness and incumbency play a strong role in shaping coverage. To assess the effects of competitiveness, we relied on the *Cook Political Report* to divide races into two categories: safe seats and those with at least some degree of uncertainty in the month before the election.[28] In all eight cases – four measures of coverage in 2010 and four in 2014 – candidates in competitive races received more attention. The way to get more gendered coverage in a race is not to have a female candidate; it's to have a close contest, which generates more coverage of all sorts. And while incumbency didn't affect the overall volume of coverage or gender mentions, it did increase the amount of trait coverage and issue mentions in both 2010 and 2014.

We also examined the extent to which candidate sex, competitiveness, and incumbency affect the coverage of specific traits and issues – the categories we presented in Figures 4.2 and 4.3. This amounted to thirty-six additional dependent variables (eight trait categories and ten issue categories in both 2010 and 2014). In those models, we found only four instances, all in 2014, in which the variable for female candidate was statistically significant. Women received more coverage in the Race and social groups issue category and less negative competence, empathy, and integrity coverage. By contrast, candidates in competitive races received more trait or issue coverage in twenty-one models, and incumbency was significant in twenty-six models. These results provide further evidence that competitiveness and incumbency are far more important than candidate sex in structuring coverage. (Tables A4.2 – A4.5 in the Appendix present these thirty-six regression equations.)[29]

---

[28] We consider seats that Cook rated as "toss-ups," "leaning" toward one party, and "likely" to go for one party as competitive. The results are virtually identical when we use Cook's full scale. But by creating a dummy variable for competitiveness, we can more easily compare the magnitude of the effects on all three of our key independent variables, since candidate sex and incumbency are also dichotomous.

[29] We conducted a series of supplemental analyses to consider alternative explanations for our findings:

(1) We examined whether candidate sex has different effects depending on the competitiveness of a race. To do so, we ran our regression models two ways. In one set of models, we interacted competitiveness with candidate sex. The interaction term was never significant. In a second set, we separated the data into competitive and non-competitive contests, and then ran the same models we presented in Figure 4.4 (absent the variable for competitiveness, of course). In neither competitive nor uncompetitive races did candidate sex influence coverage. In other words, we found no gender effects, regardless of a race's competitive status.

(2) We considered whether candidate quality affects our results. After all, a question that naturally arises is whether the similarities in coverage for men and women might be due to the fact that women have been found to be higher-quality candidates (Anzia and Berry 2011; Fulton 2012; Pearson and McGhee 2013). If that is true, then our findings might indicate gender bias, given that we would expect higher-quality candidates to get more favorable coverage. But we suspect that journalists' tendency to seek balance in their coverage works

WHEN CAN GENDER BE RELEVANT FOR CAMPAIGN NEWS COVERAGE?

All of this suggests that candidate sex is not routinely relevant for the coverage of U.S. House races. But that doesn't mean it can't be important. In fact, the journalists we interviewed mentioned two circumstances under which they might draw attention to the presence of a woman in the race: (1) in the increasingly rare case that a female candidate is novel, or (2) when gender features heavily in a candidate's own messaging.

Because the unusual is more newsworthy than the run of the mill, candidate sex can make its way into news coverage when a woman runs for office in a district that is not accustomed to seeing female candidates. Several reporters mentioned that when a female candidate is on the ballot in a district that has never sent a woman to Congress, the prospect of a historical "first" can prompt some coverage. "Generally, any kind of first gets coverage, either because it's

against such a pattern, and the empirical evidence supports this perspective. Using Gary Jacobson's data from 2010, we found that 65 percent of women and 60 percent of men were incumbents or candidates who previously held elective office (i.e., quality candidates). The quality advantage for women, however, was only on the Democratic side (74 percent of women compared to 66 percent of men). On the Republican side, men were more likely to be quality candidates (55 percent of men compared to 47 percent of women). The fact that our results do not differ by partisanship (see, for example, Table 4.2) is one piece of evidence that candidate quality cannot explain the similar media coverage for male and female candidates. In addition, when we included candidate quality in the models we report in Figure 4.4, we found no consistent evidence that candidate quality related to news coverage. Candidate quality was significant only in the model for the number of stories – on average, quality candidates got more coverage – but it did not play a role in the gender, trait, or issue models (including the specific trait and issue models we report in the Appendix). Finally, when we included an interaction term between candidate sex and candidate quality, the effect was not significant. In sum, candidate quality does not appear to provide an alternative explanation for the equivalent news coverage we find.

(3) Because women run in more urban districts, they are also more likely to run in districts with larger-circulation newspapers. This is relevant for our purposes because as a newspaper's circulation grows – increasing the likelihood of having readers in multiple congressional districts – the amount of campaign coverage of any one district served by that paper falls (Gershon 2012; Goldenberg and Traugott 1984; Hayes and Lawless 2015a; Tidmarch and Karp 1983; Vinson 2003). Indeed, when we included a control for newspaper circulation in our 2010 and 2014 models, we found a negative, statistically significant coefficient. Even with the circulation control, however, the findings from Figure 4.4 were the same.

(4) We examined whether coverage of male and female candidates in 2014 differed depending on the sex of a story's author or authors. We found that when a byline featured at least one female reporter, stories about female Democrats were marginally more likely to include a gender mention than when the story was written by a man or men only. We also found the same pattern for "women's" issues coverage of female Republican candidates. The differences, however, were slight and thus inconsequential for the overall patterns we report here. Nonetheless, the relationship between coverage of female candidates and reporter sex may be a useful area for future research.

newsworthy in itself or because the candidates do everything they can to make it newsworthy," explained Kathie Obradovich, who has covered politics for the *Des Moines Register* for twenty-two years as both a reporter and a columnist. She noted, for example, that the 2014 election cycle in Iowa included "an element of gender politics that we don't usually see." Because the state had a chance to send its first woman to the U.S. Senate (Republican Joni Ernst) and the House of Representatives (Democrat Staci Appel), there was "a layer of reporting about candidates being women that is usually absent from the coverage." Kelley Allen, who covered politics for the *Star Democrat* in Maryland in 2010, made the same point. "Anything that's a little bit unusual is newsworthy," she said. "So if you have a seat that's been held by men forever, and you have a woman running, you're going to give that attention."

In the current era, however, few "firsts" remain. A reporter who covered campaigns and elections for a paper in the South for seventeen years referred to this changing dynamic as she recalled one of her first assignments as a journalist:

When I was in college, I interned at [a magazine] ... and worked on a guide to women candidates in 1993. The whole summer, I interviewed female candidates around the country ... The kind of coverage female candidates were getting was still some of that "the first woman in such and such county." But I think we've moved past that, it's less of a factor because it's so common to have female candidates running.

Ventura County Star reporter Timm Herdt agreed. "I wouldn't be surprised if candidate gender doesn't really get covered anywhere," he said. But in the 26th District in California in 2014, the fact that the House race involved a female candidate – Julia Brownley – was particularly unremarkable:

It certainly isn't something newsworthy in this market. We have two women in the U. S. Senate. We have a bunch of women in Congress and in state government. And there were multiple women running for office this time around. Most of our hotly contested races have women ... Thinking back, 20 or 30 years ago, I used to write these "first" stories. The first woman this or that. No more. There are no more firsts around here.

Indeed, in the 2010 and 2014 midterms combined, only seventeen congressional districts saw a female candidate for the first time in at least twenty years. So even though reporters might be inclined to focus on candidate sex when it's unusual for a woman to appear on the ballot, there are few opportunities for such a storyline.

Beyond occasional cases of novelty, the very norm that encourages journalists to reflect what the campaigns are communicating can lead to stories that highlight sex and gender. Sometimes, a campaign will determine that it is strategically advantageous to call attention to the fact that a woman is in the race. And when they do, reporters may follow.

Consider Republican Martha McSally's 2014 campaign in Arizona's 2nd District. Early in the race, McSally, according to *Arizona Daily Star* reporter Joe Ferguson, "played up her accomplishments as a woman." The bio page of her campaign website read, "She is the first female fighter pilot to fly in combat, and first to command a fighter squadron in combat in United States history."[30] A press release announcing that McSally would keynote the Hawaii Republican Party's annual Lincoln Day Dinner noted that "since Martha flew her first combat mission over Iraq in 1995, she has been a woman of many 'firsts' – breaking gender barriers for women time after time."[31] And in an interview with *Self* magazine, McSally talked about how serving as the first female pilot to fly in combat (as well as completing the Hawaii Ironman, racing "too many marathons to list," and climbing Mt. Kilimanjaro) prepared her for the challenge of running for Congress.[32] Ferguson said that because McSally "decided to make being a woman something she wanted to talk about," he covered it. "Just to be clear, though, she pointed it out," he said. "It was her. She decided it was something she wanted in the news ... We never made that decision on our own."

A campaign might also decide to inject gender into its communications not to highlight the candidate's bio or credentials, but to draw media attention to the race. Virginia's 1st District in 2010, where Democrat Krystal Ball challenged Republican incumbent Rob Wittman, is a good example. A few weeks before the election, a right-wing blog uncovered and posted photos of Ball dressed as a "sexy Santa" and posing with sex toys at a costume party years earlier. The salacious nature of the story provided a platform for Ball to allege sexism on the part of her opponent and garner national attention while doing so. "Of course I am embarrassed by these photos; that was the whole point of these political operatives when they put them up," she said in a statement picked up by *Time* magazine. "But more than just embarrassed, I'm angry! It's sexist and it's wrong, regardless of political party."[33] According to a person connected to the Wittman campaign, "Every time it would die down, she'd put it right back in the media's attention ... She got a ton of national attention and raised lots of money because of what happened. She very proactively made sexism an issue." And the local media felt they had no choice but to cover it. "The race wound up

---

[30] "About Martha," McSallyforCongress.com. Accessed at: https://mcsallyforcongress.com/about-martha/ (August 1, 2015).
[31] "Colonel Martha McSally to Headline Lincoln Day Dinner," Hawaii Republican Party, January 26, 2014. Accessed at: www.hawaiifreepress.com/ArticlesMain/tabid/56/ID/11734/Col-Martha-McSally-to-Headline-Lincoln-Day-Dinner.aspx (August 1, 2015).
[32] "Running... And Running for Office," *Self*, June 25, 2014. Accessed at: www.self.com/work/2014/06/political-candidates/ (August 1, 2015).
[33] Nate Jones, "Candidate's Sexy Santa Photos Leaked: Sexism in Action?" *Time*, October 7, 2010. Accessed at: http://newsfeed.time.com/2010/10/07/candidates-sexy-santa-photos-leaked-sexism-in-action/ (August 1, 2015).

getting national attention, way more than it deserved. It wasn't a competitive race. She wasn't going to win," said one of the many local reporters familiar with it. When we asked why she wrote a story about it, she replied, "I had to – it was national news."

Then there was Republican Steve Southerland's "Men Only" fundraiser during his 2014 race against Democrat Gwen Graham. Invitees were encouraged to "tell the misses [sic] not to wait up" because "the after dinner whiskey and cigars will be smooth and the issues to discuss are many."[34] After national media outlets got wind of the invitation, Southerland doubled-down. He defended the event to the *Tampa Bay Times* as analogous to the lingerie parties he perceived as prevalent in women's social circles: "Has Gwen Graham ever been to a lingerie shower? Ask her. And how many men were there?"[35] Graham's campaign manager framed the comments as evidence of Southerland's "fundamental disrespect for women":

Only if Southerland disrespects women could he hold an official, Men-Only Southerland campaign fundraiser and laugh it off after the fact. Only if Southerland disrespects women could he air TV ads claiming to have voted for the Violence Against Women Act while he actually voted against it in Congress. Only if Southerland disrespects women could he make this insulting "lingerie party" comment about a woman like Gwen Graham.[36]

The incident opened the door for more coverage of sexism and "women's" issues than would otherwise have been the case.

While these three examples demonstrate that highly gendered campaign coverage can occur, it is important to underscore how unusual these cases are. As is clear from our data, attention to gender and to "women's" issues comprise just a tiny fraction of the overall media coverage candidates – male and female alike – receive. Nonetheless, if the small subset of races that do generate gendered coverage or call heightened attention to "women's" issues are more likely to include female candidates, then that is an important aspect of the media environment women who run for office must consider.

We test this proposition in two ways, yet can muster only the thinnest of evidence to support it. First, we identified in both 2010 and 2014 the ten

[34] Kate Nocera, "A Florida Congressman Had a Men-Only Fundraiser," *Buzzfeed*, September 3, 2014. Accessed at: www.buzzfeed.com/katenocera/a-florida-congressman-had-a-strange-men-only-fundraiser#.qoGEwY6E (August 3, 2015).

[35] Steve Bousquet, "In Southerland–Graham Race, the Subject Turns to Lingerie," *Tampa Bay Times*, September 12, 2014. Accessed at: www.tampabay.com/blogs/the-buzz-florida-politics/in-southerland-graham-race-the-subject-turns-to-lingerie/2197410 (August 3, 2015).

[36] Page Lavender, "Rep. Steve Southerland Wonders if his Female Opponent Has 'Ever Been to a Lingerie Shower,'" *Huffington Post*, September 12, 2014. Accessed at: www.huffingtonpost.com/2014/09/12/steve-southerland-lingerie_n_5812378.html (August 3, 2015).

TABLE 4.3. *Most gender mentions in local news coverage*

2010			
Democrats		**Republicans**	
John Tierney (MA-6)	90	Joseph Cao (LA-2)	21
Krystal Ball (VA-1)	20	Glenn Urquhart (DE-AL)	16
Travis Childers (MS-1)	15	Alan Nunnelee (MS-1)	14
Cedric Richmond (LA-2)	14	Scott DesJarlais (TN-4)	11
John Carney (DE-AL)	13	Todd Lally (KY-3)	10
John Boccieri (OH-16)	11	Mo Brooks (AL-5)	9
Stephanie Sandlin (SD-AL)	10	James Scott (GA-8)	9
Sanford Bishop (GA-2)	10	Justin Amash (MI-3)	8
Rick Larsen (WA-2)	10	Steven Palazzo (MS-4)	8
David Melville (LA-4)	8	John Koster (WA-2)	8
		Eric Cantor (VA-7)	8
2014			
Democrats		**Republicans**	
Dan Maffei (NY-24)	32	John Katko (NY-24)	31
Bill Bailey (IN-9)	21	Carlos Curbelo (FL-26)	22
Mark Harris (WI-6)	13	Scott DesJarlais (TN-4)	18
Sean Eldridge (NY-19)	11	Mike Bost (IL-12)	16
Patrick Hays (AR-2)	10	French Hill (AR-2)	14
Scott Peters (CA-52)	10	Carl Demaio (CA-52)	13
Doug Owens (UT-4)	9	Lee Terry (NE-2)	13
Edwin Edwards (LA-6)	9	Stewart Mills (MN-8)	11
Nancy Pelosi (CA-12)	9	Three candidates tied	9
Three candidates tied	8		

Notes: Each column lists the ten candidates in each election cycle who received the most gender mentions in their campaign news coverage (for Republican men in 2010, the gender mentions list includes eleven candidates, because four candidates tied with eight mentions). Entries are raw mentions, not percentages.

candidates in each political party who received the most gender mentions in their overall coverage. These include any references to a candidate's sex, family roles, appearance, appeals to female voters, and so forth. Table 4.3 displays the candidates who made the top-ten list for each cycle, along with the raw number of mentions each received. Note that these are total mentions, not percentages of overall coverage.

The most striking finding to emerge from the table is that women (in bold) are under-represented relative to their proportions as candidates in both cycles and across parties. On the Republican side, no women made the list in either year. Among Democrats, fewer women appeared than their numbers within the party's candidates would predict. Even Krystal Ball's place on the list wasn't due to reporters devoting significant coverage to gender; the majority of those mentions came from an October 14, 2010 *Free-Lance Star* piece she wrote about the photo scandal. Without the gender references from her own op-ed, Ball would not have made the top ten.

These data make it difficult to argue that a woman in the race is a prerequisite for a reporter to devote higher-than-usual attention to candidate sex or gender.[37] A reporter who covered congressional races for a decade before leaving the newsroom after the 2010 cycle offered a similar observation: "Candidates run the campaigns they're going to run. So if a candidate talked about being a woman, or being a mother, then I covered it. It's part of who they are and how they're communicating what they think is important." He added that he did "the exact same thing" when a male candidate talked about his bio that way. "If a man running for office kept saying, 'As a young father, I'm going to …' or 'As a father with young children, I know …,' then that'd get into my coverage." Indeed, John Tierney's astronomical number of gender mentions in 2010 were almost all about his wife, whose financial dealings were the subject of an ongoing scandal the Massachusetts Democrat couldn't avoid.

We conducted a similar analysis for coverage of women's issues. We rank-ordered the candidates in each party for each election cycle based on the number of references to "women's" issues they received in their overall campaign coverage (see Table 4.4). For the most part, the results are consistent with the (null) gender mentions findings. In 2010, two women made the list of Democrats, which is less than their share among Democratic candidates that year. No women appeared on the Republican top-ten list. In 2014, Democratic women occupied three slots, which is commensurate with their overall representation as Democratic candidates.[38] The data do indicate, however, that in 2014, the Republican candidates whose coverage focused most heavily on "women's" issues were disproportionately women. Whereas women constituted just 13 percent of GOP candidates in the general election, they were four of the ten who received the most "women's" issues coverage. In addition, Scott DesJarlais, who occupied a place on the list, competed against a woman (as did Marilinda Garcia and Lynn Jenkins). All told, this means that half of the ten Republican

---

[37] The men whose coverage was most likely to include mentions of sex and gender were not especially likely to run against women. On the GOP side, only one candidate – Scott DesJarlais – faced a female opponent (Lenda Sherrell in 2014). Among the male Democrats on the list, none ran against women in 2010 (although Stephanie Sandlin did), and only Doug Owens did in 2014 (Mia Love).

[38] Of the men who appeared on the 2010 lists, Democrat Joe Donnelly and Republicans David Reichart, Joseph Heck, and Peter Scontras ran against women. Given the proportions of female candidates on both sides of the aisle, the men who garnered the most "women's" issues coverage were no more likely to compete with a woman than the men who did not make the list. In 2014, only one male Democrat (Bill Foster) faced a female opponent (Darlene Senger).

TABLE 4.4. *Most "women's" issues mentions in local news coverage*

2010			
Democrats		**Republicans**	
Daniel Seals (IL-10)	11	Robert Dold (IL-10)	19
Tom White (NE-2)	11	Daniel Webster (FL-8)	12
Chellie Pingree (ME-1)	8	Joseph Cao (LA-2)	10
John Yarmuth (KY-3)	7	Todd Lally (KY-3)	10
James Oberstar (MN-8)	7	David Reichert (WA-8)	9
Kathy Dahlkemper (PA-3)	7	Glenn Urquhart (DE-AL)	7
Cedric Richmond (LA-2)	6	Joseph Heck (NV-3)	7
John Carney (DE-AL)	5	Peter Scontras (ME-1)	6
Travis Childers (MS-1)	5	Keith Fimian (VA-11)	6
Joe Donnelly (IN-2)	5	Dennis Rehberg (MT-AL)	6
Patrick Miles (MI-3)	5	Christopher Smith (NJ-4)	6
2014			
Democrats		**Republicans**	
Terri Sewell (AL-7)	13	John Katko (NY-24)	27
Brad Ashford (NE-2)	11	**Marilinda Garcia (NH-2)**	15
Aimee Belgard (NJ-3)	10	Doug Ose (CA-7)	13
Ann Kuster (NH-2)	10	Mike Coffman (CO-6)	11
Bill Foster (IL-11)	8	**Jackie Walorski (IN-2)**	11
Bill Keating (MA-9)	8	Scott DesJarlais (TN-4)	10
Bill Enyart (IL-12)	7	**Lynn Jenkins (KS-2)**	9
Steve Israel (NY-3)	7	**Darlene Senger (IL-11)**	9
Dan Maffei (NY-24)	7	Chris Gibson (NY-19)	8
Six candidates tied	6	Richard Tisei (MA-6)	8

Notes: Each column lists the ten candidates in each party who received the most mentions of "women's" issues in their campaign news coverage. Entries are raw mentions, not percentages. See Appendix 2 for issue coding.

candidates whose coverage focused most heavily on "women's" issues included at least one woman in the race.

What to make of this finding is not entirely clear, especially given that we did not uncover similar results for either party in 2010 or for Democrats in 2014. It could be that GOP women in 2014 drew reporters' attention to these issues. Garcia, for example, was among the Republicans who tweeted most frequently about "women's" issues (see Chapter 3). The national party's strategy could also have played a role. According to a political consultant who advised several female Republican candidates in 2014, the GOP "spent months researching, working with the Republican National Committee, looking into specific "women's" issues messaging." He told us that they anticipated that the Democrats would try to resurrect the "War on

Women" messaging that worked for them in 2012. So the Republicans ran focus groups, conducted polls, and tested messages early in the 2014 cycle and worked with their candidates to say, "Look, here's what we think is coming." It is also possible that journalists in 2014 found it easier to craft a narrative about "women's" issues when there was a woman in the race.

But it is important to place this finding in context. The raw numbers in Tables 4.3 and 4.4 translate into tiny percentages of overall coverage. For instance, although Garcia received the most coverage of "women's" issues among female GOP candidates, that constituted just 17 percent of her issue mentions in the local media. Most of her coverage, as for other candidates, was about Obamacare, the economy, and national security, the topics dominating the 2014 midterms nationwide. Moreover, the results show – unequivocally – that female candidates are not disproportionately likely to be discussed with regard to their gender (the gender mentions findings are null for both parties in both election cycles). And the "women's" issues finding is limited to one party, in one election cycle, in a narrow set of races using an approach that involves a deep search for gender inequities in political reporting. Overall, we have scant evidence that reporters rely on traditional gender conceptions when covering congressional campaigns.

CONCLUSION

Our exhaustive content analysis demonstrates that the media cover male and female congressional candidates very similarly. We found little in the way of gender differences in the volume or substance of coverage men and women receive. Journalists' tendency to reflect candidates' campaign messages (and disputes with their opponents), electoral competitiveness, and incumbency shape political reporting and affect the amount of attention devoted to gender, traits, and issues. In almost all cases, candidate sex does not. Coupled with the results we presented in Chapter 3 – which made clear that male and female candidates communicate similar messages on the campaign trail – the findings round out a depiction of an information environment in which candidate sex is not particularly salient.

But that does not eliminate the possibility that voters assess candidates in ways that could pose challenges for women pursuing elective office. Past research has found that gender stereotypes shape citizens' evaluations of candidates' traits and issue-handling abilities, sometimes eroding support for female candidates. And even though the small amount of news coverage about gender or appearance is equally likely to be directed at men, it could be that such media attention plays a stronger role in shaping voters' impressions when that kind of coverage focuses on women. Thus, we turn now to national survey data designed to examine whether and how candidate sex influences voter attitudes and behavior. Do traditional gender stereotypes drive voters' attitudes about candidates? Or, as we expect, do citizens see candidates primarily as Republicans and Democrats, leaving relatively little room for gender to affect public opinion?

5

The party, not the person

By the time the polls closed on November 4, 2014, hundreds of U.S. House candidates across the country had spent millions trying to persuade voters to send them to Washington.[1] For months, they had sparred in debates, held rallies, hosted public forums, knocked on doors, marched in parades, shaken hands, and done everything they could to convince their fellow citizens that they were the best people to represent them. But to hear the voters tell it come Election Day, the midterms' most important political figures weren't even on the ballot. The election was less about the candidates in their districts than it was about President Obama, his Democratic allies, and the Republican opposition in Washington.

Coming out of his polling place at a volunteer fire department, Powhatan County resident Mike Crist told a local reporter that he voted for Republican Randy Forbes in Virginia's 4th Congressional District race. The salesman's support of the seven-term incumbent, however, seemed to be more a statement about the Obama Administration's failed economic policies than anything else. "We need," Crist said in a dig at the president's 2008 campaign slogan, "change that you can really jiggle in your pocket."[2]

In New York's 18th Congressional District, Ken Moore told the *Poughkeepsie Journal* that his vote was motivated by concerns about the leftward turn of the country's fiscal policies. Moore hoped Republican Nan Hayworth's conservatism would serve as a bulwark against the Democrats' economic agenda – especially

---

[1] "Election to Cost Nearly $4 Billion, CRP Projects, Topping Previous Midterms," *OpenSecrets. org*, October 22, 2014. Accessed at: www.opensecrets.org/news/2014/10/election-to-cost-nearly -4-billion-crp-projects-topping-previous-midterms/ (August 18, 2015).

[2] "Check Out Who Your Neighbors Voted for on Election Day 2014," *CBS News 6*, November 4, 2014. Accessed at: http://wtvr.com/2014/11/04/election-day-2014-voters-ipadjournos/ (August 18, 2015).

what he saw as likely "taxation and big government, none of which I am in favor of."[3]

And when Willy Hughes cast his ballot for Republican incumbent Blake Farenthold at King High School in Corpus Christi, Texas, he felt no need to be polite: "All I know is he's working to beat back most of the garbage that's going on in Washington," Hughes told the *Caller-Times*.[4]

Democratic voters were frustrated too, but the target of their anger was the GOP. "I want to get all those Republicans out of there," Melvenia Myles said, explaining to the *Miami Herald* why she voted for Congresswoman Frederica Wilson and other local Democrats.[5] Others were fed up with what they saw as the Republican Party's obstructionism. In Connecticut's 2nd District, Harley Stiggle told *The Day* that sending incumbent Joe Courtney and his Democratic colleagues back to Congress was the only way to give Obama a chance at passing any legislation during the final two years of his term. "We won't get anything done with [Republicans] in office," he said. "Look at the president, they don't give him credit for the good he does. No one is perfect but they don't give him credit for anything."[6] Urbana, Maryland, resident Sophia Ewing told the *Baltimore Sun* that she supported Democrat John Delaney in the state's 6th Congressional District for a similar reason. If Delaney lost, she said, his Republican opponent, Dan Bongino, was sure to make "Obama's job just that much more difficult."[7]

These accounts exemplify the story we tell in this chapter: Although previous research has often found that assessments of candidates are shaped by gender stereotypes, we find that voters' attitudes have little to do with whether candidates are men or women and everything to do with whether they are Republicans or Democrats. Using survey data from the 2010 and 2014 midterms, we demonstrate that candidate sex plays only a minor role in the way that voters think about politicians. Citizens almost never mention gender, family roles, or appearance when offering their impressions of candidates. They assess men and women similarly when it comes to

[3] John Ferro, "Maloney Wins 18th CD; Hayworth Concedes," *Poughkeepsie Journal*, November 5, 2014. Accessed at: www.poughkeepsiejournal.com/story/news/local/2014/11/04/elections-2014-18th-congressional/18428285/ (August 18, 2015).

[4] Michael Zamora, "Farenthold Retains Congressional Seat," *Caller-Times*, November 4, 2014. Accessed: www.caller.com/news/politics/national/farenthold-retains-congressional-seat-ep-742751141.html (August 18, 2015).

[5] David Smiley, "Live Election Day Blog: Polls Close, Crist Campaign Calls for Extended Voting Hours," *Miami Herald*, November 4, 2014. Accessed at: www.miamiherald.com/news/politics-government/article3551446.html (August 18, 2015).

[6] Rick Koster, "Voters Out Early at Local Polling Places," *The Day*, November 4, 2014. Accessed at: www.theday.com/article/20141104/NWS01/141109937 (August 18, 2015).

[7] John Fritze, "House Incumbents in Maryland Favored for Re-Election Despite National Headwinds," *Baltimore Sun*, November 5, 2014. Accessed at: www.baltimoresun.com/news/maryland/politics/latest/bs-md-maryland-congress-20141104-story.html (August 18, 2015).

important character traits like leadership and empathy. And they judge male and female candidates to be equally capable of handling a wide range of public policy issues. We do identify a faint residue of traditional gender stereotypes, but the effects – which actually provide women an advantage – are small and hardly consequential.

Instead, partisanship dominates voters' evaluations of candidates and virtually dictates their vote choice. This is exactly what we would expect given that people tend to make political judgments based on considerations that are most easily accessible to them. Because the information environment does not encourage voters to think about candidate sex, and because campaign discourse and news coverage highlight the divisions between the parties, citizens view the political world through a partisan lens. It has long been a cliché for Americans to say they vote for the "person, not the party." But we show that in our modern era of polarized politics, the reverse is true. Voters care far more about the party than the person.

MEN AND WOMEN ON THE BALLOT: VOTERS' EVALUATIONS OF THEIR U.S. HOUSE CANDIDATES

As we detailed in Chapter 2, the Cooperative Congressional Election Study (CCES) provides an opportunity to collect public opinion data about congressional candidates across districts and in multiple election cycles. In both 2010 and 2014, we designed modules for the national survey that would allow us to determine whether voters assess male and female candidates differently, as well as the extent to which their evaluations are consistent with gender stereotyping. We surveyed 1,000 citizens in 2010 and 2,000 in 2014. In order to investigate different ways that candidate sex might affect voters' attitudes, we developed several types of survey questions. We asked open-ended questions about people's impressions of the candidates running in their districts. We asked citizens to assess how well a variety of politically relevant traits described the candidates. We asked voters to evaluate how well they thought the candidates would handle several issues if they were elected. And we asked respondents which candidate they planned to vote for. Although no one set of questions provides a definitive way to detect gender effects, our varied approach allows for a thorough examination of the role candidate sex plays in shaping voters' attitudes.

Let's (not) talk about sex: voters' impressions of male and female candidates

As a first cut at exploring how candidate gender might affect voters' assessments, we rely on responses to two open-ended questions we included in the 2014 survey. We asked respondents to tell us what came to mind when they thought about the Democratic House candidate in their district. We asked the same thing about the Republican candidate.[8] This was a simple processing task: we wanted voters to give us their top-of-the-head reactions without encouraging them to focus on any particular characteristics. Respondents could say anything, and as many things, that came to mind – candidates' demographics, biographies, backgrounds, party, ideology, personality traits, issue positions, and campaigns were all possibilities. By allowing for lengthy, unconstrained responses, we sought to gain a sense of what voters were thinking about when they were asked to describe candidates in their districts. To the extent that different considerations come to mind when voters think about male and female candidates, these responses can tell us that.

About two-thirds of respondents gave answers we could sensibly code (that is, responses more substantive than "I don't like politics" or, say, a respondent's description of an allegedly phallic logo at a Volvo dealership owned by Virginia Democrat Don Beyer). We classified the codable responses into eight categories: (1) gender, (2) party or ideology, (3) positive traits, (4) negative traits, (5) general positive statements, (6) general negative statements, (7) campaign-related statements, and (8) issues.[9] Table 5.1 provides a summary of the results, broken down by the party and sex of the candidate. Consistent with the findings we presented in Chapters 3 and 4, the data suggest that, just as gender is largely irrelevant for structuring campaign communications and media coverage, it is not particularly influential when we ask voters for their impressions of the candidates.

Perhaps most obviously, Table 5.1 makes clear that candidate sex is not salient to most respondents. Similar to our content analysis of media coverage in Chapter 4, we coded as a "gender mention" any open-ended response that referred to a candidate's sex, appearance, or family roles. Of the 487 comments about female candidates – Democrats and Republicans combined – only twenty-seven could be coded this way. The absence of gender mentions is even more telling when we consider that the table's entries are based on only the 64 percent of respondents who offered a substantive comment about the candidates.[10] If we

---

[8] We randomized the order of the candidates, so half the sample was asked about the Democratic candidate first and the other half was asked first about the Republican candidate. We rely exclusively on the 2014 data because we did not ask these open-ended questions in 2010.

[9] Eighty-six percent of responses about Democratic candidates and 81 percent of responses about Republican candidates fell into one of these eight categories. Many of the remaining comments dealt with politics in general and not the candidate the respondent was asked to evaluate. A handful of others – "My cousin stole one of his campaign signs," for instance – were miscellaneous responses about the candidates that did not fall into one of the eight categories.

[10] For Republican candidates, the sex of the candidate did not affect a respondent's likelihood of providing a substantive response to the open-ended question: 61 percent of people who were asked to evaluate a female GOP candidate wrote something substantive, as did 62 percent of people who were asked to evaluate a male GOP candidate. On the Democratic side, the sex of the candidate was related ($p < 0.05$) to whether the respondent offered an open-ended answer. Whereas 60 percent of people who were asked to evaluate a male Democratic candidate responded substantively, 67 percent of those asked to evaluate a female Democratic candidate did so. This is consistent with research that finds that voters are slightly more likely to know

TABLE 5.1. *Voters' impressions of House candidates in 2014, by sex and party (%)*

	Democratic candidates		Republican candidates	
	Women	*Men*	*Women*	*Men*
Gender mention	5.7*	1.4	5.3*	2.2
Party / ideology	23.5	27.8	25.8	26.3
Positive trait	23.2	20.9	19.2	15.4
Negative trait	13.7*	9.1	13.9	10.7
Positive statement (other than trait)	12.8	12.3	11.9	16.5
Negative statement (other than trait)	18.5	17.5	27.8	26.4
Campaign	5.1	4.8	3.3	4.0
Issue	4.5	6.0	3.3	4.1
N	336	794	151	979

Notes: Entries indicate the percentage of open-ended responses that fell into each category when respondents were asked: "When you think about [NAME], the Democratic/Republican candidate for the U.S. House of Representatives, what comes to mind?" Sample is restricted to respondents who provided an open-ended, substantive response (blank answers and "not sure" or "don't know" are not included in the calculation). N reflects the number of respondents. Percentages sum to more than 100 percent because respondents could offer multiple responses about a candidate. Levels of significance for gender difference: * $p < 0.05$.

include all of the (non-)responses from people who left the question blank – and, accordingly, didn't mention gender – then just 3.6 percent of reactions to female candidates in the entire sample could be classified as gender mentions.[11]

At the same time, respondents were statistically more likely to mention gender when evaluating female candidates than when assessing men. Women were more likely, for example, to be referred to with descriptors that included a reference to sex, such as "a female Republican" or "a woman who is a Democrat." We also found that five voters mentioned a female candidate's looks. Republicans Elise Stefanik and Suzanne Scholte, as well as Democrat Loretta Sanchez, were each described as "pretty" or "beautiful." One respondent referred to North Carolina Democrat Alma Adams' hats.[12] And one person noted that Nevada Democrat Erin Bilbray-Kohn was

things about female senators than about male senators (Fridkin and Kenney 2014; Jones 2014). It could also be a function of female candidates receiving slightly more news coverage than men did in 2014 (see Chapter 4).

[11] If we include in this calculation impressions of male candidates, as well as non-responses from people who left the question blank, then only 1.5 percent of responses referred to a candidate in a way that could be coded as a gender mention.

[12] According to a political strategist familiar with Adams' campaign, "Hats are part of her aesthetic. It's a known quantity about her. It's an image she cultivated herself." This is a reminder that references to a female candidate's appearance may sometimes reflect the candidate's campaign strategy.

a "middle-aged woman." (With the exception of "middle aged and grey-haired" Nevada Republican Mark Amodei, no male candidates were described this way.) Women also garnered several positive reactions because they were women. For a voter in Pennsylvania's 4th District, for instance, it was "a win win" that Linda Thompson was a woman and a Democrat. Kristen Spees appealed to a Nevada resident who thought there should be "more females in Congress." Although gender is indeed more likely to come to voters' minds when they think about female candidates, our close reading of the comments reveals little in the way of sexist or potentially damaging reactions.[13] And given that 95 percent of the comments about women were not about gender, such responses are uncommon in absolute terms.

This is largely because voters were much more likely to offer other types of reactions to the candidates. We see from the second row in Table 5.1, for example, that approximately 25 percent of responses mentioned a candidate's party or some type of ideological proclivity. Five times as many responses, in other words, described female candidates in partisan terms as they did gender terms. References to candidates' traits – positive and negative – as well as general statements about how they have performed or would perform in office also dwarfed gender mentions. When voters are asked about their initial impressions of congressional candidates, party, personality, and performance are far more salient than sex.

Equally important is that voters talk about male and female candidates very similarly. Other than the gender mentions, just one of the remaining fourteen comparisons between male and female candidates we present in Table 5.1 (seven for each party) is statistically significant. Women and men were equally likely to be described with references to their campaigns or specific policy issues. We uncovered no gender differences in positive statements about the candidates (e.g., "makes it a point to respond to my inquiries via mail, email, phone calls, etc.") or negative ones (e.g., "closed-minded, corporate bootlicker who sells his brand of social fear mongering to the petty masses"). And women were just as likely as men to be associated with positive traits. Voters considered male and female Democrats to be competent, trustworthy, hardworking, knowledgeable, grounded, and capable. They associated women and men on the GOP side with many of the same attributes, as well as determination, honesty, and compassion. The only significant difference pertains to negative traits for Democratic women, who were marginally more likely than Democratic men to be

---

[13] Most of the remaining gender mentions described women and men quite similarly. "A man for the job" and a "man in politics looking to get ahead in his party," are not substantively dissimilar to phrases like "driven, hardworking lady" or "a capable and excellent woman who can get work done." Male and female candidates were also equally (un)likely to be described in association with their families. North Dakota Republican Kevin Cramer gave the impression that he was a "family man," while GOP candidate Lori Hopkins-Cavanaugh conveyed that she was "a mom, just trying to make a difference for the people of Connecticut."

described unfavorably. We did not find a significant difference among Republicans.[14]

The similarity in the way voters talk about men and women becomes even clearer when we look more carefully at the partisan and ideological language they use. Many respondents offered just one-word descriptions for the candidates in their districts, like "Democrat," "Republican," "liberal," or "conservative." Others provided slightly more expansive responses, slamming Democrats for being "Obama puppets," "knee-jerk liberals," and "tax loving," and condemning Republicans as "narrow-minded conservatives," "Tea Party extremists," and "right-wing nut jobs." And some shared lengthier, more colorful impressions. South Boston Democrat Stephen Lynch, for example, "still has his Ironworkers' union card, hasn't forgotten where he came from . . . one of the few conservative Democrats left," one respondent said. "Definitely NOT a Chardonnay-sipping, parlor hanging, trust-funded hobby Bolshevik." Upstate New York Republican Jim Fischer, on the other hand, didn't fare as well. "I am a liberal. The Republicans are reactionaries and the Tea Party is full on crazy," noted a respondent from his district. "How do you think I feel about Jim Fischer?" Despite variation in the level of detail, the responses sounded the same regardless of the sex of the candidate.

Consider first these comments and the Democratic men they described:

A godless dumb-ocrat. (Neal Marchbanks, TX-19)

A Harry Reid, Nancy Pelosi, Obama Democrat. (Ken Dious, GA-10)

He only votes with Obama . . . Whatever the party does, he does. (Joe Courtney, CT-2)

Liberal, just another Pelosi foot soldier. (Ami Bera, CA-7)

Liberal loudmouth commie masquerading as a Democrat. (Wesley Neuman, FL-7)

He's a Democrat, so I don't know much other than the usual liberal views, supporting the gay agenda, raising taxes, and baby killing. (Robert Montigel, GA-6)

It is difficult to distinguish these remarks from those directed at female Democrats, whom voters also linked to Barack Obama, a liberal agenda, and the national Democratic Party:

A liberal Obama-ite who will continue the Democratic Party push for socialism. (Erin Bilbray-Kohn, NV-3)

---

[14] Associating Democratic women with negative traits might be driven not by candidate sex, but rather by the districts in which these women sought congressional seats. Women are more likely to emerge as candidates in districts with higher-income, highly educated, and ethnically and racially diverse electorates (Palmer and Simon 2008), which tend to be liberal. Republican voters in those districts, therefore, are – on average – less ideologically in sync with Democratic candidates than in the districts where women are less likely to run. This may make GOP voters in those districts more likely to assess Democratic candidates unfavorably.

A little Obama clone and cheerleader. (Linda Sanchez, CA-38)

Follows the Democratic orders ... No mind of her own. (Niki Tsongas, MA-3)

Just another socialist liberal who wants to destroy this country and state by making us more dependent on the government. (Suzanne Bonamici, OR-1)

Nancy Pelosi follower. No mind of her own. (Chellie Pingree, ME-1)

Very liberal and too willing to vote with her party and support increases in taxes and spending. (Ann Kuster, NH-2)

Voters' partisan reactions to Republican candidates also did not vary by sex. In Virginia's 11th District, Suzanne Scholte instilled little confidence in a voter who didn't "know much about her," but doesn't "trust Republicans." Paul Chabot faced a voter who felt the same way in California's 31st District. According to the respondent, "You can't trust any Republicans. They don't care about the majority of Americans." New Hampshire Republican Marilinda Garcia was described as "too conservative and backwards with women's issues," much like New Mexico Republican Mike Frese, who "does not care about women's equality in the workplace." And even though Barbara Comstock was seen as "weak" by a voter in VA-10, she was "better than a lock step Democrat." In OH-14, a voter expressed similarly tepid support for David Joyce: "The Democrats are not doing much to impress me, so I hope the Republicans can change it."

If we take voters at their word – or words – then it is hard to conclude that candidate sex shapes their impressions of congressional candidates. Whether a politician is a man or a woman seems not to be at the forefront of citizens' minds when they offer reactions to the people running in their districts.

A non-gendered lens: voters' assessments of candidates' traits and issue competencies

Responses to open-ended questions, of course, may not necessarily reflect the considerations that actually drive voters' evaluations.[15] Voters might censor themselves because they do not feel comfortable expressing reservations about female candidates. And gender stereotyping might make its way into citizens' assessments in more subconscious and indirect ways than open-ended responses can capture. As we summarized in Chapter 2, a central finding in the existing literature is that voters tend to associate male and female candidates with different character traits and issue strengths. Many studies find that citizens view female politicians as more compassionate and empathetic than men, but also as less competent and as weaker leaders. These trait inferences are important not only in their own right, but also because they often serve as a source of issue stereotypes. For instance, because female politicians are likely to be seen as possessing empathy, they might be stereotyped as adept at handling

---

[15] For perspectives on the utility and meaning of open-ended responses, see Hayes (2009), Lau (1989), Rahn, Krosnick, and Breuning (1994), and Smith (1989), among others.

"compassion" issues, especially those relating to women, families, and children. And because male politicians are often seen as strong leaders, voters might perceive them as better able than women to handle foreign policy, defense, and crime. Examining whether voters evaluate candidates' personality traits and issue competencies in ways that reflect gender stereotypes, therefore, is another way – beyond the open-ended responses – to detect potentially gendered attitudes.

We begin by focusing on a series of politically relevant traits. In 2010 and 2014, we asked our national sample of voters to rate both the Democratic and Republican House candidates in their districts on four traits. Two are ostensibly "masculine" attributes: "competent" and "provides strong leadership." The other two – "really cares about people like me" (which we refer to as empathy) and "trustworthy" – are considered "feminine" traits. In Washington's 5th District in 2014, for example, the question read this way: "Think about Joe Pakootas, the Democratic candidate for the U.S. House of Representatives. In your opinion, how well does the phrase 'provides strong leadership' describe Joe Pakootas?" Respondents could answer "extremely well," "quite well," "not too well," or "not well at all." They were also asked about Pakootas' competence, empathy, and trustworthiness.[16] We then repeated the battery of questions about Cathy McMorris Rodgers, the Republican incumbent running for reelection in WA-5.[17]

If traditional gender stereotypes affect the way citizens evaluate candidates, then women should outperform their male co-partisans on empathy and trustworthiness, but fare less well when it comes to competence and leadership. Figure 5.1, which presents the mean trait ratings, broken down by candidate sex, political party, and election cycle, reveals no such pattern. For all four traits, the mean evaluation for Democratic and Republican candidates fell in between "not too well" and "quite well."[18] We find slight variation by party and across election cycle, but none of the results suggests that voters associate different traits with male and female candidates.[19]

[16] The question wording follows the standard trait batteries in the American National Election Studies. We assigned responses a numerical value, with 1 representing "not well at all" and 4 representing "extremely well." In 2010, the competence question was asked using a seven-point scale that ranged from "extremely weak" to "extremely strong" and included a "not sure" option. We rescaled the measure so that it was comparable to the four-point scales for the other traits, dropping respondents who said "not sure." The substantive result is the same regardless of the scale or how we treat "not sure" responses (see Hayes and Lawless 2015b, note 78).

[17] We randomized whether the respondent was asked first about the Democratic or Republican candidate, as well as the order of the traits for each.

[18] For ease of presentation, we truncated the four-point scale so that the X-axis in each panel of Figure 5.1 ranges from just 2 ("not too well") to 3 ("quite well"). Every mean evaluation and confidence interval fell within this range. The wider confidence intervals in 2010 are a result of a smaller sample size (1,000 respondents in 2010 and 2,000 in 2014).

[19] Although not a trait linked to gender stereotypes, we also asked respondents how well the word "qualified" described their House candidates. Once again, we found no gender differences. On the four-point scale, the average rating was 2.58 for Democratic men and 2.57 for

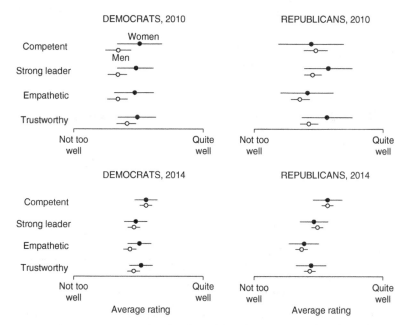

FIGURE 5.1. Voters' assessments of male and female House candidates' traits.
Notes: Dots indicate the mean rating on a 1–4 scale (with 95 percent confidence intervals). For presentation purposes, the figure displays only the middle two points of the scale. N varies slightly across traits, as some respondents did not answer all four questions. In 2010, N ranges from 650 to 896. In 2014, N ranges from 1,803 to 1,817.

Indeed, not one of the sixteen comparisons between women and men is statistically significant.[20]

When we consider how voters judge candidates' abilities to handle a series of important public policy issues, the story is again one of no gender differences. We included in the 2014 survey ten questions aimed at uncovering whether voters assess male and female candidates' issue strengths differently. Respondents were asked to rate, on a scale from 0 to 10, how capable they thought the candidates in their districts would be at dealing with issues ranging

Democratic women. For Republicans, the averages were 2.60 for men and 2.56 for women. Neither gender difference is statistically significant.

20 Our CCES modules included just a handful of respondents from any single House district. But two trait measures – competence and integrity – were administered to all 50,000 respondents as part of the larger "Common Content" survey in 2010. Even with an unusually large sample of respondents, we uncovered no statistically significant gender differences in the mean ratings for these two traits, either for Democrats or Republicans. The 2014 CCES Common Content did not include any candidate trait questions we could analyze as a robustness check.

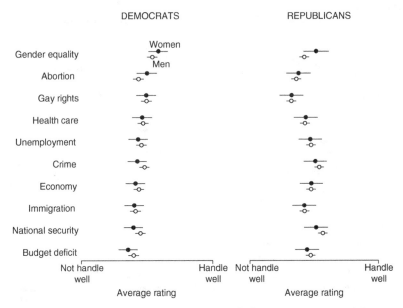

FIGURE 5.2. Voters' assessments of male and female House candidates' issue competencies, 2014.
Notes: Dots indicate the mean rating on a 0–10 scale (with 95 percent confidence intervals). For presentation purposes, the graph ranges only from 4 to 8. N varies slightly across issues, as some respondents did not answer all ten questions. N ranges from 1,817 to 1,833.

from gender equality to unemployment to national security. Higher scores indicate more favorable evaluations.[21]

The left-hand panel of Figure 5.2 presents the mean evaluations for male and female Democrats; the right-hand panel presents the data for Republicans. To provide some semblance of ordering to the graph, we present the issues in order from the most to the least favorable evaluations for Democrats overall. Across all twenty comparisons – from abortion and health care to unemployment and immigration – the gender difference never meets conventional levels of statistical significance; on all ten issues, women and men within each party are statistically indistinguishable from one another.[22] These results are not surprising

[21] The question was: "Below you will see a list of issues. On a scale from 0 to 10, how capable do you think [NAME], the Democratic candidate for the U.S. House of Representatives, would be at handling each issue? On this scale, 0 means that [NAME] would not handle the issue well at all, and 10 means that [NAME] would handle the issue very well." We then asked respondents to complete the same battery about the Republican House candidate. As with the traits, we randomized the order of the candidates and the issues in each battery of questions. We rely exclusively on the 2014 data because we did not include issue questions in the 2010 survey.

[22] For presentation purposes, we truncated the eleven-point scale so that the X-axis in each panel of Figure 5.2 ranges from 4 to 8. Every mean evaluation and confidence interval fell within this range of the scale.

given that trait assessments – where we found no gender differences – often serve as the foundation for issue stereotypes. We do note women in both parties received slightly higher ratings than men on the traditional "women's" issues of gender equality and abortion. Male Democrats and Republicans, meanwhile, fared a bit better than women on crime and national security, two stereotypic "men's" issues. Though not statistically significant, these differences may reflect some mild vestiges of gender stereotypes, a point we return to in the analysis below.

Regardless of how we ask the question, we uncover virtually no evidence that voters evaluate male and female candidates differently, or that they rely on gender stereotypes to arrive at their assessments. From open-ended responses to more conventional survey questions about personality traits and issue-handling capabilities, voters do not view the candidates in their districts through a gendered lens. The places where gender may have been salient or gender differences may have manifested themselves in the past no longer seem to emerge.

POWER OF THE PARTY: EXPLAINING WHY CANDIDATE SEX DOESN'T SHAPE VOTER EVALUATIONS

Why does gender matter only in the faintest of ways when it comes to voters' evaluations of candidates? To be sure, one reason is the information that voters encounter in campaigns. The evidence throughout this book suggests that neither the candidates nor the media encourage citizens to think about elections in gendered terms. But as we noted in Chapter 2, and as the open-ended survey responses foreshadowed, another likely explanation is the power of partisanship. To the extent that voters view the world through a partisan lens – evaluating candidates first and foremost on the basis of their party label – we would expect the sex of a candidate to play only a minimal role in shaping assessments and vote choice.

To test this expectation, we turn first to a series of regression models that predict individuals' evaluations of candidates' traits and issue-handling abilities. We focus on two key variables. First, we include in each model a variable indicating whether the candidate is a woman. If women are evaluated less favorably than men on any given trait or issue, the coefficient for sex will be negative; a positive coefficient indicates a more favorable assessment. Second, we include a variable indicating whether the respondent shares the candidate's party affiliation. (In the models for Democratic candidates, the variable indicates whether the respondent is a Democrat. In the models for Republican candidates, it indicates whether the respondent is a Republican.)[23] If a shared party affiliation between voters and candidates leads to more favorable evaluations, as we anticipate, then the party coefficient will be positive. We also include in each model a number of other variables that

---

[23] We code independents who say they lean toward one of the parties as partisans, for all of the well-known reasons (e.g., Keith *et al.* 1992).

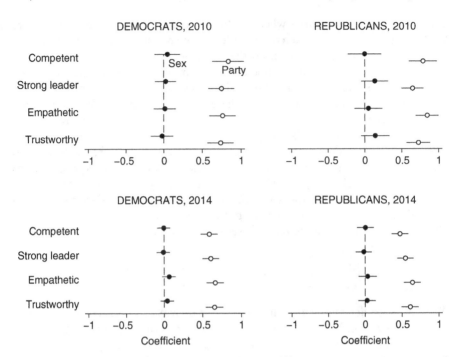

FIGURE 5.3. The effects of candidate sex and party affiliation on voters' assessments of House candidates' traits.
Notes: Dots represent unstandardized OLS regression coefficients, with 95 percent confidence intervals. See Tables A5.1 and A5.2 for the full regression equations.

could affect assessments, including whether the candidate is an incumbent, as well as the respondent's sex, ideology, and other characteristics.[24]

Figure 5.3 displays the coefficients (and 95 percent confidence intervals) for our key variables – candidate sex and shared party affiliation – from the regression models predicting trait evaluations. Once again, coefficients whose confidence intervals cross the dotted zero line are not statistically significant; their impact is effectively zero. Coefficients whose confidence intervals do not overlap the dotted line are significant and exert either a positive or negative effect.

The results indicate that in no case does candidate sex affect voters' evaluations. This is true in 2010 and 2014, for Democratic and Republican candidates, and on both "masculine" and "feminine" traits. In all sixteen models, the coefficient on candidate sex fails to reach statistical significance. The only case in which the variable even approaches significance is in 2010 for Republicans, where voters gave women slightly more favorable assessments than men on trustworthiness (a feminine trait) and leadership (a masculine one).

[24] The full regression models appear in Tables A5.1–A5.4 in the Appendix.

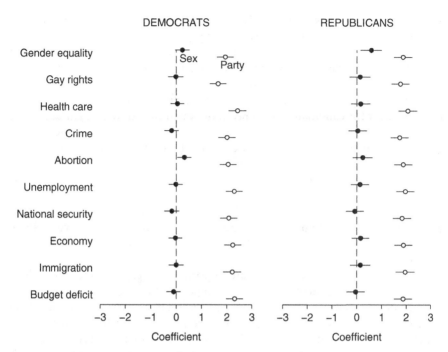

FIGURE 5.4. The effects of candidate sex and party affiliation on voters' assessments of House candidates' issue competencies, 2014.
Notes: Dots represent unstandardized OLS regression coefficients, with 95 percent confidence intervals. See Tables A5.3 and table A5.4 for the full regression equations.

By contrast, partisanship is consistently and substantively influential. On all four traits, across election cycles and party, sharing a candidate's partisanship leads to significantly more favorable evaluations. On average, the party coefficient is 0.68. To translate that into a meaningful quantity, the typical effect of sharing a candidate's partisanship moves a respondent more than two-thirds of the way from a "not too well" to a "quite well" evaluation on the trait scale. Given that the range of the scale is just four points and that, across all traits, more than 65 percent of responses fall in this narrow band between "not too well" and "quite well," this is a very large effect.

When we turn to issue-handling abilities, the story is mostly the same. Figure 5.4 presents the candidate sex and party coefficients and confidence intervals for the ten issues we asked voters to consider in 2014. In eighteen of the twenty models (nine for Democrats and nine for Republicans), candidate sex has no effect on how well a voter thinks a candidate will deal with the issue. Voters view female and male candidates as equally capable of handling a wide range of issues, from health care and gay rights, to crime and national security, to unemployment and the budget. And just as with traits, partisanship has a very large effect on voters' assessments of candidates' issue competencies. In all twenty models, shared party affiliation is statistically significant and positive. Across all issues and both parties, the party coefficient averages 2.0. On the eleven-point scale, that means that sharing the candidate's party affiliation leads to a two-point – or 18 percent – increase in assessments of issue-handling. By contrast, even setting aside statistical significance, the average size of the absolute value of the coefficient for candidate sex is only about one-fifteenth the magnitude.

In two of the twenty models, however, we do find a detectable residue of gender stereotypes. Democratic women receive significantly higher ratings on abortion than do Democratic men. And Republican women receive significantly higher ratings on gender equality than do their male GOP counterparts. (The gender equality coefficient for candidate sex among Democrats approaches significance, with a p-value of 0.07.) These results suggest that female candidates of both parties may have a small advantage on policy issues that have particular consequences for women themselves.

But two things about this result are important to keep in mind. First, these favorable assessments do not come at the expense of ratings on "men's" issues. Women do just as well as men on crime and national security, for instance. That is, the differential issue-handling ratings are positive-sum for women – they benefit female candidates, but do not harm them. Second, the effect of candidate sex even on abortion and gender equality ratings is dwarfed by the impact of party. Respondents see female candidates as better able to handle policy issues that have a direct connection to women, but the main driver of how well they perceive that a candidate will handle these issues is whether they share the candidate's party affiliation.

Given that voters evaluate male and female candidates similarly on both trait and issue dimensions, it is not surprising that candidate sex does not affect vote choice. We draw that conclusion from vote choice models from the 2010 and 2014 midterms. These are different from the trait and issue models, in that the dependent variable is whether the respondent reported in the preelection survey the intent to vote for the Democratic candidate. Thus, the equations reflect a choice between a Democrat and a Republican.[25] The key variables are whether the Democratic candidate is a woman, and whether the Republican candidate is a woman. If the coefficient for female Democratic candidate is negative, then that indicates that voters are less likely to cast ballots for the Democrat when the party's nominee is a woman. Similarly, if the coefficient for female Republican candidate is positive, that means that the presence of a GOP woman in a race drives up support for the Democrat. Both scenarios would

[25] We use the pre-election vote intention question because of panel attrition that reduces our sample size in the post-election survey. But because the two measures are correlated at 0.93, our results are the same regardless of which question we rely on. The analysis does not include the 21 percent of respondents in the pre-election survey who said they were "not sure" which candidate they would vote for.

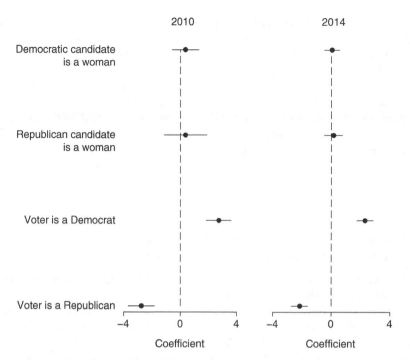

FIGURE 5.5. The effects of candidate sex and party affiliation on voting for the Democrat.
Notes: Dots represent logistic regression coefficients, with 95 percent confidence intervals. See Tables A5.5 for the full regression equation.

reflect a disadvantage for female candidates. We also include variables indicating whether the respondent is a Democrat or a Republican. Of course, we expect the Democratic variable to be positive – indicating a greater likelihood of voting for the Democrat – and the Republican indicator to be negative.[26]

The results presented in Figure 5.5 make clear that in both 2010 and 2014, the sex of the candidate has no bearing on whether the respondent planned to cast a ballot for the Democratic candidate. With confidence intervals overlapping the dotted line, the effect of candidate sex is zero. On the other hand, partisanship has a significant effect on vote choice. Democratic respondents are significantly more likely than non-Democrats to vote for the Democrat, and Republicans are less likely to do so. An even simpler way to illustrate how party identification virtually determines voting behavior is to calculate the percentage of partisans who said they would vote for their own party's House candidate. In 2010, 94 percent of Democrats and 97 percent of Republicans voted for the candidate who shared their party affiliation. In 2014, 92 percent of Democrats and 93 percent of Republicans voted for their own

[26] The reference category is independents who said they did not lean toward one of the parties.

party's candidates. With such high party loyalty rates and the fact that only between 10 and 15 percent of Americans are truly politically independent, it is no surprise that little else about candidates, including their sex, seems to shape voting behavior or election outcomes.

Taken together, the evidence from these analyses is straightforward. In thirty-four out of thirty-six models, the sex of the candidate did not affect voters' evaluations of traits, issue competencies, or vote choice. And in the two cases where we uncovered small gender differences, both conferred an advantage to women running for office. In all thirty-six cases, however, shared party affiliation exerted a significant and substantive impact. When voters assess candidates' personality traits and issue-handling abilities, and when they cast their votes, it's partisanship – not candidate sex – that guides their judgments.[27]

WHEN SEX MATTERS: WOMEN AND MEN'S (OCCASIONALLY) DIFFERENT VIEWS OF FEMALE CANDIDATES

One limitation of our analyses thus far is that they lump all voters together, reporting the average effect of candidate sex and partisanship across our entire group of respondents. It is plausible, however, that female voters might respond more favorably than men to female candidates. Indeed, some research suggests that voters support candidates who elicit group identification (Chaney and Sinclair 1994; Plutzer and Zipp 1996; Smith and Fox 2001). According to Sue Tolleson-Rinehart (1992: 14), gender consciousness – "the recognition that one's relation to the political world is shaped in important ways by the physical fact of one's sex" – is a potentially empowering cognitive evaluation. Although the evidence for a "gender affinity" effect varies (e.g., Dolan 2008; Goodyear-Grant and Croskill 2011; Lawless 2004a; Rosenthal 1995), it can lead women to evaluate female candidates more favorably.[28]

In order to examine whether candidate sex differentially affects male and female voters' evaluations and vote choice, we supplemented all of our models with an interaction between the sex of the respondent and the sex of the candidate. This allows us to determine whether there are statistical differences in the way that male and female respondents evaluate women who run for

---

[27] As in Chapters 3 and 4, our results are robust to a consideration of candidate quality. When we control for candidate quality in the 2010 analyses, it has no effect on the trait evaluation models for either Democrats or Republicans or on the vote choice model. Interacting candidate quality with candidate sex also produces no significant effect. This may seem surprising, since we would expect candidate quality to be related to voter attitudes. But the null result is probably a product of the fact that our main models already control for incumbency and vote share, which likely account for much of any candidate quality effect. The upshot is that we find no evidence that candidate quality provides an alternative explanation for our findings.

[28] Tolleson-Rinehart (1992) argues against the merits of "male gender consciousness," explaining that men tend not to assess their societal, economic, and political status relative to other groups. Rather, the status of white men tends to be the yardstick against which other groups evaluate their own fortunes.

office. If we find that female voters view women more favorably, it could suggest that female candidates may have an incentive to reach out to female voters in particular, even if the larger patterns of campaign communications are not gendered (see Chapter 3).

In the main, we find only inconsistent evidence that female and male voters evaluate female candidates differently. When we focus on Republican candidates, we find no evidence of a gender affinity effect. Men and women assess male and female GOP candidates' personal attributes in an identical fashion in both 2010 and 2014. As far as issue competency is concerned, only in one regression equation – for the economy – is the interaction significant. But the effect is not consistent with what we might expect: female voters gave female Republican candidates slightly *lower* ratings than they gave male candidates. In the other nine issue models, there are no differences in the way that men and women assessed male and female candidates.

Turning to Democratic candidates, we find some evidence, albeit not uniform, that female and male voters evaluate women slightly differently. In 2010, the interaction between voter sex and candidate sex is insignificant in all of the trait models. But in 2014, female voters evaluated Democratic women more favorably than Democratic men on competence, empathy, and trustworthiness. Male voters, on the other hand, evaluated Democratic men slightly more favorably than Democratic women on those measures. The same pattern emerged on eight of the ten issue-handling questions, with female voters giving Democratic women slightly more favorable evaluations. (We found no differences on crime and health care.)

A more thorough explication of the data reveals that these results stem primarily from Democrats, and generally more liberal Democrats. When we restrict the analysis to Republican identifiers only, we find no effects. That is, Republican men and women evaluated male and female Democrats the same way – negatively. Among left-of-center Democratic respondents, though, women gave Democratic female candidates a boost. This is not unimportant. From the perspective of understanding how citizens evaluate candidates, it tells us that some women (liberal Democrats) may have somewhat more favorable attitudes toward some female candidates (Democrats).

But these small variations are likely to be inconsequential when we turn to the outcome that ultimately matters most – whether someone votes for a female candidate. After all, left-of-center Democrats are the very people who are almost certainly going to vote for Democratic candidates in the first place. As we did with the traits and issues, we interacted the candidate sex variables with the sex of the respondent in our vote choice models. We found no effects whatsoever.[29] Candidate sex may lead some women to more favorable evaluations of female Democratic candidates' traits or issue-handling abilities,

---

[29] We also explored whether Democrats and Republicans evaluate female candidates differently – controlling for the candidates' partisanship, of course. We found no evidence that partisans evaluated male and female candidates differently.

but that does not translate into differential behavior on Election Day. Presented with an either–or choice between a Democrat and a Republican, voters rely predominantly on their partisanship to guide their decision. The voting booth, at least in U.S. House races, appears to be blind to gender.

CONCLUSION

Our analysis of two election cycles of national survey data shows that voters are just as unlikely as journalists to assess candidates in traditionally gendered terms. Instead, partisanship – long identified as a central force in congressional elections – shapes voters' overall impressions of candidates, as well as evaluations of their personal attributes and issue-handling abilities. Candidate sex, for the most part, does not. What's more, in the very rare cases when voters do offer differential assessments of male and female candidates, women are consistently advantaged. When it comes to casting a ballot, candidate sex never matters. In these hyper-partisan times, voters favor candidates – men and women alike – who share their party affiliation.

The findings presented in this chapter make a compelling case that candidate sex is neither salient nor influential for voters. The same was true for journalists covering House races (Chapter 4) and for candidates competing in them (Chapter 3). Yet perceptions of bias against women in the political arena are widespread, and the notion that female candidates face sexism, discrimination, and a harsher political playing field is commonly held. How can we reconcile these perceptions with the findings we've presented throughout this book? Shedding light on this critical puzzle is the topic for our next and final chapter.

6

The origins and implications of perceptions of gender bias

Five chapters, 110 pages, and dozens of tables and figures ago, we laid out an argument that challenges the conventional wisdom about gender and political campaigns. Despite the view – widely held by the press, politicians, political scientists, and the public – that women who run for office face a systematically more challenging or fundamentally different political environment than men, we contended that two features of politics in the twenty-first century have helped level the playing field. The declining novelty of women in politics and the polarization of the Republican and Democratic parties have left little space for the sex of a candidate to influence modern campaigns. In U.S. House elections across the entire country, and likely in the thousands of down-ballot races that reflect similar conditions, women and men face similar electoral landscapes.

This argument naturally meets skepticism. Although we have known for decades that women win elections at the same rate as men, the sense in public discourse and much of the scholarly literature is that women achieve these victories in spite of a more onerous and inhospitable campaign trail. This is undoubtedly an understandable perspective. Women have had the right to vote for less than a hundred years, and the quest for women's representation has been long, bumpy, and difficult. It wasn't until 1978 that a woman who wasn't replacing her deceased husband was elected to the U.S. Senate. Not until 1993 did more than two women serve in the chamber simultaneously. And women continue to make up less than one-quarter of the elected officials in Congress, state capitols, and city halls. The campaign trail seems a logical culprit.

But when we consider the electoral environment's key components, there is reason to doubt that the campaign trail systematically differs for women and men. First, the main imperative for candidates – male and female alike – is to portray themselves as embodying the personal characteristics and prioritizing the issues that voters value. This creates commonality, not divergence, in men's and women's campaigns. In an era in which partisanship is the chief factor that differentiates opposing candidates, whether in television advertising or social media, campaigns will reflect a clash of the partisans, not a battle of the sexes. Second, because press coverage of campaigns strongly corresponds to candidate messages, reporters will cover men and women similarly. Journalistic norms further demand that the most newsworthy features of campaigns get the most attention. Partisan conflict between candidates in competitive races generates headlines; the fact that a candidate happens to be a woman typically does not. Third, voters will not evaluate male and female candidates differently because candidate communications and press coverage do not prime them to do so, and because their partisan attachments are so strong. They assess and vote for the party, not the person. Only rarely will the sex of a candidate affect candidate, journalist, or voter behavior.

The evidence supporting this argument is substantial and wide-ranging. Throughout Chapters 3, 4, and 5, we found that whether a candidate is a man or a woman exerts very little influence in contemporary congressional elections. Male and female House candidates communicate similar messages on the campaign trail, receive similar coverage in the local press, and garner similar evaluations from voters in their districts. We conducted hundreds of statistical tests based on data from more than 400,000 campaign ads, 50,000 tweets, 10,000 newspaper articles, and 3,000 survey respondents. And no matter where we looked or how we analyzed the data, we found only the scarcest of evidence to support the prevailing view that women who run for Congress face a significantly different or more treacherous campaign environment than men.

In an attempt to summarize our sprawling results, Table 6.1 provides an overview of the statistical evidence. The first column presents, by chapter, the categories where we looked for gender differences or effects. For each, we list the total number of analyses we conducted, either in bivariate or multivariate tests.[1] The entries in the table's final column indicate the number of statistically significant results – that is, gender differences – we uncovered in each category. Consider the top third of the table, which displays the evidence from Chapter 3. Overall, we offered 117 comparisons of how women and men communicate on the campaign trail. In only five cases were their campaign communications statistically distinguishable from each other (at $p < 0.05$). In the other 96 percent of comparisons, the volume and content of male and female candidates' campaign ads and social media messages were identical. The middle third of the table makes a similar point about local news coverage. In just nine of the ninety-six tests pertaining to the volume and content of campaign stories did statistically significant gender differences emerge. The dearth of significant results is comparable in our analysis of voters. We looked in ninety-five places for differences in the public's impressions of male and female candidates, assessments of their traits and

---

[1] We do not include the gender comparisons mentioned only in footnotes. The proportion of statistically significant gender differences in the notes throughout the book, though, is even smaller than the percentage presented in Table 6.1.

TABLE 6.1. *Summary of the statistical evidence*

	Number of gender comparisons	Number of gender differences
Chapter 3: Candidate communications		
Volume of campaign ads, 2010	2	0
Volume of tweets, 2014	1	0
Issue content in candidates' campaign ads, 2010	40	1
Issue content in candidates' tweets, 2014	40	2
Effect of sex on issue content in campaign ads, 2010	10	0
Effect of sex on word usage in campaign ads, 2010	6	0
Effect of sex on issue content in tweets, 2014	10	2
Effect of sex on trait content in tweets, 2014	8	0
Chapter 4: Media coverage of candidates' campaigns		
Volume of overall coverage, 2010 and 2014	2	1
Gender mentions in news coverage, 2014	6	0
Volume and content of trait coverage, 2010 and 2014	18	1
Volume and content of issue coverage, 2010 and 2014	22	2
Convergence of candidate communications and media coverage, 2010 and 2014	4	0
Effect of sex on volume of coverage, 2010 and 2014	8	1
Effect of sex on trait coverage, 2010 and 2014	16	3
Effect of sex on issue coverage, 2010 and 2014	20	1
Chapter 5: Voters' evaluations of candidates		
Voters' overall impressions of candidates, 2014	16	3
Voters' evaluations of candidates' traits, 2010 and 2014	16	0
Voters' evaluations of candidates' issue competence, 2014	20	0
Effect of candidate sex on voters' evaluations of traits, 2010 and 2014	16	0
Effect of candidate sex on voters' evaluations of issue competence, 2014	20	2
Effect of candidate sex on vote choice, 2010 and 2014	4	0
TOTAL	**305**	**19 (6.2%)**
TOTAL consistent with gender stereotypes	**305**	**13 (4.2%)**

Note: The "Number of gender comparisons" column includes all bivariate and multivariate tests presented in the text, tables, figures, or appendices in Chapters 3, 4, and 5. Gender comparisons mentioned only in footnotes are not included. The "Number of gender differences" column indicates the number of comparisons in which the gender difference (in bivariate tests) or the coefficient on candidate sex (in multivariate analyses) was statistically significant at $p < 0.05$.

issue competencies, and intentions to vote for them. In ninety, we found nothing. Combined, the analyses amount to a total of nineteen statistically significant gender differences out of a possible 305.

Because so much of the discussion about female candidates' fortunes focuses on the challenges presented by social stereotypes of women, we also calculated the number of statistically significant differences consistent with gender stereotypes. For example, our finding from Chapter 5 that Republican women in 2014 received more favorable ratings than Republican men on gender equality – traditionally seen as a "women's" issue – is in line with gender stereotyping. The finding from Chapter 4 that female candidates in 2014 garnered more news coverage than men is not. In the 6 percent of results where gender differences did emerge, only thirteen of the nineteen are consistent with gender stereotypes. In the other six, the differences run counter to what the conventional wisdom would predict or are not directly related to gender stereotypes. All told, a mere 4 percent of our results could be interpreted as evidence that gender stereotypes directly affect candidates' campaign communication, news coverage, or voter assessments.

The strongest evidence that candidate sex can shape campaigns comes not from the quantitative data, but from the interviews we conducted with campaign professionals and newspaper reporters. Campaign managers told us that men who run against women must take care not to be portrayed as overly aggressive, particularly in campaign debates. Although this consideration can influence the tone of races involving female candidates, we found no evidence that it alters what candidates talk about. Indeed, even the campaign managers themselves said that these concerns did not affect the substance of what the candidates communicated to voters or the media. We also learned from campaign managers and journalists that candidate sex can shape media coverage in the rare cases that candidates decide to emphasize gender. But as an empirical matter, we could marshal only the thinnest of evidence that campaigns involving women were more likely than contests with only male candidates to do so. Quantitative or qualitative, our data reveal very few meaningful gender differences in the campaign environment.

These results are perhaps even more convincing alongside voters' impressions of these same campaigns. In the post-election wave of the 2014 Cooperative Congressional Election Study, we asked respondents to assess how the media covered the House candidates in their districts and how the voters treated them.[2] Perceptions of equitable treatment by the media and the electorate were far more common than perceptions of poor treatment. Just

---

[2] The question read: "Thinking back to the U.S. House elections in your district, what is your level of agreement with each of the following statements: (1) [NAME], the Democratic candidate, was treated fairly by the media; (2) [NAME], the Republican candidate, was treated fairly by the media; (3) [NAME], the Democratic candidate, was treated poorly by the voters; and (4) [NAME], the Republican candidate, was treated poorly by the voters." Respondents selected their level of agreement on a five-point scale that ranged from "strongly agree" to "strongly

15 percent of citizens thought that the Republican House candidate in their district was not treated fairly by the press, and the number for Democratic candidates was even lower (about 9 percent).[3] Ten percent of respondents reported that their GOP House candidate was treated poorly by the voters, and 13 percent of respondents thought the same about the Democratic candidate.[4]

As we might expect, a respondent's party identification and whether the candidate won the race were related to perceptions of treatment by the media and voters. There is no evidence, however, that voters thought female candidates were treated worse than men. In two regression models – one for Democratic candidates and the other for Republicans – we predict whether a respondent "agreed" or "strongly agreed" that the candidate received fair treatment by the media throughout the campaign. In another two, we predict whether a respondent "agreed" or "strongly agreed" that the major-party candidates in the district were treated poorly by the voters.[5] Figure 6.1 presents the coefficients (and 95 percent confidence intervals) for the key variable in these four models: whether the candidate was a woman. As usual, coefficients with confidence intervals that cross the dotted zero line are not statistically significant: their impact is zero. Coefficients whose confidence intervals do not overlap the dotted line are significant and exert either a positive or a negative effect.

In three of the four models, candidate sex does not affect voters' impressions of how the candidates were treated. Respondents believed that female Republican candidates were just as likely as male Republican candidates to be treated fairly by the press. Their assessments of voters' reactions also did not vary based on the sex of the candidate, regardless of political party. The only statistically significant result suggests a perceived advantage for female candidates. When considering Democratic candidates' campaigns, respondents had the sense that women were treated more fairly by the media than men were. We cannot say for sure why this is, although it could reflect our finding from Chapter 4 that races involving female candidates in 2014 received more coverage than races involving only men. Nonetheless, the key point is that what we found in our analyses is the same thing that Americans saw in their congressional districts.

---

disagree." We randomized the order of the candidates and the order of the questions within the battery.

[3] Twenty-nine percent of respondents, on the other hand, "agreed" or "strongly agreed" that the GOP candidate was treated fairly in the media, and 36 percent thought the same about the Democratic candidate. The remaining 50 percent of respondents neither agreed nor disagreed with the statement.

[4] On the other side of the spectrum, 35 percent of respondents "disagreed" or "strongly disagreed" that the GOP candidate was treated poorly by the voters, as did 33 percent of respondents reflecting on the Democratic candidates' treatment. The remaining 50 percent of respondents neither agreed nor disagreed with the statement.

[5] We cast the media question in positive terms and the voters' question in negative terms to try to reduce the likelihood that respondents would mechanically answer both questions the same way.

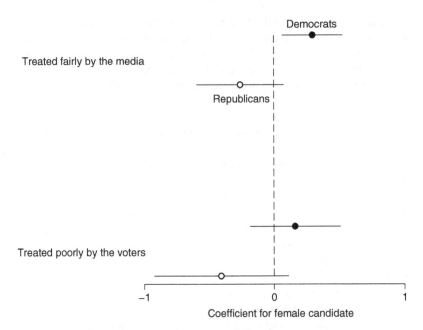

FIGURE 6.1. Voters' impressions of House candidates' treatment in 2014.
Notes: Dots represent logistic regression coefficients, with 95 percent confidence intervals. See Table A6.1 for the full regression equations.

All of this raises a profound puzzle, however. If our findings accurately portray congressional campaigns, and if voters' impressions of those campaigns dovetail with our data, then how can we account for the widespread perceptions of electoral bias we presented in Chapter 1? How is it that 60 percent of these same survey respondents believe that the media focus too much on female candidates' appearance and cover women in sexist ways? Why do nearly half believe that when women run for office, they face bias from voters? Why do almost one-third think that women don't win elections as often as men? As we suggest in the next section, these beliefs appear to arise from sources well beyond what people actually observe in their own districts.[6]

---

[6] The question was: "What is your level of agreement with each of the following statements?" Respondents were presented with six statements, with their order randomized. They could indicate that they strongly agreed, agreed, neither agreed nor disagreed, disagreed, or strongly disagreed. In our analyses, we collapse together respondents who agreed and strongly agreed, as well as those who disagreed and strongly disagreed. See Chapter 1, Figure 1.1.

It is not unreasonable to wonder whether people would perceive as much gender bias if we had asked these questions specifically about congressional elections. Although we can't say for sure, we do know that only 25 percent of our respondents "disagreed" or "strongly disagreed" with the following statement: "The experiences of high-profile women in politics, like those who run for president, governor, or the U.S. Senate, are similar to the experiences of other women who run for lower level offices, like Congress." The remaining respondents either saw no distinctions between

EXPLAINING PERCEPTIONS OF GENDER BIAS IN ELECTIONS

Why do substantial portions of the public believe that women receive sexist media coverage, face bias from voters, and have a harder time than men getting elected? We don't claim to have definitive answers, besides being confident that these perceptions do not arise from what citizens see in campaigns close to home. Instead, in the short time we have left together (this book has to end at some point), our aim is more modest: to offer some informed speculation and preliminary data about the origins of these beliefs. Although we do not intend here to articulate a theory or formally test hypotheses, we hope our data-driven conjecture can lay a foundation to understand the origins and persistence of perceptions of electoral bias against women.

Social identity

Social identity is a natural place to start. A long line of research has shown that people's group "memberships" – gender, race, religion, and so forth – can be relevant for understanding political attitudes (see Huddy 2001 for a review). Social identity theory (Tajfel 1981; Turner 1996) has helped explain attitudes related to national identity and culture (e.g., Citrin, Reingold, and Green 1990), political conflict between groups (e.g., Gibson and Gouws 2000), and political behavior (e.g., Fowler and Kam 2007; Sanchez 2006). We suspect that two social identities – gender and partisanship – may help explain people's perceptions of bias against female candidates.

Our first supposition is that women will be more likely than men to be cognizant of sexism and gender discrimination in politics. Because women in the electorate share a gender identity with a minority group – in this case, female politicians – that group membership might make bias against the group particularly salient. For instance, women's significant under-representation in politics may be more noticeable and concerning to women than to men. And when episodes of sexism in politics occur, they may be more likely to shape women's perceptions. Combined with women's experience with sexism in their own lives (more on this below), this may naturally and understandably lead to the view that the campaign trail creates unique barriers for female candidates. These perceptions, of course, will vary by an individual's level of group identification – the attitudes of those with a high level of gender consciousness may differ from those with a lower level of group identity (Gurin 1985; Miller *et al.* 1981; Tolleson-Rinehart 1992). But, on average, we would expect women to be more likely than men to sense that female politicians face additional obstacles in their campaigns for office.

Our second expectation is that, since partisanship in our polarized era has effectively become a social identity (Green, Palmquist, and Schickler 2002; Greene 1999), Democrats should be more likely than Republicans to perceive

women's experiences in the two types of campaigns, or neither agreed nor disagreed with the statement.

TABLE 6.2. *Voters' perceptions of female candidates' experiences, by respondent sex and party (%)*

	Democrats		Republicans	
	Women	Men	Women	Men
Women who run for office are subjected to sexist media coverage	73*	64	61*	38
Too much attention is paid to women's appearance when they run for office	71*	63	61*	50
Women who run for office face significant bias from voters on Election Day	64*	53	50*	22
To win their elections, women have to be better qualified than men do	68*	51	51*	26
Women who run for office do not raise as much money as men	35	38	31*	23
Women who run for office do not win as often as men	43*	32	35*	16
N	530	385	307	381

Notes: Entries indicate the percentage of respondents who agreed or strongly agreed with each statement. Party differences are statistically significant at $p < 0.05$ in all comparisons. Levels of significance of gender differences: * $p < 0.05$. Sample sizes vary slightly across questions, as some respondents did not provide answers. Democrats and Republicans include independents who lean Democratic or Republican.

bias against female candidates. After all, the vast majority of female candidates are Democrats. Of the women serving in the U.S. Congress in 2015, 73 percent were Democrats. Sixty percent of women serving in state legislatures are Democrats. And 59 percent of female governors have been Democrats.[7] This imbalance may produce in-group favoritism in which Democratic voters are more likely to see the political system as biased against female candidates, who they know are likely to be Democrats.

The data support our expectations. In Table 6.2, we present the percentage of respondents, broken down by sex and partisanship, that agreed with each of the six statements about electoral bias against female candidates.[8] Turning first to gender differences, among Democrats, women were statistically more likely than men to agree that female candidates face bias on five of the six measures. Averaging across all six items, the gender gap among Democrats is 9 percentage points. On the GOP side, the gender gap is even larger. In all six comparisons, female Republicans were more likely than male Republicans to perceive

[7] These numbers come from the Center for American Women and Politics at Rutgers University. See www.cawp.rutgers.edu/ (September 26, 2015).

[8] For the purposes of exploring partisanship as a social identity, we do not consider pure independents. The percentage of independents seeing bias ranges from 25 percent to 52 percent on the various measures.

electoral bias against women. The average difference across all measures is a substantial 19 percentage points. This large gender gap stems from the fact that Republican men are substantially less likely than any of the other three groups to view women as facing systematic disadvantages.

The partisan divide is just as large as the gender gap. The average size of the partisan gap among women is 9 percentage points, with Democrats significantly more likely than Republicans to report perceptions of bias against female candidates. Among men, the partisan gap averages 19 points. Here, too, Democrats are always significantly more likely than Republicans to see women as facing disadvantages. Combined, the effects of sex and partisanship are striking: compared to female Democrats, male Republicans are only about half as likely to perceive that women who run for office face a tougher road to office than men. This preliminary evidence suggests that sex and partisanship can affect how citizens construe social reality and lead to divergent judgments about the political system more broadly.

National discussions about gender in politics

Besides social identity, exposure to national discussions about gender in politics may also shape people's perceptions of female candidates' experiences. This expectation stems from two features of media coverage of high-profile women in politics. First, national news coverage regularly frames female candidates as facing sexism, if not outright discrimination. A *Boston Globe* story in September 2015 serves as a case in point. Readers were told that a woman aspiring to the White House would have to "overcome obstacles that male candidates do not face" and live up to "higher standards of ethical behavior than male candidates."[9] Stories referencing the press's purported tendency to emphasize female candidates' appearance – thus creating obstacles to their election – have also been a prominent feature of recent election cycles.[10] In October 2015, a *Washington Post* article noted that "all female politicians" receive "enormous scrutiny" of the way they look.[11] Talking

[9] Annie Linsky, "In Swing States, Clinton May Face Gender Bias," *Boston Globe*, September 9, 2015. Accessed at: www.bostonglobe.com/news/nation/2015/09/09/hillary-clinton-faces-challenges-unique-woman-running-for-office/Zkv99eyLTzAVzskuGnvRPN/story.html (September 26, 2015).

[10] See Elizabeth Flock, "Study: Female Candidates Become Less Electable When Media Mention Their Appearance," *U.S. News & World Report*, April 8, 2013. Accessed at: www.usnews.com/news/blogs/washington-whispers/2013/04/08/study-female-candidates-become-less-electable-when-medi a-mention-their-appearance (October 2, 2015); Diana Reese, "News Coverage of Female Candidate's Appearance Damages Her Chance of Winning," *Washington Post*, April 8, 2013. Accessed at: www.washingtonpost.com/blogs/she-the-people/wp/2013/04/08/news-coverage-of -female-candidates-appearance-damages-her-chance-of-winning/ (October 2, 2015).

[11] Paul Farhi, "Why Does Bernie Sanders Dress Like That? Because He Can," *Washington Post*, October 13, 2015. Accessed at: www.washingtonpost.com/lifestyle/style/why-does-bernie-sanders -dress-like-that-because-he-can/2015/10/12/55ca840e-6141-11e5-b38e-06883aacba64_story .html (October 23, 2015).

heads and political pundits often state as simple fact that the political environment is biased against women.[12]

Second, episodes of sexism are often sensationalized in a way that over-represents their prevalence and influence on women's political fortunes. When U.S. Senator Kirsten Gillibrand released her memoir in 2014, for example, the vast majority of news coverage focused on several anecdotes she relayed about male Senate colleagues' comments about her weight. The point of the book, according to Gillibrand, was "to elevate women's voices in the public sphere and bring women more fully into making the decisions that shape our country."[13] Yet the national headlines were "Senator Says Male Colleague Told Her, 'You're Even Pretty When You're Fat,'" "Senator Gillibrand Talks Weight Struggles, Sexism in New Book," and the like.[14] Segments about the book on national television newscasts opened with lines like, "The Senate's longstanding rules of decorum apparently don't apply to a woman's weight."[15] In the fall of 2015, Donald Trump's boorish remarks in *Rolling Stone* about fellow Republican presidential candidate Carly Fiorina's looks generated a similar deluge of news coverage (not to mention a response ad by Fiorina and a confrontation between the two in the second Republican presidential debate).[16]

One reason such bad behavior gets so much attention from the media and political commentators is precisely because it's unusual – controversial, dramatic, and anomalous events are virtually irresistible to reporters. But lost in virtually all of the discussion is the important distinction between offensive behavior by, say, a billionaire real estate developer who seems stuck in junior high and the systematic dynamics of political campaigns. While episodes of sexism do occur – and should be publicized and denounced when they do – people may infer from the widespread national news attention devoted to these unusual

---

[12] "Is the Political Media Biased against Women," *Politico*, June 26, 2012. Accessed at: www .politico.com/arena/archive/is-the-political-media-biased-against-women.html (October 23, 2015).

[13] Jennifer Senior, "Mother of Two, Senator of 20 Million," *New York Times*, October 9, 2014. Accessed at: www.nytimes.com/2014/10/12/books/review/kirsten-gillibrands-off-the-sidelines .html (September 27, 2015).

[14] Maya Rhodan, "Senator Says Male Colleague Told Her, 'You're Pretty Even When You're Fat,'" *Time*, August 27, 2014. Accessed at: http://time.com/3197103/kirsten-gillibrand-senate -sexism/ (September 27, 2015); and Glenn Blain, "Senator Gillibrand Talks Weight Struggles, Sexism in New Book," *New York Daily News*, August 27, 2014. Accessed at: www.nydailynews .com/news/politics/sen-kirsten-gillibrand-talks-weight-struggles-sexism-new-book-article-1.191 9242 (September 28, 2015).

[15] Jake Miller, "Senator Kirsten Gillibrand: Male Colleague Called Me Porky," *CBS News*, August 27, 2014. Accessed at: www.cbsnews.com/news/sen-kirsten-gilllibrand-male-colleague -called-me-porky/ (September 27, 2015).

[16] Paul Solotaroff, "Trump Seriously: On the Trail with the GOP's Tough Guy," *Rolling Stone*, September 9, 2015. Accessed at: www.rollingstone.com/politics/news/trump-seriously-20150909? page=13 (September 27, 2015).

incidents that gender bias is pervasive and consequential for all levels of office, in all realms of politics, including at the polls.

One way to test this expectation is by drawing on CCES respondents' impressions of the way that Hillary Clinton and Sarah Palin were treated by the media and voters during the 2008 presidential campaign. Overall, 43 percent of respondents believed that Hillary Clinton faced sexist media coverage, and nearly two-thirds thought the same about Sarah Palin. Perceptions of bias from the voters were less prevalent, but still common (38 percent thought Clinton faced voter bias, and 54 percent believed that Palin did).[17]

We use these as proxies for attentiveness to national political conversations about women in politics for three reasons. First, public discussions and press accounts of the 2008 campaign regularly focused on, and sometimes even contributed to, the sexism that both candidates faced.[18] Second, because so much discussion of gender and politics has focused on Clinton and Palin, people might be particularly likely to extrapolate from these two women's experiences to women in politics generally (Dowling and Miller 2015). Third, perceptions of bias against Clinton and Palin are positively associated with national news consumption, which affirms that national media discussions about women in politics often highlight examples of sexism and discrimination.[19]

To explore the relationship between perceptions of Clinton and Palin's experiences and perceptions of electoral bias against women generally, we created two measures. The first is a scale for perceptions of the way Clinton and

[17] We asked respondents: "Thinking back to the 2008 presidential election, what is your level of agreement with each of the following statements? (1) Hillary Clinton was subjected to sexist media coverage when she ran for president in 2008; (2) Sarah Palin was subjected to sexist media coverage when she ran for vice president in 2008; (3) Hillary Clinton faced significant gender bias from voters during her 2008 campaign; and (4) Sarah Palin faced significant gender bias from voters during her 2008 campaign." We randomized the order of the questions. Respondents could indicate that they strongly agreed, agreed, neither agreed nor disagreed, disagreed, or strongly disagreed. In our analyses, we collapse together respondents who agreed and strongly agreed, as well as those who disagreed and strongly disagreed. These, of course, are not the only measures one could use to gauge people's exposure to discussions of women in national politics. But they strike us as attitudes that are likely to reflect attentiveness to debates about women in politics (see Dowling and Miller 2015).

[18] Recounting the incident in which Clinton became slightly choked up when discussing the humbling yet harrowing experience of running for president in 2008, for example, Bill Maher said, "The first thing a woman does, of course, is cry" (*Real Time with Bill Maher*, Episode 608, February 29, 2008). MSNBC's Chris Matthews used the words "stripteaser" and "witchy" to describe Clinton (*The Chris Matthews Show*, November 18, 2007). On Fox News, Tucker Carlson praised the creation of a Hillary Clinton nutcracker, saying, "That is so perfect. I have often said, when she comes on television, I involuntarily cross my legs" (*Tucker*, July 16, 2007). See also Matea Gold, "Media on the Defensive over Palin Coverage," *Los Angeles Times*, September 5, 2008. Accessed at: http://articles.latimes.com/2008/sep/05/nation/na-mediaattacks5 (October 24, 2015).

[19] Controlling for a respondent's sex and partisanship, national news consumption is a statistically significant predictor of perceptions of the way Clinton and Palin were treated in 2008. The more national news a respondent consumed, the more likely he or she was to believe that Clinton and Palin faced bias from the media and the voters.

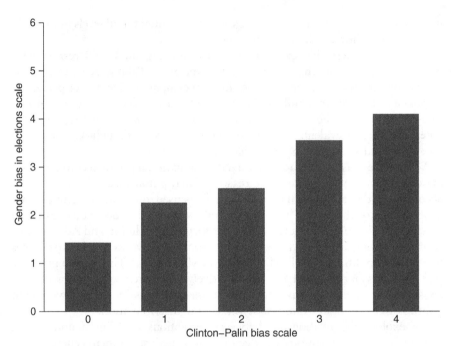

FIGURE 6.2. The relationship between perceptions of bias against Hillary Clinton and Sarah Palin and perceptions of gender bias in elections.
Notes: The X-axis represents the total number of ways respondents believed that Clinton and Palin faced bias in 2008. The bars represent that number of statements respondents agreed with about bias against women in politics more generally (see Table 6.2).

Palin were treated. It ranges from 0 to 4 and represents the total number of statements with which a respondent agreed (or strongly agreed) when reflecting on the treatment Clinton and Palin received in 2008. Higher scores indicate more perceived bias. The second measure is an index of perceptions of bias against women in politics more generally. Here, we summed up the number of statements from Table 6.2 that each respondent agreed (or strongly agreed) with when considering female candidates' experiences in the political arena. This scale ranges from 0 (a respondent agreed with none of the statements) to 6 (a respondent agreed with all of them). Higher numbers indicate more perceptions of electoral bias.[20]

Figure 6.2 displays the relationship between the two scales. The X-axis indicates the number of ways respondents thought Clinton and Palin faced bias. At each number on the scale, the bar represents the average number of statements about

[20] Reliability analysis confirmed the appropriateness of scaling the items. For the four-point Clinton–Palin scale, Cronbach's alpha is 0.71. For the seven-point perceptions of bias of scale, Cronbach's alpha is 0.74.

electoral bias against women that respondents agreed with. For example, people who agreed with three of the Clinton–Palin bias statements on average agreed with 3.6 of the more general bias statements.[21] The pattern is straightforward: Respondents who saw more bias against Clinton and Palin also perceived more bias against women in politics in general.[22] In other words, as exposure to conversations about female candidates in the national media – mainstream and otherwise – increases, so does the sense that women experience bias on the campaign trail. People's impressions of what it's like for a woman to run for office are shaped far more by the high-profile and highly unusual candidacies of women seeking national office than by direct observations of candidates' experiences in their districts.

Perceptions of workplace and societal bias

In addition to social identity and attention to national conversations about women in politics, views about bias in the workplace and society may be related to people's assessment of the political environment. People who experience, are attentive to, or are exposed to gender bias in other contexts, such as the professional world, might extrapolate that women in politics face many of the same challenges. This strikes us as quite plausible at a time when gender bias in corporate America and the workplace more generally has received sustained public attention.[23]

As an initial way to test this possibility, we asked respondents whether they had read or were familiar with Facebook executive Sheryl Sandberg's *Lean In: Women, Work, and the Will to Lead*. Released in 2013, the book, in the words of its publisher, "examines why women's progress in achieving leadership roles has stalled, explains the root causes, and offers compelling, commonsense

---

[21] We would of course imagine that these two batteries are correlated and that they tap similar considerations. But our analysis indicates that they are measuring somewhat different concepts. In no case is the correlation between any of the Clinton–Palin items and any of the electoral bias items greater than 0.46. The two scales are also significantly correlated (at 0.49), but the relationship is far from perfect. In fact, 45 percent of respondents who saw absolutely no bias against Clinton or Palin agreed with at least one of the statements about bias against female candidates in general, and 24 percent agreed with all of them.

[22] Certainly, party identification influences assessments of gender bias faced by Hillary Clinton and Sarah Palin. For instance, 59 percent of Democrats, compared to only 30 percent of Republicans and independents, believed Hillary Clinton received sexist media coverage (difference significant at p < 0.05). On the other end of the spectrum, whereas 84 percent of Republicans identified sexist media treatment directed at Sarah Palin, 57 percent of·Democrats and independents did so (difference significant at p < 0.05). Still, sizeable portions of respondents perceived gender bias across party lines.

[23] See Nikki Waller and Joann S. Lublin, "What's Holding Women Back in the Workplace?" *Wall Street Journal*, September 30, 2015. Accessed at: www.wsj.com/articles/whats-holding-women-back-in-the-workplace-1443600242 (October 2, 2015); and Rachel Emma Silverman, "Gender Bias at Work Turns Up in Feedback," *Wall Street Journal*, September 30, 2015. Accessed at: www.wsj.com/articles/gender-bias-at-work-turns-up-in-feedback-1443600759 (October 2, 2015).

solutions that can empower women to achieve their full potential."[24] *Lean In*'s publication, along with a 2012 essay in *The Atlantic* by former Obama Administration official Anne-Marie Slaughter, sparked a public debate about the sources of and solutions to gender bias in the professional world.[25]

We expect that people who are at least familiar with the book, and thus familiar with the national discussion of challenges faced by professional women that Sandberg and Slaughter spurred, may be more likely to perceive bias against female candidates. And this is what we find. The 21 percent of individuals who had read or were familiar with *Lean In* were twice as likely as those who were not (16 percent compared to 8 percent) to agree with all six statements about electoral bias. At the other end of the spectrum, respondents who were unfamiliar with the book were almost twice as likely as those who knew about *Lean In* to agree with none of the electoral bias statements (19 percent compared to 11 percent). On average, people who read or were familiar with the book agreed with 3.3 of the electoral bias statements, while those who were unfamiliar agreed with 2.6. All of these differences are statistically significant (p < 0.05).

Of course, people do not have to follow national conversations about bias in the workplace to form opinions about its prevalence or applicability to politics. Most citizens have firsthand experience navigating the working world; those who don't undoubtedly know many people who do. In our survey, 52 percent of women reported having been treated in a sexist way, and 36 percent said they had been discriminated against at work because of their gender. Among men, 49 percent said they knew a woman who had been treated in a sexist way and 28 percent said they knew a woman who had been discriminated against at work.

People who experience or see examples of workplace and broader societal discrimination against women may assume that women face similar barriers when they run for office. So we also included on the CCES survey two additional sets of questions. First, we asked respondents whether they believe that women have fewer opportunities in the workplace, earn less money than men for doing the same job, or have more difficulty climbing the corporate ladder.[26] Second,

---

[24] Sheryl Sandberg, *Lean In: Women, Work, and the Will to Lead*, New York: Alfred A. Knopf, 2013. Accessed at: www.amazon.com/Lean-In-Women-Work-Will/dp/0385349947 (October 2, 2015).

[25] Anne-Marie Slaughter, "Why Women Still Can't Have It All," *The Atlantic*, July/August 2012. Accessed at: www.theatlantic.com/magazine/archive/2012/07/why-women-still-cant-have-it-all /309020/ (October 2, 2015). Slaughter later published a book based on the article: *Unfinished Business: Women, Men, Work, Family*, New York: Random House, 2015.

[26] We also asked respondents about whether these dynamics characterized their own workplace. But using these responses would force us to drop all respondents (about 600) who were either unemployed or did not work outside the home. Accordingly, we rely only on the questions that applied to all respondents. This decision is not substantively consequential. When we restrict our analysis to respondents who were employed outside the home and ask about their perceptions of sexism in their workplace, the results are very similar to those from the full sample.

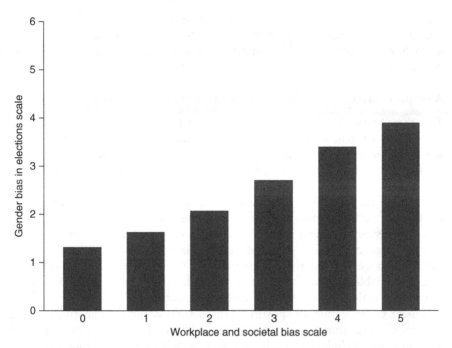

FIGURE 6.3. The relationship between perceptions of workplace and societal bias and perceptions of gender bias in elections.

Notes: The X-axis represents the total number of ways respondents believed that women face sexism and discrimination in the business world and in society at large. The bars represent the number of statements respondents agreed or strongly agreed with about bias against women in politics more generally (see Table 6.2).

we asked whether they know a woman who has been discriminated against at work, or who has been treated in a sexist way outside of work.[27] As before, we created a scale – this one ranging from 0 to 5 – to gauge the level of professional and societal gender bias a respondent reported.[28] We show in Figure 6.3 that these attitudes correlate with perceptions of electoral bias.

The X-axis presents the number of items in which respondents indicated perceptions of, or exposure to, sexism or discrimination. The bars represent the average number of statements about electoral bias against women that respondents agreed with. Again, as people report more bias in the workplace and society, the average number of responses indicating electoral bias against women increases. Gender bias in realms outside of politics fuel, or at least reinforce, beliefs that female candidates face bias on the campaign trail. And

[27] The measure of whether a female respondent faced sexism herself performs similarly to the measure that taps whether respondents know someone who has faced sexism. So again, to preserve the full sample size, we rely on the questions asked of both male and female respondents.

[28] Combining these five items into one scale is statistically appropriate; Cronbach's alpha is 0.71.

perhaps because women are more under-represented in politics than in other traditionally male-dominated career fields – like law, business, medicine, and journalism – people reasonably assume that women's experiences in politics will be even worse (see Figure 1.2).

A simple model of perceptions of gender bias in campaigns and elections

The three correlates of gender bias we just presented – social identity, perceptions of gender in national politics, and people's perceptions of the workplace and society – are, as our preceding discussion has indicated, related. Thus, showing that all of these indicators correlate to perceptions of bias against female candidates does not mean that they each independently affect those attitudes. With regression analysis, though, we can examine the influence of each explanation while holding the others constant.

The dependent variable in our model is the seven-point scale (ranging from 0 to 6) of perceptions of electoral gender bias. We include as independent variables gauges of our three explanations. To measure social identity, we include variables for whether the respondent is a woman or a Democrat. We use the scale measuring a respondent's perceptions of Clinton and Palin's treatment to tap national exposure to discussions about women and politics. And to capture attitudes about sexism and discrimination in non-political domains, we include a variable indicating whether the respondent was familiar with *Lean In*, as well as the societal and workplace bias scale.

In Figure 6.4, we show the independent effect of each variable by plotting its coefficient and 95 percent confidence interval. Consistent with the descriptive findings, every variable is a statistically significant predictor of perceptions of gender bias in elections. The coefficients are always positive, and the confidence intervals do not cross the zero line. Because the variables are measured on different scales, we cannot simply compare the size of their coefficients to determine which explanation exerts the strongest relative effect. But we can use the regression equation to generate predicted values on the perceptions of electoral bias scale.

Consider social identity. The positive coefficients indicate that women and Democrats are more likely to see bias against female candidates than are men and non-Democrats. All else equal, a female Democrat will agree with 0.72 more of the statements that comprise the seven-point electoral bias scale than will a male independent or Republican. Considering that the average respondent agreed with 2.74 statements, a shift of nearly three-quarters of a statement is notable.

The other factors confer even more explanatory power. Holding all other variables constant, individuals who believed that Clinton and Palin in 2008 were treated unfairly by the media and voters are a full two points more likely to perceive that female candidates in general experience bias when they run for office than are people who did not think that Clinton or Palin suffered in the

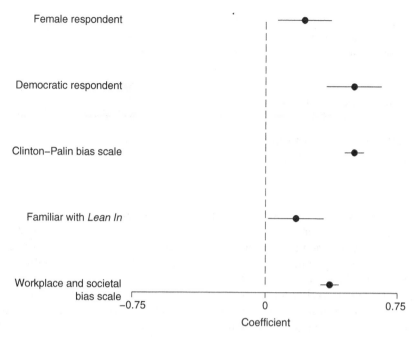

FIGURE 6.4. Influences on perceptions of gender bias in elections.
Notes: Dots represent OLS regression coefficients, with 95 percent confidence intervals. See Table A6.2 (full sample model) for the full regression equation.

press or at the polls. The same is true of those who were familiar with *Lean In*, or who reported gender bias in the workplace and society. These individuals "score" approximately 2.3 points higher on the perceptions of electoral bias scale than respondents who weren't familiar with Sandberg's book and who did not see workplace or societal sexism.[29]

Although this analysis represents only a first cut, it begins to reconcile the empirical absence of systematic bias against female candidates with widespread perceptions of a political landscape rife with sexism and gender discrimination. People's assessments of what it's like for women who run for office are not

[29] For the most part, these factors operate similarly for male and female respondents. Views of Clinton and Palin, as well as perceptions of workplace and societal bias, have similar effects when we run the analysis separately for men and women (see Table A6.2, columns 2 and 3). Only familiarity with *Lean In* loses significance in the model for male respondents. Perhaps this is a result of women's heightened gender consciousness, which serves as the mechanism that leads them to extrapolate from the book to the political arena. Men might need more proximate experiences with workplace or societal gender discrimination to make the leap to the political sphere. We also find that partisanship plays a stronger role among men than among women, largely owing to the fact that Republican men are much less likely to see gender bias in elections than other individuals. Thus, the partisan gap among men is far larger than the partisan gap among women.

rooted in the level playing fields they observe in their districts. Instead, these perceptions appear to derive, at least in part, from social identities, national portrayals of women in politics, and exposure to bias in non-political environments. This serves as the backdrop as we conclude the book with a series of implications of our findings and prescriptions for the press, practitioners, and political scientists.

WOMEN'S UNDER-REPRESENTATION AND THE IMPLICATIONS FOR THE MEDIA, POLITICAL ORGANIZATIONS, AND POLITICAL SCIENTISTS

Establishing the disconnect between an environment that does not systematically differ for male and female candidates and the public perception that gender bias pervades the electoral arena is more than an academic enterprise. It is fundamental for understanding the roots of women's under-representation: these misperceptions likely contribute to women's self-doubts about their ability to run for office. And because these doubts contribute to women's lower likelihood of running for office, the conventional wisdom ultimately makes it more difficult to close the gender gap in political ambition.

In making this argument, we want to be clear about two things: First, we do not, in any way, think it is unreasonable to see the electoral environment this way. As this chapter suggests, national conversations about women in politics, women's under-representation in our political institutions, and gender bias in realms outside of the political arena make it entirely plausible to hold this view. And every time a journalist writes a story about gender discrimination in politics, every time a female politician highlights an episode of sexism, every time a political scientist portrays the experiences of a limited number of high-profile female candidates as typical, those perceptions are reinforced. Second, we do not mean to diminish any instance of gender bias, question its veracity, or suggest that episodes of sexism should go unspoken, unreported, or undenounced. The sexism that women experience in the workplace, that female candidates and elected officials encounter in the political arena, and that journalists chronicle in the stories they write is real and unfortunate. But when political organizations rely on hashtags like #CertifiedSexism and #ReadyForSexism,[30] or chronicle references to media mentions of female candidates' appearance,[31] they validate the notion that the campaign trail is biased and discriminatory. As a result, unrepresentative, uncommon instances of sexism aggregate up to a sense that elections are systematically harder for women.

---

[30] The Women's Campaign Fund, a bipartisan national organization, regularly sends emails and online briefings in this vein. See www.wcfonline.org/msrepresentation (October 3, 2015).
[31] "Name It. Change It.," a project sponsored by the Women's Media Center, She Should Run, and the Political Parity Project, exists to "end sexist and misogynistic coverage of women candidates by all members of the press." See www.nameitchangeit.org/pages/about (October 3, 2015).

And that has an impact on women who might think about running for office. When assessing their potential as candidates, perceptions of electoral bias and more challenging campaign dynamics lead many women to conclude that they have to be better than the average man to succeed.[32] National surveys of potential candidates – lawyers, business leaders, educators, and political activists – consistently reveal that men and women with the same professional, educational, and political credentials do not assess their political qualifications the same way (see Lawless and Fox 2005, 2010, 2012). They look the same on paper, but men are roughly 50 percent more likely than women to consider themselves "very qualified" to seek an elective position. Women are twice as likely as men to assert that they are "not at all qualified" to run for office.[33] Whether a candidate self-assesses as "qualified" is one of the most important predictors not only of considering a candidacy, but also eventually launching an actual campaign.

Importantly, this gap in self-assessments does not derive from differences in women's and men's actual credentials. Rather, it stems in large part from how women perceive the electoral environment. Like the general public, many women in the pool of potential candidates do not believe that women who run for office perform as well as men. Most think that female candidates are subjected to sexist media coverage. Seven out of ten doubt that women can raise as much money as men. And the majority contend that women running for office face discrimination from voters. It's hardly a surprise that female potential candidates are about two-thirds more likely than men to doubt that they have thick enough skin to run for office, and are significantly more likely to question their ability to engage in the mechanics and withstand the rigors of a campaign (Lawless and Fox 2012). Experimental research has shown that media coverage suggesting that women face electoral bias drives down young women's confidence in their ability to mount a future political campaign (Brooks and Hayes 2015). These views might also contribute to the gender gap in political recruitment (Fox and Lawless 2010). Party leaders, elected officials, and political activists who think that women will face obstacles that men will not encounter may be less likely to encourage women to run for office.

If misperceptions about the electoral environment contribute to women's under-representation – both directly and indirectly – what is to be done? How can these views be altered? We think the solution lies, at least in part, with

---

[32] We are certainly not the first people to make this argument. Scholars have long argued that traditional gender socialization – women's historical exclusion from the political sphere, coupled with tenacious traditional gender role expectations – fosters a masculinized ethos in electoral politics (e.g., Enloe 2004; Flammang 1997; Lawless and Fox 2010). A political consequence of these patterns of gender socialization is that, over time, men have developed a greater sense of comfort and familiarity in the political sphere (see Thomas 2005). But we are the first to provide such thorough, systematic evidence that these perceptions do not reflect the empirical reality of a very similar electoral landscape for women and men.

[33] This gender gap in self-efficacy, which exists across professions, is roughly equal for Democrats and Republicans (Fox and Lawless 2011).

modifying the way the national media cover women in politics, the strategies groups advocating for women's representation employ, and the research agenda political scientists pursue.

The media

As with everything in politics, most Americans' exposure to women in the political realm occurs through the media. And as our data have suggested, voters' perceptions of electoral bias seem to be fed by portrayals of high-profile female politicians facing sexism. This likely occurs because news stories regularly state that women in American elections face a more difficult road to office than do men, and because widespread coverage of unusual episodes of sexism sends a signal that they are run of the mill. This dynamic is exacerbated in an environment where traditional reporting is accompanied by a seemingly endless stream of commentary – occasionally of questionable veracity – on cable television and the internet. This helps paint a picture of an electoral system more riven by gender bias than it actually is.

We offer two recommendations for how the media can help chip away at the existing (mis)perceptions. One is that reporters, pundits, and commentators familiarize themselves with contemporary research on women in elections. To the extent that coverage of gender and elections engages academic scholarship, it often seems to be rooted in findings from the 1980s and 1990s, an era in which social attitudes and norms – and the relative novelty of women in politics – may very well have created a more difficult landscape for female candidates. More recent research, however, finds little evidence of bias, sexism, or disadvantages arising from gender stereotypes, especially when we look beyond presidential politics. Yet relatively little news reporting makes mention of this changing context. This is not to say that there are no exceptions. It is possible to find an occasional article about what constitutes sexist coverage,[34] whether sexism played a role in a female candidate's loss,[35] or the evolution of female politicians' experiences.[36] But too much political reporting continues to make vague references to unique challenges that a candidate will face "as a woman," including suggestions that gender stereotypes pose obstacles.

[34] Molly Ball, "No, It's Not Sexist to Describe Women Politicians' Clothes," *The Atlantic*, July 2, 2013. Accessed at: www.theatlantic.com/politics/archive/2013/07/no-its-not-sexist-to-describe -women-politicians-clothes/277460/ (October 4, 2015).

[35] Jodi Kantor and Kate Taylor, "In Quinn's Loss, Questions about Role of Gender and Sexuality," *New York Times*, September 11, 2013. Accessed at: www.nytimes.com/2013/09 /12/nyregion/in-quinns-loss-questions-about-role-of-gender-and-sexuality.html?pagewanted =1&smid=tw-share (October 4, 2015).

[36] Liza Mundy, "The Secret History of Women in the Senate," *Politico Magazine*, January/ February 2015. Accessed at: www.politico.com/magazine/story/2015/01/senate-women -secret-history-113908 (October 4, 2015).

To be clear, we aren't suggesting that reporters or talking heads be able to craft a literature review or pick apart a regression model.[37] But journalists who cover gender in politics, and pundits who analyze it, should be attentive to the scholarship that shows the conditions under which gender matters, the conditions under which it doesn't, and the implications for women's fortunes when they run. As we have shown throughout this book, the campaign trail can on occasion present slightly different challenges and opportunities for women. But these circumstances are unusual. And even the few differences we found have little to do with outcomes – either in terms of the kind of coverage women receive, the way voters assess them, or their likelihood of winning. Because academic research is now increasingly accessible through blogs, websites, webinars, and ungated versions of papers, the barriers to learning about this emerging research are relatively low.

Our second recommendation involves the way the media cover high-profile episodes of sexism. Whether it's Donald Trump talking about Carly Fiorina's face, President Obama calling California's Kamala Harris the country's "best looking attorney general," the late Daniel Inouye encouraging fellow U.S. Senator Kirsten Gillibrand to remain "chubby," or former U.S. Senator Tom Harkin comparing Senator Joni Ernst to Taylor Swift, the coverage is immediate and relentless. And in one respect, it's salutary. One way to drive sexism out of public discourse is to "name and shame" – call it out and highlight its inappropriateness. Media coverage of these incidents can help make sexism, in politics and elsewhere, socially unacceptable.

At the same time, we encourage journalists to put such episodes in context. Sexism no doubt occurs, as these examples make clear. But the presence of sexism from colleagues or fellow candidates is far from ubiquitous. Moreover, even when it does happen, it does not mean that women will face bias from voters or the media on the campaign trail. As we have explained, a variety of forces – such as journalistic norms and party polarization – operate to reduce gender bias in the electoral environment. Yet the coverage of these incidents often implies that they are representative of what women encounter in all realms of political life. And that's just not true. Simple modifications to stories about sexism and bias, therefore, could go a long way. Merely introducing some of these incidents by highlighting how unusual they are could remind people that despite the behavior of some bad actors, women do not systematically have a harder time getting elected or face discrimination when they run for office.

We are not fooling ourselves. In a click-bait headline world, we are not so naïve as to think that "Five of the Most Sexist Moments in Politics" is likely to be replaced by "Five of the Most Sexist Moments in Politics That Don't Diminish Women's Chances of Winning Elections."[38] But these two simple

---

[37] That, of course, is up to Reviewer 2.
[38] Valentina Zarya, "Playing the Gender Card: Five of the Most Sexist Moments in Politics," *Fortune*, July 22, 2015. Accessed at: http://fortune.com/2015/07/22/sexist-moments-politics/ (October 4, 2015).

recommendations – that journalists consider the current state of research on women in politics and that they cover episodes of sexism with some broader context – strike us as practical. They would produce better reporting without sacrificing the ability for news outlets to cater to the market demand for stories about gender in politics.

Political organizations and politicians

When women run for office, they do just as well as men. They raise just as much money, receive the same amount of news coverage, and win elections at equal rates. These equitable outcomes are the result, in significant measure, of the efforts of many political organizations and female politicians. Partisan, bipartisan, and non-partisan groups – Emily's List, Emerge America, VoteRunLead, and others – train female candidates and prepare them to succeed. They help combat women's tendency to doubt their qualifications to run, familiarize them with the nuts and bolts of campaigning, and help women develop donor and supporter networks. Prominent female politicians – through public speeches, memoirs, and political action committees – also regularly encourage women to take the plunge. These organizations and individuals, by recruiting and training women to run for office, not only help level the playing field for women, but also do unparalleled work closing the gender gap in political ambition.

These groups, though, often find themselves stuck between a rock and a hard place. Although their mission is to encourage women to run for office and support those who do, money is required to do the work. And showcasing egregious incidents of sexism is a tried and true way to motivate donors. In early 2014, for example, The Hillary Project, an anti-Clinton super-PAC, released an online game that gave players an opportunity to slap Clinton across the face. In response, Ready for Hillary, the super-PAC that supported Clinton's 2016 presidential candidacy prior to her announcement, sent an email to its hundreds of thousands of supporters and solicited donations. The result? A 40 percent increase in web traffic and online contributions.[39] In 2012, the Turn Right USA super-PAC ran an ad that depicted Democratic congressional candidate Janice Hahn as a pole dancer. The Democratic Congressional Campaign Committee launched an immediate online response, and expected to raise $150,000 in less than five days.[40] During the 2014 Texas governor's race, Democratic candidate Wendy Davis, who was catapulted into the national spotlighting for her eleven-hour filibuster of an anti-abortion bill, was dubbed "Abortion Barbie" by

[39] Amy Chozick, "Outrage over Sexist Remarks Turns into a Political Fundraising Tool," *New York Times*, February 27, 2014. Accessed at: www.nytimes.com/2014/02/28/us/politics/outrage-over-sexist-remarks-turns-into-a-political-fund-raising-tool.html (October 4, 2015).
[40] Catalina Camia, "Dems Raise Money Off Vile Ad Attacking House Candidate," *U.S. News & World Report*, June 15, 2011. Accessed at: http://content.usatoday.com/communities/onpolitics/post/2011/06/janice-hahn-video-gangsters-craig-huey-/1#.VhHIWitK-aY (October 4, 2015).

a small group of conservative critics. When her campaign discovered life-size posters of Davis's head on a naked, pregnant Barbie doll's body, scissors hanging in the background, they responded by sending out five fundraising emails.[41] Rather than fear sexist attacks, explained a former Emily's List communications director, "We gleefully wait for the next one."[42]

We understand the incentives to publicize uncivil and sexist attacks on women. And not only because it can be an effective and efficient way to raise money. Denouncing episodes of sexism is part of the mission of many of these groups. By calling out examples of sexist reporting, bias on the campaign trail, or obstacles female candidates confront, they highlight the importance of their own work and demonstrate that more needs to be done.[43] These are the very things these groups should do. But we think it might be possible to do so without inadvertently discouraging women from running for office. Most obviously, context is key. Rather than portray these rare episodes as typical, can-you-believe-they're-at-it-again moments, why not frame them as unusual? Why not take credit for the fact that blatant sexism is far less prevalent than it once was, in large part because of the work these organizations do? Why not tweak the message so as to characterize the incident as sexist, but not the overall political environment? That way, donors would remain motivated, but the collateral damage associated with portraying the electoral environment as rife with sexism would be minimized.

Context also matters when encouraging women to run for office and providing campaign training. Informing potential candidates of the current political landscape and the latest research findings could quell their concerns about the electoral environment. Differentiating between presidential campaigns and contests for the other 500,000 political positions could mitigate women's reticence to put themselves forward. Asking elected officials and former candidates who tell their "war stories" to share not only examples of the sexism they encountered, but also its typically low prevalence, could give women a better sense of the infrequency with which women encounter bias on the campaign trail. Here too, we are not recommending that political organizations conduct business in a fundamentally different way. We're simply suggesting that, in the course of leveling the playing field for female

---

[41] Jay Newton-Small, "Davis Campaign Seizes on 'Abortion Barbie' Posters in Texas," *Time*, May 28, 2014. Accessed at: http://time.com/132067/wendy-davis-texas-abortion-barbie/ (October 5, 2015).

[42] Amy Chozick, "Outrage over Sexist Remarks Turns into a Political Fundraising Tool," *New York Times*, February 27, 2014. Accessed at: www.nytimes.com/2014/02/28/us/politics/outrage-over-sexist-remarks-turns-into-a-political-fund-raising-tool.html (October 4, 2015).

[43] A video produced by the Women's Media Center serves as a perfect example. In "Sexism Sells, but We're Not Buying It," the organization presents a six-minute stream of sexist comments that pundits and political commentators made about Hillary Clinton, Nancy Pelosi, and Sarah Palin. At the end of the video, viewers are encouraged to join the organization if they want to change the status quo. See "Sexism Sells, but We're Not Buying It." Women's Media Center. Accessed at: www.youtube.com/watch?v=U-k0IY5CuGI (October 5, 2015).

candidates, they should not – even inadvertently – portray that playing field as more systematically inhospitable than it actually is.

Political scientists

What do our findings suggest for researchers interested in women's under-representation? In the broadest terms, we think there are diminishing returns from looking at the campaign trail, especially in general elections. Our multifaceted approach, fine-grained coding scheme, and extensive data analysis turned up virtually nothing in the way of gender differences. From our vantage point, it is clear that the congressional campaign environment is very similar for female and male candidates, and that what's holding women back is not a discriminatory or more challenging electoral landscape. This is a clearly positive development in the pursuit of political equality.

This is not to say, however, that we think the search for gender effects in elections is altogether moribund. Our argument implies that candidate sex may play a more prominent role in contexts in which female candidates are novel (such as presidential elections) and where partisanship is less important (such as primary or non-partisan elections). Thus, studying gender dynamics in these circumstances may yield valuable theoretical and empirical insights (e.g., Crowder-Meyer, Gadarian, and Trounstine 2015). Similarly, our media argument rests heavily on adherence to journalistic norms, which limit the influence of candidate sex in news coverage. But we know little about whether these patterns prevail in newer partisan or ideological outlets, where the traditional standards of journalism are far less influential. The caveat is that the audiences for these venues remain small (Lawrence, Sides, and Farrell 2010; Prior 2013), and very little of their coverage focuses on anything other than presidential or Senate contests. Nonetheless, there remain opportunities for discerning the conditions under which candidate sex matters, and whether such dynamics affect women's path to office. If, as many political consultants think, women make better candidates, then we may actually find that gender works in female candidates' favor, especially at a time of public discontent with the political process.[44]

Regardless of the findings, gender differences that emerge must – and we apologize for sounding like a broken record – be placed in context. All social scientists seek generalizability in their research. That is, we all want our findings to apply as broadly as possible. But we must use caution when extrapolating from the results of case studies or context-dependent findings. Studies of Geraldine Ferraro, Elizabeth Dole, Sarah Palin, and Hillary Clinton no doubt have helped us understand the way that these women – and potentially others – may be covered by the press or viewed by voters on the biggest stage. But their

---

[44] Molly Ball, "A Woman's Edge: Why Both the Dems and the GOP Think Voters Prefer Female Candidates," *The Atlantic*, May 2013. Accessed at: www.theatlantic.com/magazine /archive/2013/05/a-womans-edge/309284/ (October 7, 2015).

experiences, and the experiences of other high-profile candidates running for statewide office, may not always generalize to the experiences of the vast majority of women running for office in the United States. This is particularly true in the case of Clinton, about whom studies are sure to proliferate in the coming years.[45] Research should be clear about the scope and limits of any empirical findings or theoretical frameworks. Just as the media and political organizations should consider the bigger picture, so should political scientists.

Context matters not only for the generalizability of research findings, but also for how we interpret the results in any one study. Emphasizing one or a handful of gender differences amid an array of statistically insignificant findings can be tempting, especially given the conventional wisdom. But if such a difference stands out in a larger sea of similarity, what is the real story? Take, for instance, the nineteen significant gender differences in the summary of the statistical evidence we presented at the beginning of this chapter. We could have written a book, or at the very least an article, about these few ways that the campaign environment varies for women and men. But that would hardly be an accurate description of the electoral landscape, as it ignores the 286 places where we found no differences. There must be a commitment from scholars, reviewers, and editors to write up and publish well-executed research, regardless of the findings. The move toward pre-registration – in which scholars publish their hypotheses and research designs before executing a study – may be one potential solution (Monogan 2013; Nyhan 2015).

In a similar vein, it is critical that studies of gender and elections should not fall victim to the "file drawer" problem – the tendency of research that doesn't have statistically significant findings to be rejected in the academic review process or never to be written up at all (e.g., Franco, Malhotra, and Simonovits 2014; Rosenthal 1979). This form of publication bias tends to over-represent conclusions that are consistent with the direction of statistically significant results. In the study of women and elections, this means that evidence of gender differences tends to be easier to publish than results finding no differences. To be sure, the file drawer problem can be overcome by diligent researchers who pose a question in such a way as to make null findings interesting and important. But on average, "non-results" have a harder time finding their way to publication, even if they are no less "true."

Political scientists probably know more systematically about women's electoral experiences and fortunes than anyone else. Whereas practitioners, pollsters, and politicians are familiar with the nuances of many individual campaigns, it's political scientists who provide theoretical arguments and empirical evidence for campaign dynamics more generally. To the extent that the academic community is committed to contextualizing and publicizing

---

[45] Linda Feldman, "Hillary Clinton's Challenge: Sexism or 'Clinton-ism'?" *Christian Science Monitor*, September 30, 2015. Accessed at: www.csmonitor.com/USA/Politics/2015/0930/Hillary-Clinton-s-challenge-Sexism-or-Clinton-ism (October 8, 2015).

research about gender and elections, we can play a central role in closing the gap between the public's perceptions of gender bias and the reality of gender equity in most cases.

A FINAL WORD

This is an optimistic book. Our findings reveal a remarkably level playing field for women running in the most recent U.S. House races. The fact that these contests share characteristics with the thousands of other state legislative and down-ballot elections across the country suggests favorable terrain for future generations of female candidates in the vast majority of American campaigns. Had we been writing twenty years ago, we would likely not have found the same thing. Our results reflect in large part the efforts of many female politicians who, by seeking office themselves, have made women's presence in politics far less novel. And while challenges for women remain – particularly in the candidate emergence process – there are fewer barriers to political success today than ever before. The challenge that lies ahead is to let people know.

Appendices

APPENDIX 1. *Issue classifications based on coding from the 2010 Wesleyan Media Project campaign ad data*

Race and social groups	Foreign affairs	Defense and security	Taxes and spending	"Women's" issues
affirmative action, homosexuality/gay and lesbian rights, race relations/civil rights	China, foreign aid, foreign policy, Israel, Middle East	Afghanistan/war in Afghanistan, Iran, Iraq/war in Iraq, military, nuclear proliferation, September 11, terror/terrorism/terrorists, veterans	deficit/budget/debts, government spending, taxes	abortion, child care, women's health

Civil and social order	Social welfare	Economy	Government functioning	"Men's" issues
abortion, assisted suicide/euthanasia, capital punishment, civil liberties/privacy, crime, gambling, gun control, moral/family/religious values, narcotics/illegal drugs, pledge of allegiance	BP oil spill, child care, education/schools, energy policy, environment, global warming, health care, lottery for education, Medicare, prescription drugs, social security, tobacco, welfare, women's health	business, economic stimulus, economy, employment/jobs, farming, housing/subprime mortgages, minimum wage, poverty, recession, trade/globalization, unions	campaign finance reform, corporate fraud, government ethics/scandals, Supreme Court/judiciary, term limits	Afghanistan/war in Afghanistan, capital punishment, crime, gun control, Iran, Iraq/war in Iraq, military, nuclear proliferation, September 11, terror/terrorism/terrorists

APPENDIX 2. *Issue classifications for coding of candidate tweets in 2014*

Race and social groups	Foreign affairs	Defense and security	Taxes and spending	"Women's" issues
advocacy for women, affirmative action, Alaskan natives, civil rights, Don't Ask Don't Tell, ERA, gay rights, marriage equality, minority students, Native American issues, pay equity, race advocacy, racial equality, Redskins football team, seniors, workplace discrimination, workplace diversity	Africa, Arctic, China, diplomacy, foreign policy, genocide, human rights, international adoption, international issues in health, Israel, kidnapping of girls in Nigeria, Mexico, Middle East, other specific country, spending on foreign aid, trade	Afghanistan, Benghazi, defense, defense spending, GI bill, Guantanamo Bay, intelligence, Iran, Iraq, military, NASA/space, national security, nuclear weapons, Pakistan, Patriot Act, radical Islam, security, terrorism, torture, veterans' affairs, war	arts programs, balanced budget, budget/spending, Bush tax cuts, business, debt ceiling, debt or deficit, earmarks/pork, eminent domain, funding for local projects, funding for memorials, funding for NPR, government size/power, oil subsidies, other program funding, research and development, spending, taxes/tax breaks	abortion, advocacy for women, birth control/contraception, children's issues/child care, crimes to a fetus, domestic violence, ERA, family planning, kidnapping of girls in Nigeria, maternity leave, pay equity, pornography, sexual assault, women's health care

Civil and social order	Social welfare	Economy	Government functioning	"Men's" issues
abortion, alcohol, assisted suicide, bullying, civil liberties, crime, crimes to a fetus, criminal justice system, death penalty, domestic violence, drug	9/11 workers' health plan, birth control/contraception, BP oil spill, cap and trade, children's issues/ child care, climate change, cloning, conservation,	agriculture, auto industry, bailout, banks, business, Cash for Clunkers, consumer protection, credit card reform, economy, ethanol subsidies, farms,	campaign finance reform, constitutional amendments, decreasing partisanship in Congress, disaster relief/ FEMA, ethics, FDA, government	Afghanistan, Benghazi, crime, criminal justice system, death penalty, defense, defense spending, Ferguson, Guantanamo Bay, guns, hunting rights,

rehab programs, English as the national language, Ferguson, gambling/casinos, guns, hate crimes, hunting rights, illegal drugs, immigration, legalization of marijuana, legalization of medical marijuana, police brutality, pornography, privacy, public safety, religion/religious issues/creationism taught in schools, religious freedom, school prayer, seatbelt laws, securing the border, separation of church and state, sex education, sexual assault, social issues, stem cell research, tobacco/smoking

Ebola, education, endangered animals, energy/electricity/coal/nuclear power, entitlements, environment, family leave, family planning, fires, health/health care/health insurance/Obamacare, Hobby Lobby case, homelessness, maternity leave, Medicaid, medical research, Medicare, mental health, mining, natural gas, oil drilling, oil pipelines, paid sick leave, pilot safety, prescription drugs, recycling, school vouchers, social security, social services, student loans, teacher salaries, teen pregnancy, utilities, water, welfare, wildlife/forests, women's health, work safety, workers' compensation

federal employee wages, fishing, Freddie Mac/Fannie Mae, free enterprise, gas prices, global currency, housing/foreclosures, inequality (economic), infrastructure, jobs, labor, local development, manufacturing, merchant marines, minimum wage, mortgage rates, net neutrality, outsourcing, patent protection, personal finances, poverty, redistribution of wealth, regulations, retirement, stimulus, TARP, technology, tourism, transportation, unemployment, unions, Wall Street reform

functioning/reform/transparency, insurance reform (not health care), IRS, lobbying, PACs, personal scandal, postal service, reforms to congressional campaigns, secret service, state secession, term limits, tort reform, wages for members of Congress and other elected officials

intelligence, Iran, Iraq, military, national security, nuclear weapons, Pakistan, Patriot Act, public safety, radical Islam, securing the border, security, terrorism, torture, war

APPENDIX 3. *Trait classifications for coding of candidate tweets in 2014*

	Competence	Leadership	Integrity	Empathy
Positive traits	accomplished, articulate, assertive, capable, careful, cautious, clever, collaborative, committed, competent, consistent, contemplative, creative, dedicated, determined, diligent, effective, eloquent, experienced, focused, good speaker/orator, hardworking, has common-sense, intelligent, knowledgeable, nerd, open-minded, polished, pragmatic, proactive, problem solver, quick thinker, quick-witted, rational, reasonable, reliable, responsible, savvy, sharp, talented, thorough, thoughtful, understated, wonky	active, ambitious, brave, committed, confident, consistent, courageous, decisive, direct, effective, energetic, enthusiastic, entrepreneurial, fearless, feisty, fighter, formidable, idealistic, independent, independent thinker, maverick, optimistic, passionate, persistent, powerful, principled, straight shooter, strong, strong leader, team player, tough, unapologetic, unifier	decent, earnest, ethical, has integrity, honest, honorable, principled, reliable, sincere, trustworthy	accessible, affable, approachable, caring, compassionate, concerned with needs of district, courteous, disarming, down to earth, empathetic, engaging, friendly, gentle, good listener, in touch, kind, laid back, likeable, listens to constituents, low-key, nice, outgoing, patient, personable, selfless, sensitive, sympathetic, tactful, talkative

Negative traits	absent-minded, bizarre, careless, clueless, crazy, incompetent, ineffective, inelegant, inexperienced, irrational, irresponsible, not collaborative, not knowledgeable, not dedicated, not polished, not pragmatic, not serious, not smooth, party animal, reactive, senile, superficial, unfit, uninformed, unintelligent, unprofessional, unreliable	abrasive, adversarial, afraid, argumentative, blunt, boring, brash, caustic, combative, coward, cynical, difficult, fearful, flashy, flip-flopper, inconsistent, lack of confidence, lackadaisical, lacks vision, naïve, not confident, not independent, not a leader, obnoxious, opportunistic, party puppet/lapdog, passive, rabble rouser, reserved, rigid, scared, showboat, unreasonable, unsure, useless crank, weak, weak leader	dirty fighter, disgraceful, dishonest, disingenuous, evasive, greedy, hypocritical, immoral, lacks integrity, liar, malicious, manipulative, not trustworthy, unethical	aloof, bigoted, condescending, cranky, elitist, insensitive, not caring, not engaged, not warm, not nice, out of touch, self-serving, tactless

TABLE A3.1. *The effects of candidate sex and party on issue content in 2010 campaign ads*

	Economy	Social welfare	Taxes & spending	Defense & security	Civil & social order	Govt. functioning	Foreign affairs	Race & social groups	"Men's" issues	"Women's" issues
Female	-0.008	0.180	0.255	0.104	-0.070	-0.600	-0.453	—	-0.417	0.262
	(0.178)	(0.178)	(0.173)	(0.341)	(0.317)	(0.313)	(0.409)		(0.473)	(0.461)
Democrat	-0.970*	-0.556*	-1.385*	1.382*	1.104*	0.384	0.318	1.824	1.260*	1.506*
	(0.141)	(0.131)	(0.145)	(0.335)	(0.258)	(0.228)	(0.247)	(1.106)	(0.360)	(0.396)
Constant	0.887*	0.077	1.112*	-3.465*	-3.233*	-2.565*	-2.619*	-7.038*	-3.415*	-4.372*
	(0.128)	(0.111)	(0.119)	(0.303)	(0.207)	(0.199)	(0.183)	(0.846)	(0.309)	(0.350)
N	478,495	478,495	478,495	478,495	478,495	478,495	478,495	478,495	478,495	478,495
Pseudo R^2	0.040	0.014	0.079	0.048	0.033	0.009	0.006	0.039	0.042	0.047
Log likelihood	-325,270	-329,243	-325,097	-128,523	-127,669	-136,602	-129,605	-9,302	-119,482	-75,478
χ^2	47.972	18.249	90.726	17.245	18.446	7.090	2.453	2.720	12.902	15.776

Note: Dependent variables are whether a campaign ad mentioned that particular issue. Cell entries are logistic regression coefficients with robust standard errors clustered on congressional district in parentheses. Level of significance: * $p < 0.05$.

TABLE A3.2. *The effects of candidate sex and party on word usage in 2010 campaign ads*

	Liberal	Change	Dirty	Conservative	Special interests	Wall Street	Fighter
Female	-0.453	0.430	-0.121	-0.057	-0.962	-0.122	0.219
	(0.661)	(0.361)	(0.414)	(0.463)	(0.660)	(0.250)	(0.329)
Democrat	-2.800*	-1.731*	-1.246*	-0.681	0.239	0.480*	0.849*
	(0.618)	(0.523)	(0.352)	(0.449)	(0.343)	(0.234)	(0.214)
Constant	-2.572*	-2.713*	-3.007*	-3.296*	-3.646*	-2.319*	-2.744*
	(0.181)	(0.151)	(0.192)	(0.261)	(0.225)	(0.195)	(0.182)
N	478,495	478,495	478,495	478,495	478,495	478,495	478,495
Pseudo R^2	0.125	0.071	0.038	0.012	0.009	0.008	0.023
Log likelihood	-68,744	-74,966	-61,712	-57,527	-58,748	-170,054	-157,907
χ^2	22.557	11.674	13.210	2.308	2.269	4.476	16.691

Note: Dependent variables are whether a campaign ad mentioned that particular word. Cell entries are logistic regression coefficients with robust standard errors clustered on congressional district in parentheses. Level of significance: * $p < 0.05$.

TABLE A3.3. *The effects of candidate sex and party on issue content in 2014 tweets*

	Economy	Social welfare	Taxes & spending	Defense & security	Civil & social order	Govt. func-tioning	Foreign affairs	Race & social groups	"Men's" issues	"Women's" issues
Female	−0.148	−0.404	−0.051	0.119	0.180	−0.750*	−0.398	0.182	0.342	0.635*
	(0.154)	(0.212)	(0.196)	(0.461)	(0.391)	(0.285)	(0.348)	(0.171)	(0.331)	(0.259)
Democrat	0.631*	−0.240	0.003	−0.784*	0.195	0.120	−0.172	1.348*	−0.866*	1.74*
	(0.168)	(0.228)	(0.168)	(0.303)	(0.333)	(0.247)	(0.319)	(0.221)	(0.239)	(0.271)
Constant	−3.624*	−2.594*	−3.846*	−3.443*	−4.262*	−5.249*	−4.559*	−5.765*	−3.312*	−7.059*
	(0.147)	(0.240)	(0.147)	(0.275)	(0.192)	(0.222)	(0.217)	(0.213)	(0.227)	(0.240)
N	54,083	54,083	54,083	54,083	54,083	54,083	54,083	54,083	54,083	54,083
Pseudo R^2	0.011	0.005	0.000	0.015	0.002	0.006	0.003	0.032	0.020	0.048
Log likelihood	−8,364	−11,911	−5,450	−5,948	−4,468	−1,657	−2,722	−2,526	−6,742	−1,291
χ^2	14.395	3.733	0.069	6.941	2.556	7.767	1.663	37.777	13.240	55.584

Note: Dependent variables are whether a tweet mentioned that particular issue. Cell entries are logistic regression coefficients with robust standard errors clustered on congressional district in parentheses. Level of significance: * $p < 0.05$.

TABLE A3.4. *The effects of candidate sex and party on trait content in 2014 tweets*

	Positive leadership	Positive competence	Positive empathy	Positive integrity	Negative leadership	Negative competence	Negative empathy	Negative integrity
Female	-0.048	0.063	-0.024	-0.352	-0.754	-0.508	-0.383	-0.007
	(0.174)	(0.182)	(0.356)	(0.368)	(0.413)	(0.430)	(0.531)	(0.655)
Democrat	-0.298	0.354*	-0.066	-0.308	-0.677	0.426	-0.175	0.098
	(0.154)	(0.167)	(0.355)	(0.270)	(0.377)	(0.360)	(0.481)	(0.504)
Constant	-3.550*	-4.647*	-4.272*	-5.793*	-5.147*	-7.450*	-7.400*	-7.233*
	(0.156)	(0.151)	(0.378)	(0.236)	(0.382)	(0.28)	(0.441)	(0.435)
N	54,083	54,083	54,083	54,083	54,083	54,083	54,083	54,083
Pseudo R^2	0.002	0.003	0.000	0.003	0.015	0.005	0.002	0.000
Log likelihood	-6,395	-3,449	-3,807	-925	-1,347	-299	-239	-335
χ^2	3.741	4.735	0.039	1.581	4.579	2.483	0.523	0.050

Note: Dependent variables are whether a tweet mentioned that particular trait. Cell entries are logistic regression coefficients with robust standard errors clustered on congressional district in parentheses. Level of significance: * $p < 0.05$.

TABLE A4.1. *The effects of candidate sex, electoral competitiveness, and incumbency on volume of coverage*

	2010				2014			
	Total stories	Gender mentions	Trait mentions	Issue mentions	Total stories	Gender mentions	Trait mentions	Issue mentions
Female	0.182	0.042	-0.000	0.159	1.765*	0.000	-0.010	0.078
	(1.038)	(0.029)	(0.029)	(0.153)	(0.881)	(0.020)	(0.021)	(0.158)
Competitiveness	12.790*	0.061*	0.164*	0.912*	13.105*	0.078*	0.197*	0.918*
	(1.573)	(0.021)	(0.042)	(0.153)	(1.786)	(0.029)	(0.048)	(0.199)
Incumbent	0.361	0.007	0.104*	0.899*	-0.510	-0.002	0.078*	0.810*
	(0.458)	(0.012)	(0.018)	(0.085)	(0.395)	(0.015)	(0.020)	(0.093)
Democrat	-0.033	-0.004	-0.019	-0.291*	0.051	-0.006	-0.026	-0.168*
	(0.153)	(0.013)	(0.019)	(0.075)	(0.130)	(0.015)	(0.018)	(0.080)
Female opponent	0.409	-0.019*	-0.005	-0.095	1.836*	0.001	0.003	0.029
	(1.045)	(0.008)	(0.026)	(0.110)	(0.882)	(0.032)	(0.027)	(0.151)
Constant	10.473*	0.034*	0.087*	0.987*	9.168*	0.100*	0.104*	1.454*
	(0.718)	(0.007)	(0.013)	(0.097)	(0.557)	(0.016)	(0.017)	(0.116)
N	787	787	787	787	763	763	763	763
R^2	0.190	0.029	0.061	0.133	0.249	0.008	0.069	0.072

Notes: The dependent variable in the "Total stories" equations is the total number of stories that mentioned a candidate. The "Gender mentions," "Trait mentions," and "Issues mentions" dependent variables are scaled by the number of stories in a district. Cell entries are unstandardized OLS regression coefficients with robust standard errors clustered on congressional district in parentheses. Level of significance: * $p < 0.05$.

TABLE A4.2. *The effects of candidate sex, electoral competitiveness, and incumbency on trait coverage in 2010*

	Positive leadership	Positive competence	Positive empathy	Positive integrity	Negative leadership	Negative competence	Negative empathy	Negative integrity
Female	0.002	−0.005	−0.001	−0.004	−0.000	−0.002	0.009	0.001
	(0.008)	(0.008)	(0.005)	(0.005)	(0.004)	(0.005)	(0.009)	(0.016)
Competitiveness	0.025*	0.018	0.001	0.007	0.011*	0.018*	0.008	0.076*
	(0.008)	(0.010)	(0.003)	(0.009)	(0.003)	(0.009)	(0.006)	(0.017)
Incumbent	0.017*	0.014*	0.012*	0.004	0.011*	0.006	0.017*	0.023*
	(0.006)	(0.007)	(0.004)	(0.005)	(0.003)	(0.006)	(0.005)	(0.009)
Democrat	0.008	0.007	0.001	−0.005	−0.004	−0.005	−0.010*	−0.011
	(0.006)	(0.008)	(0.004)	(0.006)	(0.003)	(0.005)	(0.005)	(0.010)
Female opponent	−0.000	−0.015*	0.010	−0.006	0.002	0.008	−0.002	−0.002
	(0.010)	(0.007)	(0.007)	(0.006)	(0.005)	(0.006)	(0.005)	(0.013)
Constant	0.010	0.022*	0.004	0.015*	0.004*	0.005	0.004*	0.023*
	(0.005)	(0.006)	(0.002)	(0.005)	(0.002)	(0.004)	(0.002)	(0.005)
N	787	787	787	787	787	787	787	787
R^2	0.025	0.009	0.016	0.003	0.022	0.007	0.030	0.050

Notes: Each dependent variable is scaled by the number of stories in a district. Cell entries are unstandardized OLS regression coefficients with robust standard errors clustered on congressional district in parentheses. Levels of significance: * $p < 0.05$.

TABLE A4.3. *The effects of candidate sex, electoral competitiveness, and incumbency on trait coverage in 2014*

	Positive leadership	Positive competence	Positive empathy	Positive integrity	Negative leadership	Negative competence	Negative empathy	Negative integrity
Female	0.002	0.021	-0.001	-0.001	-0.003	-0.007*	-0.005*	-0.016*
	(0.006)	(0.014)	(0.003)	(0.002)	(0.003)	(0.003)	(0.002)	(0.006)
Competitiveness	0.036*	0.036*	0.004	0.015*	0.017*	0.012*	0.010*	0.068*
	(0.008)	(0.012)	(0.004)	(0.005)	(0.006)	(0.005)	(0.005)	(0.033)
Incumbent	0.009	0.037*	-0.001	0.002	0.001	0.005	0.009*	0.016
	(0.005)	(0.010)	(0.003)	(0.002)	(0.003)	(0.003)	(0.003)	(0.013)
Democrat	-0.006	0.010	0.001	-0.005*	-0.006*	-0.002	-0.006	-0.011
	(0.006)	(0.010)	(0.003)	(0.002)	(0.003)	(0.003)	(0.003)	(0.010)
Female opponent	-0.008	0.016	0.004	-0.002	-0.002	0.001	-0.000	-0.005
	(0.006)	(0.016)	(0.004)	(0.003)	(0.003)	(0.004)	(0.005)	(0.013)
Constant	0.023*	0.028*	0.007*	0.008*	0.010*	0.009*	0.008*	0.011*
	(0.005)	(0.010)	(0.002)	(0.002)	(0.003)	(0.003)	(0.003)	(0.004)
N	763	763	763	763	763	763	763	763
R²	0.030	0.022	-0.003	0.028	0.024	0.012	0.014	0.025

Notes: Each dependent variable is scaled by the number of stories in a district. Cell entries are unstandardized OLS regression coefficients with robust standard errors clustered on congressional district in parentheses. Levels of significance: * p < 0.05.

TABLE A4.4. *The effects of candidate sex, electoral competitiveness, and incumbency on issue coverage in 2010*

	Economy	Social welfare	Taxes & spending	Defense & security	Civil & social order	Govt. func- tioning	Foreign affairs	Race & social groups	"Men's" issues	"Women's" issues
Female	0.061	0.024	−0.001	0.011	0.007	0.030	0.009	0.018	0.007	0.004
	(0.068)	(0.043)	(0.039)	(0.021)	(0.019)	(0.021)	(0.012)	(0.010)	(0.008)	(0.019)
Competitiveness	0.287*	0.276*	0.233*	0.036	0.061*	0.009	0.001	0.007	0.024*	0.030
	(0.057)	(0.047)	(0.047)	(0.020)	(0.022)	(0.011)	(0.008)	(0.007)	(0.010)	(0.016)
Incumbent	0.332*	0.206*	0.135*	0.118*	0.031*	0.036*	0.031*	0.011*	−0.001	0.075*
	(0.038)	(0.026)	(0.028)	(0.015)	(0.013)	(0.011)	(0.007)	(0.005)	(0.006)	(0.012)
Democrat	0.056	−0.054*	−0.227*	−0.031*	−0.013	−0.005	−0.017*	−0.001	−0.011*	−0.016
	(0.035)	(0.022)	(0.025)	(0.015)	(0.011)	(0.010)	(0.007)	(0.004)	(0.005)	(0.011)
Female opponent	−0.010	−0.024	−0.065	−0.018	0.024	0.005	−0.003	−0.003	−0.002	−0.018
	(0.044)	(0.032)	(0.038)	(0.019)	(0.023)	(0.019)	(0.008)	(0.006)	(0.009)	(0.015)
Constant	0.190*	0.235*	0.366*	0.057*	0.077*	0.022*	0.024*	0.014*	0.023*	0.065*
	(0.035)	(0.027)	(0.032)	(0.012)	(0.012)	(0.009)	(0.007)	(0.004)	(0.006)	(0.010)
N	787	787	787	787	787	787	787	787	787	787
R^2	0.113	0.110	0.096	0.067	0.017	0.015	0.015	0.009	0.012	0.039

Notes: Each dependent variable is scaled by the number of stories in a district. Cell entries are unstandardized OLS regression coefficients with robust standard errors clustered on congressional district in parentheses. Levels of significance: * $p < 0.05$.

TABLE A4.5. *The effects of candidate sex, electoral competitiveness, and incumbency on issue coverage in 2014*

	Economy	Social welfare	Taxes & spending	Defense & security	Civil & social order	Govt. functioning	Foreign affairs	Race & social groups	"Men's" issues	"Women's" issues
Female	−0.041	0.097	−0.032	0.002	0.045	−0.023	0.006	0.024*	0.125	−0.055
	(0.049)	(0.062)	(0.025)	(0.031)	(0.085)	(0.023)	(0.019)	(0.011)	(0.083)	(0.030)
Competitiveness	0.138*	0.356*	0.143*	0.109*	0.134*	−0.019	0.024	0.033*	0.031	0.115*
	(0.069)	(0.085)	(0.039)	(0.039)	(0.046)	(0.017)	(0.019)	(0.014)	(0.026)	(0.042)
Incumbent	0.192*	0.233*	0.051*	0.164*	0.082	0.052*	0.043*	−0.008	0.043	0.121*
	(0.037)	(0.040)	(0.021)	(0.020)	(0.044)	(0.022)	(0.012)	(0.008)	(0.040)	(0.022)
Democrat	0.029	−0.089*	−0.116*	−0.033	−0.004	0.043	−0.008	0.010	0.024	−0.047*
	(0.035)	(0.037)	(0.018)	(0.020)	(0.031)	(0.023)	(0.010)	(0.007)	(0.026)	(0.022)
Female opponent	0.084	−0.053	0.037	−0.040	−0.015	0.002	0.002	0.012	0.002	−0.043
	(0.060)	(0.056)	(0.037)	(0.030)	(0.038)	(0.020)	(0.017)	(0.011)	(0.022)	(0.032)
Constant	0.312*	0.449*	0.252*	0.143*	0.185*	0.040*	0.037*	0.037*	0.019	0.191*
	(0.038)	(0.044)	(0.025)	(0.024)	(0.037)	(0.015)	(0.010)	(0.009)	(0.027)	(0.024)
N	763	763	763	763	763	763	763	763	763	763
R^2	0.026	0.057	0.050	0.051	0.005	0.007	0.011	0.016	0.007	0.037

Notes: Each dependent variable is scaled by the number of stories in a district. Cell entries are unstandardized OLS regression coefficients with robust standard errors clustered on congressional district in parentheses. Levels of significance: * $p < 0.05$.

TABLE A5.1. *The impact of candidate sex on evaluations of Democratic U.S. House candidates' traits*

	2010				2014			
	Competent	Strong leader	Empathetic	Trustworthy	Competent	Strong leader	Empathetic	Trustworthy
Female candidate	0.047	0.025	0.014	-0.022	-0.005	-0.010	0.061	0.040
	(0.083)	(0.069)	(0.072)	(0.073)	(0.043)	(0.043)	(0.044)	(0.044)
Democrat	0.834*	0.747*	0.761*	0.735*	0.585*	0.606*	0.661*	0.652*
	(0.104)	(0.084)	(0.087)	(0.086)	(0.055)	(0.054)	(0.056)	(0.057)
Incumbent	0.195*	0.118	0.083	0.138	0.007	0.001	0.016	-0.060
	(0.092)	(0.075)	(0.081)	(0.081)	(0.059)	(0.060)	(0.066)	(0.065)
Vote share	0.191	0.433	0.064	0.228	0.002	0.003	0.003	0.004*
	(0.282)	(0.249)	(0.268)	(0.284)	(0.002)	(0.002)	(0.002)	(0.002)
Ideology	-0.262*	-0.182*	-0.277*	-0.216*	-0.215*	-0.184*	-0.212*	-0.195*
	(0.041)	(0.036)	(0.035)	(0.035)	(0.024)	(0.024)	(0.024)	(0.025)
Sex (female)	0.069	0.005	-0.018	-0.059	0.093*	0.106*	0.089*	0.071
	(0.074)	(0.058)	(0.058)	(0.059)	(0.041)	(0.039)	(0.042)	(0.042)
Race (white)	-0.103	-0.006	0.001	0.071	-0.136*	-0.190*	-0.104	-0.105
	(0.085)	(0.077)	(0.078)	(0.081)	(0.053)	(0.054)	(0.055)	(0.055)
News interest	-0.005	0.013	0.052	0.050	0.007	-0.027	-0.030	0.009
	(0.052)	(0.038)	(0.041)	(0.038)	(0.023)	(0.025)	(0.025)	(0.024)
Education	0.026	-0.049*	-0.001	-0.009	0.004	-0.013	-0.011	0.002
	(0.024)	(0.021)	(0.020)	(0.020)	(0.015)	(0.015)	(0.015)	(0.015)
Age	0.001	0.000	0.001	0.002	0.002	0.001	0.003	0.003*
	(0.003)	(0.002)	(0.002)	(0.002)	(0.001)	(0.001)	(0.001)	(0.001)
Constant	2.463*	2.439*	2.592*	2.312*	2.771*	2.794*	2.655*	2.450*
	(0.314)	(0.277)	(0.268)	(0.267)	(0.151)	(0.153)	(0.156)	(0.160)
N	627	826	827	819	1571	1575	1574	1576
R^2	0.407	0.338	0.384	0.337	0.305	0.300	0.320	0.300

Note: Cell entries are OLS coefficients with robust standard errors clustered on congressional district in parentheses. Level of significance: * $p < 0.05$.

TABLE A5.2. *The impact of candidate sex on evaluations of Republican U.S. House candidates' traits*

	2010				2014			
	Competent	Strong leader	Empathetic	Trustworthy	Competent	Strong leader	Empathetic	Trustworthy
Female candidate	-0.002	0.136	0.049	0.143	0.007	-0.018	0.034	0.027
	(0.115)	(0.093)	(0.096)	(0.098)	(0.058)	(0.055)	(0.063)	(0.060)
Republican	0.788*	0.647*	0.846*	0.726*	0.475*	0.547*	0.640*	0.609*
	(0.097)	(0.076)	(0.078)	(0.082)	(0.058)	(0.056)	(0.059)	(0.059)
Incumbent	0.068	0.116	0.118	0.155*	0.014	0.013	0.052	0.005
	(0.098)	(0.076)	(0.080)	(0.077)	(0.060)	(0.063)	(0.061)	(0.061)
Vote share	0.107	0.028	-0.290	-0.299	0.002	0.001	-0.001	0.000
	(0.294)	(0.213)	(0.231)	(0.229)	(0.002)	(0.002)	(0.001)	(0.002)
Ideology	0.318*	0.242*	0.275*	0.224*	0.255*	0.237*	0.267*	0.229*
	(0.041)	(0.033)	(0.033)	(0.035)	(0.025)	(0.024)	(0.024)	(0.025)
Sex (female)	-0.084	0.034	0.082	-0.011	0.055	0.112*	0.102*	0.049
	(0.075)	(0.058)	(0.058)	(0.060)	(0.041)	(0.039)	(0.042)	(0.040)
Race (white)	-0.076	0.052	-0.033	0.017	-0.160*	-0.144*	-0.132*	-0.159*
	(0.097)	(0.072)	(0.075)	(0.074)	(0.058)	(0.054)	(0.053)	(0.054)
News interest	-0.036	-0.000	-0.015	0.007	0.022	-0.004	-0.028	-0.010
	(0.058)	(0.045)	(0.041)	(0.041)	(0.025)	(0.024)	(0.025)	(0.024)
Education	0.015	-0.014	0.000	-0.004	-0.021	-0.028*	-0.042*	-0.015
	(0.025)	(0.021)	(0.020)	(0.021)	(0.015)	(0.014)	(0.015)	(0.014)
Age	-0.001	-0.001	-0.000	0.002	-0.001	-0.002	-0.002	0.002
	(0.003)	(0.002)	(0.002)	(0.002)	(0.001)	(0.001)	(0.001)	(0.001)
Constant	1.161*	1.422*	1.278*	1.384*	1.715*	1.768*	1.736*	1.610*
	(0.340)	(0.237)	(0.238)	(0.233)	(0.145)	(0.137)	(0.147)	(0.143)
N	629	842	840	829	1540	1541	1547	1541
R²	0.399	0.333	0.404	0.330	0.265	0.280	0.323	0.283

Note: Cell entries are OLS coefficients with robust standard errors clustered on congressional district in parentheses. Level of significance: * $p < 0.05$.

TABLE A5.3. *The impact of candidate sex on evaluations of Democratic U.S. House candidates' issue competencies, 2014*

	Gender equality	Gay rights	Health care	Crime	Abortion	Unemployment	National security	Economy	Immigration	Budget deficit
Female candidate	0.243 (0.145)	-0.014 (0.154)	0.050 (0.135)	-0.182 (0.140)	0.321* (0.141)	-0.016 (0.139)	-0.171 (0.147)	-0.028 (0.135)	0.001 (0.148)	-0.098 (0.139)
Democrat	1.943* (0.168)	1.656* (0.166)	2.430* (0.181)	2.009* (0.173)	2.052* (0.170)	2.296* (0.170)	2.079* (0.172)	2.239* (0.174)	2.216* (0.182)	2.311* (0.171)
Incumbent	0.358 (0.211)	0.500* (0.236)	0.267 (0.199)	0.010 (0.199)	0.247 (0.212)	0.060 (0.188)	0.032 (0.207)	0.027 (0.194)	0.118 (0.213)	0.021 (0.199)
Vote share	0.004 (0.005)	0.002 (0.005)	0.007 (0.005)	0.009* (0.005)	0.006 (0.005)	0.009* (0.005)	0.011* (0.005)	0.011* (0.005)	0.011* (0.005)	0.010* (0.005)
Ideology	-0.681* (0.075)	-0.821* (0.076)	-0.738* (0.079)	-0.554* (0.075)	-0.771* (0.076)	-0.638* (0.075)	-0.614* (0.072)	-0.702* (0.076)	-0.674* (0.077)	-0.669* (0.073)
Sex (female)	0.166 (0.129)	0.221 (0.133)	0.303* (0.130)	0.295* (0.125)	0.181 (0.133)	0.306* (0.133)	0.238 (0.129)	0.333* (0.127)	0.279* (0.129)	0.356* (0.126)
Race (white)	0.026 (0.170)	0.311 (0.180)	-0.132 (0.172)	-0.248 (0.168)	-0.037 (0.177)	-0.251 (0.165)	-0.242 (0.170)	-0.090 (0.168)	-0.060 (0.175)	-0.220 (0.171)
News interest	-0.019 (0.073)	-0.007 (0.074)	-0.147 (0.075)	-0.101 (0.070)	-0.196* (0.077)	-0.187* (0.073)	-0.184* (0.073)	-0.218* (0.070)	-0.190* (0.075)	-0.257* (0.071)
Education	0.089 (0.051)	0.122* (0.049)	0.050 (0.048)	0.048 (0.048)	0.072 (0.051)	0.048 (0.048)	0.064 (0.046)	0.045 (0.046)	0.061 (0.047)	0.028 (0.044)
Age	0.005 (0.004)	0.007 (0.004)	0.005 (0.004)	0.013* (0.004)	0.007 (0.004)	0.006 (0.004)	0.011* (0.004)	0.007 (0.004)	0.004 (0.005)	0.009* (0.004)
Constant	6.449* (0.516)	6.357* (0.526)	6.548* (0.511)	5.759* (0.498)	6.716* (0.509)	6.360* (0.508)	6.015* (0.489)	6.342* (0.508)	6.191* (0.509)	6.302* (0.501)
N	1577	1577	1582	1579	1580	1577	1584	1584	1583	1578
R^2	0.286	0.274	0.377	0.286	0.320	0.354	0.309	0.360	0.336	0.363

Note: Cell entries are OLS regression coefficients with robust standard errors clustered on congressional district in parentheses. Level of significance:
* $p < 0.05$.

TABLE A5.4. *The impact of candidate sex on evaluations of Republican U.S. House candidates' issue competencies, 2014*

	Gender equality	Gay rights	Health care	Crime	Abortion	Unemployment	National security	Economy	Immigration	Budget deficit
Female candidate	0.573*	0.126	0.150	0.034	0.231	0.123	-0.080	0.146	0.138	-0.043
	(0.217)	(0.208)	(0.192)	(0.184)	(0.200)	(0.182)	(0.177)	(0.174)	(0.203)	(0.182)
Republican	1.870*	1.764*	2.063*	1.731*	1.877*	1.961*	1.830*	1.887*	1.959*	1.874*
	(0.187)	(0.183)	(0.192)	(0.183)	(0.186)	(0.184)	(0.186)	(0.184)	(0.193)	(0.185)
Incumbent	0.066	-0.111	-0.099	0.094	0.153	-0.101	0.024	-0.083	-0.171	-0.072
	(0.179)	(0.183)	(0.180)	(0.179)	(0.195)	(0.177)	(0.183)	(0.176)	(0.186)	(0.192)
Vote share	0.006	0.008	0.004	0.008	0.002	0.008	0.009	0.005	0.008	0.005
	(0.005)	(0.005)	(0.005)	(0.006)	(0.005)	(0.005)	(0.006)	(0.005)	(0.006)	(0.006)
Ideology	0.882*	0.875*	0.974*	0.742*	0.976*	0.872*	0.774*	0.922*	0.923*	0.849*
	(0.081)	(0.079)	(0.086)	(0.083)	(0.079)	(0.083)	(0.086)	(0.079)	(0.081)	(0.082)
Sex (female)	0.055	0.286*	0.163	0.114	0.098	0.194	0.041	0.169	0.108	0.122
	(0.135)	(0.135)	(0.139)	(0.137)	(0.144)	(0.135)	(0.137)	(0.138)	(0.137)	(0.142)
Race (white)	-0.505*	-0.410*	-0.590*	-0.393*	-0.489*	-0.417*	-0.555*	-0.507*	-0.364*	-0.528*
	(0.167)	(0.173)	(0.167)	(0.159)	(0.168)	(0.164)	(0.159)	(0.157)	(0.170)	(0.159)
News interest	-0.166*	-0.220*	-0.084	0.056	-0.183*	-0.079	0.061	0.012	-0.143	-0.022
	(0.080)	(0.076)	(0.086)	(0.081)	(0.078)	(0.082)	(0.080)	(0.081)	(0.082)	(0.083)
Education	-0.124*	-0.076	-0.115*	-0.029	-0.087	-0.065	-0.015	-0.050	-0.089	-0.056
	(0.048)	(0.048)	(0.048)	(0.045)	(0.048)	(0.046)	(0.047)	(0.046)	(0.047)	(0.047)
Age	0.004	0.005	-0.004	0.002	0.004	-0.003	0.003	-0.005	-0.001	0.000
	(0.005)	(0.004)	(0.005)	(0.005)	(0.005)	(0.005)	(0.005)	(0.005)	(0.005)	(0.005)
Constant	3.074*	2.389*	2.999*	2.858*	2.502*	2.956*	2.899*	2.866*	2.778*	2.993*
	(0.461)	(0.466)	(0.488)	(0.473)	(0.464)	(0.468)	(0.463)	(0.469)	(0.483)	(0.485)
N	1563	1563	1565	1563	1560	1562	1558	1564	1562	1565
R²	0.311	0.289	0.352	0.276	0.328	0.325	0.280	0.329	0.324	0.299

Note: Cell entries are OLS regression coefficients with robust standard errors clustered on congressional district in parentheses. Level of significance:
* p < 0.05.

TABLE A5.5. *The impact of candidate sex on voting for the Democrat*

	2010	2014
Democratic female candidate	0.354	0.050
	(0.488)	(0.262)
Republican female candidate	0.351	0.145
	(0.772)	(0.313)
Voter is a Democrat	2.710*	2.303*
	(0.464)	(0.291)
Voter is a Republican	−2.748*	−2.156*
	(0.475)	(0.296)
Democratic incumbent	0.669	0.231
	(0.542)	(0.450)
Republican incumbent	−1.202*	−0.178
	(0.580)	(0.332)
Democratic vote share	−0.452	0.021
	(1.782)	(0.012)
Ideology	−0.933*	−0.748*
	(0.204)	(0.138)
Sex (female)	0.351	−0.035
	(0.377)	(0.252)
Race (white)	0.258	−0.021
	(0.467)	(0.309)
News interest	−0.139	0.036
	(0.314)	(0.168)
Education	0.143	−0.007
	(0.123)	(0.081)
Age	0.003	0.000
	(0.013)	(0.008)
Constant	2.438	1.037
	(1.745)	(1.116)
N	694	1132
Pseudo R^2	0.755	0.640
Log likelihood	−480.972	−782.944
χ^2	249.164	424.743

Note: Dependent variables are whether a respondent planned to vote for the Democratic House candidate. Cell entries are logistic regression coefficients with robust standard errors clustered on congressional district in parentheses. Level of significance: * $p < 0.05$.

TABLE A6.1. *Voters' impressions of House candidates' treatment in 2014*

	Treated fairly by the media		Treated poorly by the voters	
	Democratic candidates	*Republican candidates*	*Democratic candidates*	*Republican candidates*
Female candidate	0.294* (0.118)	−0.259 (0.171)	0.161 (0.176)	−0.407 (0.256)
Incumbent	0.064 (0.220)	0.377 (0.196)	0.597 (0.394)	0.056 (0.306)
Won the race	−0.251 (0.219)	−0.009 (0.199)	1.607* (0.400)	1.086* (0.296)
Competiveness of race	0.054 (0.067)	0.044 (0.075)	−0.165 (0.119)	0.154 (0.098)
Democratic respondent	−0.106 (0.109)	0.536* (0.114)	1.322* (0.168)	−0.915* (0.190)
Female respondent	−0.482* (0.106)	−0.162 (0.112)	−0.415* (0.156)	−0.499* (0.174)
Constant	−0.129 (0.228)	−1.136* (0.200)	−3.614* (0.422)	−2.108* (0.299)
N	1550	1549	1546	1553
Pseudo R^2	0.034	0.030	0.113	0.088
Log likelihood	−1018.680	−945.071	−559.600	−481.283

Note: Dependent variables are whether a respondent thought the candidate running for the House in his/her district was treated fairly by the media (left-hand side of the table) and poorly by the voters (right-hand side of the table). Cell entries are logistic regression coefficients with standard errors in parentheses. Level of significance: * $p < 0.05$.

TABLE A6.2. *Influences on perceptions of gender bias in elections*

	Gender bias in elections scale (full sample)	Gender bias in elections scale (women only)	Gender bias in elections scale (men only)
Female respondent	0.221*	–	–
	(0.078)		
Democratic respondent	0.503*	0.322*	0.725*
	(0.079)	(0.106)	(0.118)
Clinton–Palin bias scale	0.504*	0.530*	0.460*
	(0.028)	(0.036)	(0.043)
Familiar with *Lean In*	0.174*	0.258*	0.085
	(0.081)	(0.112)	(0.116)
Workplace and societal bias scale	0.368*	0.406*	0.326*
	(0.026)	(0.038)	(0.035)
Constant	0.086	0.107	0.287
	(0.124)	(0.179)	(0.172)
R^2	0.383	0.383	0.319
N	1683	890	793

Note: Cell entries are OLS regression coefficients with standard errors in parentheses. Level of significance: * $p < 0.05$.

Works cited

Aday, Sean and James Devitt. 2001. "Style over Substance: Newspaper Coverage of Elizabeth Dole's Presidential Bid." *Press/Politics* 6(2): 52–73.

Alexander, Deborah and Kristi Andersen. 1993. "Gender as a Factor in the Attribution of Leadership Traits." *Political Research Quarterly* 46(3): 527–45.

Anzia, Sarah F. and Christopher R. Berry. 2011. "The Jackie (and Jill) Robinson Effect: Why Do Congresswomen Outperform Congressmen?" *American Journal of Political Science* 55(3): 478–93.

Arnold, R. Douglas. 2004. *Congress, the Press, and Political Accountability.* New York: Russell Sage Foundation; Princeton University Press.

Atkeson, Lonna Rae. 2003. "Not All Cues Are Created Equal: The Conditional Impact of Female Candidates on Political Engagement." *Journal of Politics* 65(4): 1040–61.

Atkeson, Lonna Rae and Nancy Carrillo. 2007. "More is Better: The Influence of Collective Female Descriptive Representation on External Efficacy." *Politics & Gender* 3(1): 79–101.

Atkeson, Lonna Rae and Timothy Krebs. 2008. "Press Coverage in Mayoral Elections: Is there a Gender Bias?" *Political Research Quarterly* 61(2): 239–53.

Banwart, Mary Christine. 2010. "Gender and Candidate Communication: Effects of Stereotypes in the 2008 Election." *American Behavioral Scientist* 54(3): 265–83.

Banwart, Mary Christine and Kelly L. Winfrey. 2013. "Running on the Web: Online Self-Presentation Strategies in Mixed-Gender Races." *Social Science Computer Review* 31(5): 614–24.

Bartels, Larry M. 2000. "Partisanship and Voting Behavior, 1956–1996." *American Journal of Political Science* 44(1): 35–50.

2002. "Beyond the Running Tally: Partisan Bias in Political Perceptions." *Political Behavior* 24(2): 117–50.

Bauer, Nichole M. 2015. "Emotional, Sensitive, and Unfit for Office? Gender Stereotype Activation and Support for Female Candidates." *Political Psychology* 36(6): 691–708.

Belt, Todd L., Marion R. Just, and Ann N. Crigler. 2012. "The 2008 Media Primary: Handicapping the Candidates in Newspapers, on TV, Cable and the Internet." *International Journal of Press/Politics* 17(3): 341–69.

Bennett, W. Lance. 2011. *News: The Politics of Illusion*, 9th edn. New York: Longman.

Bergbower, Matthew L., Scott D. McClurg, and Thomas M. Holbrook. 2015. "The Partisan Content of Candidate Messages in U.S. Senate Elections." *Journal of Elections, Public Opinion, and Parties* 25(3): 333–50.

Braden, Maria. 1996. *Women Politicians in the Media.* Lexington: University of Kentucky.

Brader, Ted. 2006. *Campaigning for Hearts and Minds: How Emotional Appeals in Political Ads Work.* University of Chicago Press.

Bradley, Amy M. and Robert H. Wicks. 2011. "A Gendered Blogosphere? Portrayal of Sarah Palin on Political Blogs during the 2008 Presidential Campaign." *Journalism and Mass Communication Quarterly* 88(4): 807–20.

Brooks, Deborah Jordan. 2011. "Testing the Double Standard for Candidate Emotionality: Voter Reactions to the Tears and Anger of Male and Female Politicians." *Journal of Politics* 73(2): 597–615.

2013. *He Runs, She Runs: Why Gender Stereotypes Do Not Harm Women Candidates.* Princeton University Press.

Brooks, Deborah Jordan and Danny Hayes. 2015. "Perpetuating the Problem: The Effects of Media Portrayals of Gender Bias in Elections." Prepared for the annual meeting of the American Political Science Association, San Francisco, California.

Bruni, Frank. 2002. *Ambling into History: The Unlikely Odyssey of George W. Bush.* New York: HarperCollins.

Burns, Nancy, Kay Lehman Schlozman, and Sidney Verba. 2001. *The Private Roots of Public Action: Gender, Equality, and Political Participation.* Cambridge, MA: Harvard University Press.

Burrell, Barbara. 1992. "Women Candidates in Open Seat Primaries for the U.S. House of Representatives, 1968–1990." *Legislative Studies Quarterly* 17(4): 493–508.

1994. "Campaign Finance: Women's Experience in the Modern Era." In *Women and Elective Office*, ed. Sue Thomas and Clyde Wilcox. New York: Oxford University Press.

2014. *Gender in Campaigns for the U.S. House of Representatives.* Ann Arbor: University of Michigan Press.

Bystrom, Dianne G., Mary Christine Banwart, Lynda Lee Kaid, and Terry A. Robertson. 2004. *Gender and Candidate Communication.* New York: Routledge.

Campbell, David E. and Christina Wolbrecht. 2006. "See Jane Run: Women Politicians as Role Models for Adolescents." *Journal of Politics* 68(2): 233–47.

Carlin, Diana B. and Kelly L. Winfrey. 2009. "Have You Come a Long Way, Baby? Hillary Clinton, Sarah Palin, and Sexism in 2008 Campaign Coverage." *Communication Studies* 60(4): 326–43.

Carroll, Susan J. 2009. "Reflections on Gender and Hillary Clinton's Presidential Campaign: The Good, the Bad, and the Misogynic." *Politics & Gender* 5(1): 1–20.

Carroll, Susan J. and Kira Sanbonmatsu. 2013. *More Women Can Run: Gender and Pathways to the State Legislature.* New York: Oxford University Press.

Carroll, Susan J. and Ronnee Schreiber. 1997. "Media Coverage of Women in the 103rd Congress." In *Women, Media and Politics,* ed. Pippa Norris. New York: Oxford University Press.

Chaney, Carol and Barbara Sinclair. 1994. "Women and the 1992 House Elections." In *The Year of the Woman,* ed. Elizabeth A. Cook, Sue Thomas, and Clyde Wilcox. Boulder, CO: Westview.

Citrin, Jack, Beth Reingold, and Donald P. Green. 1990. "American Identity and the Politics of Ethnic Change." *Journal of Politics* 52(4): 1124–54.

Cohen, Geoffrey L. 2003. "Party over Policy: The Dominating Impact of Group Influence on Political Beliefs." *Journal of Personality and Social Psychology* 85(5): 808–22.

Conroy, Meredith, Sarah Oliver, Ian Breckenridge-Jackson, and Caroline Heldman. 2015. "From Ferraro to Palin: Sexism in Coverage of Vice Presidential Candidates in Old and New Media." *Politics, Groups, and Identities,* special virtual issue. DOI: 10.1080/21565503.2015.1050412.

Cook, Elizabeth Adell. 1998. "Voter Reaction to Women Candidates." In *Women and Elective Office,* ed. Sue Thomas and Clyde Wilcox. New York: Oxford University Press.

Cook, Timothy E. 2005. *Governing with the News: The News Media as a Political Institution,* 2nd edn. University of Chicago Press.

Crowder-Meyer, Melody, Shana Kushner Gadarian, and Jessica Trounstine. 2015. "Electoral Institutions, Gender Stereotypes, and Women's Local Representation." *Politics, Groups, and Identities* 3(2): 318–34.

Dabelko, Kirsten La Cour and Paul S. Herrnson. 1997. "Women's and Men's Campaigns for the U.S. House of Representatives." *Political Research Quarterly* 50(1): 121–35.

Daku, Mark, Lori Young, and Stuart Soroka. 2011. Lexicoder. Version 2.0. Accessed at: www.lexicoder.com/download.html (April 2, 2015).

Dalton, Russell J., Paul Allen Beck, Robert Huckfeldt, and William Koetzle. 1998. "A Test of Media-Centered Agenda Setting: Newspaper Content and Public Interests in a Presidential Election." *Political Communication* 15(4): 463–81.

Darcy, Robert, Susan Welch, and Janet Clark. 1994. *Women, Elections, and Representation,* 2nd edn. Lincoln: University of Nebraska Press.

Devitt, James. 2002. "Framing Gender on the Campaign Trail: Female Gubernatorial Candidates and the Press." *Journalism & Mass Communication Quarterly* 79(2)445–63.

Dittmar, Kelly. 2015a. *Navigating Gendered Terrain: Stereotypes and Strategy in Political Campaigns.* Philadelphia: Temple University Press.

2015b. "How Views about Gender Shape U.S. Election Campaigns." *Scholars Strategy Network.* Accessed at: www.scholarsstrategynetwork.org/sites/default/files/ssn_key_findings_dittmar_on_how_gender_shapes_campaign_strategy.pdf (October 16, 2015).

Dodson, Debra L. 1998. "Representing Women's Interests in the U.S. House of Representatives." In *Women and Elective Office*, ed. Sue Thomas and Clyde Wilcox. New York: Oxford University Press.

Dolan, Kathleen. 2004. *Voting for Women: How the Public Evaluates Women Candidates.* Boulder, CO: Westview Press.

2005. "Do Women Candidates Play to Gender Stereotypes? Do Men Candidates Play to Women? Candidate Sex and Issues Priorities on Campaign Websites." *Political Research Quarterly* 58(1): 31–44.

2006. "Symbolic Mobilization? The Impact of Candidate Sex in American Elections." *American Politics Research* 34(6): 687–704.

2008. "Is there a Gender Affinity Effect in American Politics? Information, Affect, and Candidate Sex in U.S. House Elections." *Political Research Quarterly* 61(1): 79–89.

2010. "The Impact of Gender Stereotyped Evaluations on Support for Women Candidates." *Political Behavior* 32(1): 69–88.

2014. *When Does Gender Matter? Women Candidates and Gender Stereotypes in American Elections.* New York: Oxford University Press.

Dowling, Conor M. and Michael G. Miller. 2015. "Can Information Alter Perceptions about Women's Chances of Winning Office? Evidence from a Panel Study." *Politics & Gender* 11(1): 55–88.

Druckman, James N. 2004. "Priming the Vote." *Political Psychology* 25(4): 577–94.

2005. "Media Matter: How Newspapers and Television News Cover Campaigns and Influence Voters." *Political Communication* 22(4): 463–81.

Druckman, James N. and Michael Parkin. 2005. "The Impact of Media Bias: How Editorial Slant Affects Voters." *Journal of Politics* 67(4): 1030–49.

Druckman, James N., Martin J. Kifer, and Michael Parkin. 2014. "U.S. Congressional Campaign Communications in an Internet Age." *Journal of Elections, Public Opinion & Parties* 24(1): 20–44.

Duerst-Lahti, Georgia. 2006. "Presidential Elections: Gendered Space and the Case of 2004." In *Gender and Elections: Shaping the Future of American Politics*, ed. Susan J. Carroll and Richard L. Fox. New York: Cambridge University Press.

Dunaway, Johanna, Regina G. Lawrence, Melody Rose, and Chris Weber. 2013. "Traits versus Issues: News Coverage of Female Candidates for Senatorial and Gubernatorial Office." *Political Research Quarterly* 66(3): 715–26.

Enloe, Cynthia. 2004. *The Curious Feminist*. Berkeley: University of California Press.

Evans, Heather K., Victoria Cordova, and Savannah Sipole. 2014. "Twitter Style: An Analysis of How House Candidates Used Twitter in their 2012 Campaigns." *PS: Political Science and Politics* 47(2): 454–62.

Evans, Heather K., Joycelyn Ovalle, and Stephen Green. 2016. "Rockin' Robins: Do Congresswomen Rule the Roost in the Twittersphere?" *Journal for the Association of Information Science and Technology* 16(2): 268–75.

Falk, Erika and Kate Kenski. 2006. "Issue Saliency and Gender Stereotypes: Support for Women as Presidents in Times of War and Terrorism." *Social Science Quarterly* 87(1): 1–18.

Fazio, Russell H. and Carol J. Williams. 1986. "Attitude Accessibility as a Moderator of the Attitude-Perception and Attitude-Behavior Relations: An Investigation of the 1984 Presidential Election." *Journal of Personality and Social Psychology* 51(3): 505–14.

Fazio, Russell H., M. C. Powell, and P. M. Herr. 1983. "Toward a Process Model of the Attitude-Behavior Relation: Accessing One's Attitude upon Mere Observation of the Attitude Object." *Journal of Personality and Social Psychology* 44(4): 723–35.

Fiber, Pamela and Richard L. Fox. 2005. "A Tougher Road for Women: Assessing the Role of Gender in Congressional Elections." In *Gender and American Politics*, ed. Sue Tolleson-Rinehart and Jyl Josephson. New York: M. E. Sharpe.

Flammang, Janet. 1997. *Women's Political Voice: How Women Are Transforming the Practice and Study of Politics*. Philadelphia: Temple University.

Fowler, James H. and Cindy D. Kam. 2007. "Beyond the Self: Social Identity, Altruism, and Political Behavior." *Journal of Politics* 69(3): 813–27.

Fowler, Linda L. and Jennifer L. Lawless. 2009. "Looking for Sex in All the Wrong Places: Press Coverage and the Electoral Fortunes of Gubernatorial Candidates." *Perspectives on Politics* 7(3): 519–37.

Fox, Richard L. 1997. *Gender Dynamics in Congressional Elections*. Thousand Oaks: SAGE.

   2013. "Congressional Elections: Women's Candidacies and the Road to Gender Parity." In *Gender and Elections*, 3rd edn, ed. Susan J. Carroll and Richard L. Fox. New York: Cambridge University Press.

Fox, Richard L. and Jennifer L. Lawless. 2010. "If Only They'd Ask: Gender, Recruitment, and Political Ambition." *Journal of Politics* 72(2): 310–36.

   2011. "Gendered Perceptions and Political Candidacies: A Central Barrier to Women's Equality in Electoral Politics." *American Journal of Political Science* 55(1): 59–73.

Fox, Richard L. and Zoe Oxley. 2003. "Gender Stereotyping in State Executive Elections: Candidate Selection and Success." *Journal of Politics* 65(3): 833–50.

Franco, Annie, Neil Malhotra, and Gabor Simonovits. 2014. "Publication Bias in the Social Sciences: Unlocking the File Drawer." *Science* 345(6203): 1502–5.

Frederick, Brian. 2009. "Are Female House Members Still More Liberal in a Polarized Era? The Conditional Nature of the Relationship between Descriptive and Substantive Representation." *Congress & the Presidency* 36(2): 181–202.

Fridkin, Kim L. and Patrick J. Kenney. 2009. "The Role of Gender Stereotypes in U.S. Senate Campaigns." *Politics & Gender* 5(3): 301–24.

2014. "How the Gender of U.S. Senators Influences People's Understanding and Engagement in Politics." *Journal of Politics* 76(4): 1017–31.

Fulton, Sarah A. 2012. "Running Backwards and in High Heels: The Gendered Quality Gap and Incumbent Electoral Success." *Political Research Quarterly* 65(2): 303–14.

Gerrity, Jessica C., Tracy Osborn, and Jeanette Morehouse Mendez. 2007. "Women and Representation: A Different View of the District?" *Politics & Gender* 3(2): 179–200.

Gershon, Sarah. 2012. "When Race, Gender, and the Media Intersect: Campaign News Coverage of Minority Congresswomen." *Journal of Women, Politics, & Policy* 33(2): 105–25.

Gibson, James L. and Amanda Gouws. 2000. "Social Identities and Political Intolerance: Linkages within the South African Mass Public." *American Journal of Political Science* 44(2): 278–92.

Gidengil, Elisabeth and Joanna Everitt. 2003. "Talking Tough: Gender and Reported Speech in Campaign News Coverage." *Political Communication* 20(3): 209–32.

Gilardi, Fabrizio. 2015. "The Temporary Importance of Role Models for Women's Political Representation." *American Journal of Political Science* 59(4): 957–70.

Githens, Marianne and Jewel L. Prestage. 1977. *A Portrait of Marginality: The Political Behavior of the American Woman*. New York: Longman.

Goldenberg, Edie and Michael Traugott. 1984. *Campaigning for Congress*. Washington, DC: Congressional Quarterly Press.

Goodyear-Grant, Elizabeth and Julie Croskill. 2011. "Gender Affinity Effects in Vote Choice in Westminster Systems: Assessing 'Flexible' Voters in Canada." *Politics & Gender* 7(2): 223–50.

Gordon, Ann, David M. Shafie, and Ann N. Crigler. 2003. "Is Negative Advertising Effective for Female Candidates? An Experiment in Voters' Use of Gender Stereotypes." *International Journal of Press/Politics* 8(3): 35–53.

Graber, Doris A. 2010. *Mass Media and American Politics*, 8th edn. Washington, DC: Congressional Quarterly Press.

Graber, Doris A. and Johanna Dunaway. 2014. *Mass Media and American Politics*, 9th edn. Washington, DC: Congressional Quarterly Press.

Green, Donald, Bradley Palmquist, and Eric Schickler. 2002. *Partisan Hearts and Minds: Political Parties and the Social Identity of Voters*. New Haven, CT: Yale University Press.

Green, Jane and Sara B. Hobolt. 2008. "Owning the Issue Agenda: Party Strategies and Vote Choices in British Elections." *Electoral Studies* 27(3): 460–76.

Greene, Steven. 1999. "Understanding Party Identification: A Social Identity Approach." *Political Psychology* 20(2): 393–403.

Groseclose, Tim. 2001. "A Model of Candidate Location When One Candidate Has a Valence Advantage." *American Journal of Political Science* 45(4): 862–86.

Gulati, Girish J. and Christine B. Williams. 2013. "Social Media and Campaign 2012: Developments and Trends for Facebook Adoption." *Social Science Computer Review* 31(5): 577–88.

Gurin, Patricia. 1985. "Women's Gender Consciousness." *Public Opinion Quarterly* 49(2): 143–63.

Hansen, Susan B. 1997. "Talking About Politics: Gender and Contextual Effects on Political Proselytizing." *Journal of Politics* 59(1): 73–103.

Hayes, Danny. 2005. "Candidate Qualities through a Partisan Lens: A Theory of Trait Ownership." *American Journal of Political Science* 49(4): 908–23.

2008. "Does the Messenger Matter? Candidate–Media Agenda Convergence and its Effect on Voter Issue Salience." *Political Research Quarterly* 61(1): 134–46.

2009. "Has Television Personalized Voting Behavior?" *Political Behavior* 31(2): 231–60.

2010. "The Dynamics of Agenda Convergence and the Paradox of Competitiveness in Presidential Campaigns." *Political Research Quarterly* 63(3): 594–611.

2011. "When Gender and Party Collide: Stereotyping in Candidate Trait Attribution." *Politics & Gender* 7(2): 133–65.

Hayes, Danny and Jennifer L. Lawless. 2015a. "As Local News Goes, So Goes Citizen Engagement: Media, Knowledge, and Participation in U.S. House Elections." *Journal of Politics* 77(2): 447–62.

2015b. "A Non-Gendered Lens? Media, Voters, and Female Candidates in Contemporary Congressional Elections." *Perspectives on Politics* 13(1): 95–118.

Hayes, Danny, Jennifer L. Lawless, and Gail Baitinger. 2014. "Who Cares What They Wear? Media, Gender, and the Influence of Candidate Appearance." *Social Science Quarterly* 95(5): 1194–1212.

Heith, Diane J. 2003. "The Lipstick Watch: Media Coverage, Gender, and Presidential Campaigns." In *Anticipating Madam President*, ed. Robert P. Watson and Ann Gordon. Boulder, CO: Lynne Rienner.

Heldman, Caroline, Susan J. Carroll, and Stephanie Olson. 2005. "She Brought Only a Skirt: Print Media Coverage of Elizabeth Dole's Bid for the Republican Presidential Nomination." *Political Communication* 22(3): 315–35.

Herrnson, Paul. 2011. *Congressional Elections: Campaigning at Home and in Washington*, 6th edn. Los Angeles: SAGE/CQ Press.

Herrnson, Paul, J. Celeste Lay, and Atiya Kai Stokes. 2003. "Women Running 'as Women': Candidate Gender, Campaign Issues, and Voter Targeting Strategies." *Journal of Politics* 65(1): 244–55.

Hillygus, D. Sunshine and Todd Shields. 2009. *The Persuadable Voter: Wedge Issues in Presidential Campaigns*. Princeton University Press.

Hitchon, Jacqueline C., Chingching Chang, and Rhonda Harris. 1997. "Should Women Emote? Perceptual Bias and Opinion Change in Response to Political Ads for Candidates of Different Genders." *Political Communication* 14(1): 49–69.

Holbrook, Thomas M. 1996. *Do Campaigns Matter?* Thousand Oaks: SAGE.

Huckfeldt, Robert, Jeffrey Levine, William Morgan, and John Sprague. 1999. "Accessibility and the Political Utility of Partisan and Ideological Orientations." *American Journal of Political Science* 43(3): 888–911.

Huckfeldt, Robert, Jeffery J. Mondak, Michael Craw, and Jeanette Morehouse Mendez. 2005. "Making Sense of Candidates: Partisanship, Ideology, and Issues as Guides to Judgment." *Cognitive Brain Research* 23(1): 11–23.

Huddy, Leonie. 2001. "From Social to Political Identity: A Critical Examination of Social Identity Theory." *Political Psychology* 22(1): 127–56.

Huddy, Leonie and Theresa Capelos. 2002. "Gender Stereotyping and Candidate Evaluation: Good News and Bad News for Women Politicians." In *The Social Psychology of Politics*, ed. Victor C. Ottati, R. Scott Tindale, John Edwards, Fred B. Bryant, Linda Health, Daniel C. O'Connell, Yolanda Suarez-Balzacar, and Emil J. Posavac. New York: Kluwer Academic/Plenum Publishers.

Huddy, Leonie and Nayda Terkildsen. 1993. "Gender Stereotypes and the Perception of Male and Female Candidates." *American Journal of Political Science* 37(1): 119–47.

Iyengar, Shanto and Donald R. Kinder. 1987. *News That Matters*. University of Chicago Press.

Iyengar, Shanto, Guarav Sood, and Yphtach Lelkes. 2012. "Affect, Not Ideology: A Social Identity Perspective on Polarization." *Public Opinion Quarterly* 76(3): 405–31.

Jacobs, Lawrence R. and Robert Y. Shapiro. 1994. "Issues, Candidate Image, and Priming: The Use of Private Polls in Kennedy's 1960 Presidential Campaign." *American Political Science Review* 88(3): 527–40.

Jacobson, Gary. 2010. "The Republican Resurgence in 2010." *Political Science Quarterly* 126(1): 27–52.

2015. "It's Nothing Personal: The Decline of the Incumbency Advantage in U.S. House Elections." *Journal of Politics* 77(3): 861–73.

Jalalzai, Farida. 2006. "Women Candidates and the Media: 1992–2000 Elections." *Politics & Policy* 34(3): 606–33.

Jamieson, Kathleen Hall and Paul Waldman. 2003. *The Press Effect: Politicians, Journalists, and the Stories that Shape the Political World.* New York: Oxford University Press.

Jones, Philip E. 2014. "Does the Descriptive Representation of Gender Influence Accountability for Substantive Representation?" *Politics & Gender* 10(2): 175–99.

Just, Marion R., Ann Crigler, Dean Alger, Timothy Cook, Montague Kern, and Darrell West. 1996. *Crosstalk: Citizens, Candidates, and the Media in a Presidential Campaign.* University of Chicago Press.

Kahn, Kim Fridkin. 1992. "Does Being Male Help? An Investigation of the Effects of Candidate Gender and Campaign Coverage on Evaluations of U.S. Senate Candidates." *Journal of Politics* 54(2): 497–517.

1993. "Gender Differences in Campaign Messages: An Examination of the Political Advertisements of Men and Women Candidates for U.S. Senate." *Political Research Quarterly* 46(3): 481–502.

1994a. "The Distorted Mirror: Press Coverage of Women Candidates for Statewide Office." *Journal of Politics* 56(1): 154–73.

1994b. "Does Gender Make a Difference? An Experimental Examination of Sex Stereotypes and Press Patterns in Statewide Campaigns." *American Journal of Political Science* 38(1): 162–95.

1996. *The Political Consequences of Being a Woman.* New York: Columbia University Press.

Kahn, Kim Fridkin and Edie Goldenberg. 1991. "Women Candidates in the News: An Examination of Gender Differences in U.S. Senate Campaigns." *Public Opinion Quarterly* 55(2): 180–99.

Kahn, Kim Fridkin and Patrick J. Kenney. 1999. *The Spectacle of U.S. Senate Campaigns.* Princeton University Press.

2002. "The Slant of the News: How Editorial Endorsements Influence Campaign Coverage and Citizens' Views of Candidates." *American Political Science Review* 96(2): 381–94.

Kathlene, Lyn. 1994. "Power and Influence in State Legislatures: The Interaction of Gender and Position in Committee Hearing Debates." *American Political Science Review* 88(3): 560–76.

1995. "Alternative Views of Crime: Legislative Policymaking in Gendered Terms." *Journal of Politics* 57(3): 696–723.

Keith, Bruce E., David B. Magleby, Candice J. Nelson, Elizabeth Orr, Mark C. Westlye, and Raymond E. Wolfinger. 1992. *The Myth of the Independent Voter.* Berkeley: University of California Press.

Kinder, Donald R. 1986. "Presidential Character Revisited." In *Political Cognition: The 19th Annual Carnegie Symposium on Cognition*, ed. Richard R. Lau and David O. Sears. Hillsdale, NJ: Erlbaum.

King, David C. and Richard E. Matland. 2003. "Sex and the Grand Old Party: An Experimental Investigation of the Effect of Candidate Sex on Support for a Republican Candidate." *American Politics Research* 31(6): 595–612.

Kirkpatrick, Jeanne J. 1974. *Political Woman*. New York: Basic Books.

Kittilson, Miki Caul and Kim Fridkin. 2008. "Gender, Candidate Portrayals, and Election Campaigns: A Comparative Perspective." *Politics & Gender* 4(3): 371–92.

Koch, Jeffrey W. 2000. "Do Citizens Apply Gender Stereotypes to Infer Candidates' Ideological Orientations?" *Journal of Politics* 62(2): 414–29.

LaMarre, Heather L. and Yoshikazu Suzuki-Lambrecht. 2013. "Tweeting Democracy? Examining Twitter as an Online Public Relations Strategy for Congressional Campaigns." *Public Relations Review* 39(4): 360–8.

Larson, Stephanie Greco. 2001. "Running as Women? A Comparison of Female and Male Pennsylvania Assembly Candidates' Campaign Brochures." *Women & Politics* 22(2): 107–24.

Lau, Richard R. 1989. "Construct Accessibility and Electoral Choice." *Political Behavior* 11(1): 5–32.

Lawless, Jennifer L. 2004a. "Politics of Presence: Women in the House and Symbolic Representation." *Political Research Quarterly* 57(1): 81–99.

2004b. "Women, War, and Winning Elections: Gender Stereotyping in the Post September 11th Era." *Political Research Quarterly* 57(3): 479–90.

2009. "Sexism and Gender Bias in Election 2008: A More Complex Path for Women in Politics." *Politics & Gender* 5(1): 70–80.

2012. *Becoming a Candidate: Political Ambition and the Decision to Run for Office*. New York: Cambridge University Press.

2015. "Female Candidates and Legislators." *Annual Review of Political Science* 18: 349–66.

Lawless, Jennifer L. and Richard L. Fox. 2005. *It Takes a Candidate: Why Women Don't Run for Office*. New York: Cambridge University Press.

2010. *It Still Takes a Candidate: Why Women Don't Run for Office*. New York: Cambridge University Press.

2012. *Men Rule: The Continued Under-Representation of Women in U.S. Politics*. Washington, DC: Women & Politics Institute.

Lawless, Jennifer L. and Kathryn Pearson. 2008. "The Primary Reason for Women's Under-Representation: Re-Evaluating the Conventional Wisdom." *Journal of Politics* 70(1): 67–82.

Lawrence, Eric, John Sides, and Henry Farrell. 2010. "Self-Segregation or Deliberation? Blog Readership, Participation, and Polarization in American Politics." *Perspectives on Politics* 8(1): 141–57.

Lawrence, Regina G. and Melody Rose. 2009. *Hillary Clinton's Race for the White House: Gender Politics and the Media on the Campaign Trail.* Boulder, CO: Lynne Rienner.

Leeper, Mark. 1991. "The Impact of Prejudice on Female Candidates: An Experimental Look at Voter Inference." *American Politics Quarterly* 19(2): 248–61.

Levendusky, Matthew S. and Neil Malhotra. 2015. "Does Media Coverage of Partisan Polarization Affect Political Attitudes?" *Political Communication.* DOI: 10.1080/10584609.2015.1036455.

Mansbridge, Jane. 1999. "Should Blacks Represent Blacks and Women Represent Women? A Contingent 'Yes.'" *Journal of Politics* 61(3): 628–57.

McCarty, Nolan, Keith T. Poole, and Howard Rosenthal. 2006. *Polarized America: The Dance of Ideology and Unequal Riches.* Cambridge, MA: MIT Press.

McCombs, Maxwell E. and Donald L. Shaw. 1972. "The Agenda-Setting Function of Mass Media." *Public Opinion Quarterly* 36(2): 176–87.

McDermott, Monika L. 1997. "Voting Cues in Low-Information Elections: Candidate Gender as a Social Information Variable in Contemporary U.S. Elections." *American Journal of Political Science* 41(1): 270–83.

Miller, Arthur H., Patricia Gurin, Gerald Gurin, and Oksana Malanchuk. 1981. "Group Consciousness and Political Participation." *American Journal of Political Science* 25(3): 494–511.

Miller, Geralyn. 2001. "Newspaper Coverage and Gender: An Analysis of the 1996 Illinois State Legislative House District Races." *Women & Politics* 22(3): 83–100.

Miller, Melissa K. and Jeffrey S. Peake. 2013. "Press Effects, Public Opinion, and Gender: Coverage of Sarah Palin's Vice-Presidential Campaign." *International Journal of Press/Politics* 18(4): 482–507.

Miller, Melissa K., Jeffrey S. Peake, and Brittany Anne Boulton. 2010. "Testing the Saturday Night Live Hypothesis: Fairness and Bias in Newspaper Coverage of Hillary Clinton's Presidential Campaign." *Politics & Gender* 6(2): 169–98.

Mo, Cecilia Hyunjung. 2015. "The Consequences of Explicit and Implicit Gender Attitudes and Candidate Quality in the Calculations of Voters." *Political Behavior* 37(2): 357–95.

Monogan, James, III. 2013. "A Case for Registering Studies of Political Outcomes: An Application in the 2010 House Elections." *Political Analysis* 21(1): 21–37.

Norris, Pippa. 1997a. "Introduction: Women, Media and Politics." In *Women, Media, and Politics*, ed. Pippa Norris. New York: Oxford University Press.

    1997b. "Women Leaders Worldwide: A Splash of Color in the Photo Op." In *Women, Media, and Politics*, ed. Pippa Norris. New York: Oxford University Press.

Nyhan, Brendan. 2015. "Increasing the Credibility of Political Science Research: A Proposal for Journal Reforms." *PS: Political Science & Politics* 48(S1): 78–83.

Osborn, Tracy L. 2012. *How Women Represent Women: Political Parties, Gender, and Representation in the State Legislatures.* New York: Oxford University Press.

Palmer, Barbara and Dennis Simon. 2008. *Breaking the Political Glass Ceiling: Women and Congressional Elections,* 2nd edn. New York: Routledge.

Paolino, Phillip. 1995. "Group-Salient Issues and Group Representation: Support for Women Candidates in the 1992 Senate Elections." *American Journal of Political Science* 39(2): 294–313.

Pearson, Kathryn and Eric McGhee. 2013. "What It Takes to Win: Questioning Gender Neutral Outcomes in U.S. House Elections." *Politics & Gender* 9(4): 439–62.

Petrocik, John R. 1996. "Issue Ownership in Presidential Elections, with a 1980 Case Study." *American Journal of Political Science* 40(3): 825–50.

Phillips, Anne. 1995. *The Politics of Presence.* New York: Oxford University Press.

Pitkin, Hanna F. 1967. *The Concept of Representation.* Berkeley: University of California Press.

Plutzer, Eric and John F. Zipp. 1996. "Gender Identity and Voting for Women Candidates." *Public Opinion Quarterly* 60(1): 30–57.

Popkin, Samuel L. 1994. *The Reasoning Voter: Communication and Persuasion in Presidential Campaigns,* 2nd edn. University of Chicago Press.

Prior, Markus. 2013. "Media and Political Polarization." *Annual Review of Political Science* 16: 101–27.

Rahn, Wendy M., Jon A. Krosnick, and Marijke Breuning. 1994. "Rationalization and Derivation Processes in Survey Studies of Political Candidate Evaluation." *American Journal of Political Science* 38(3): 582–600.

Reingold, Beth and Jessica Harrell. 2010. "The Impact of Descriptive Representation on Women's Political Engagement: Does Party Matter?" *Political Research Quarterly* 63(2): 280–94.

Ridout, Travis N. and Michael M. Franz. 2011. *The Persuasive Power of Campaign Advertising.* Philadelphia: Temple University Press.

Ridout, Travis N. and Rob Mellen, Jr. 2007. "Does the Media Agenda Reflect the Candidates' Agenda?" *Harvard International Journal of Press/Politics* 12(2): 44–62.

Ritchie, Jessica. 2013. "Creating a Monster: Online Media Construction of Hillary Clinton during the Democratic Primary Campaign, 2007–2008." *Feminist Media Studies* 13(1): 102–19.

Rosenthal, Cindy Simon. 1995. "The Role of Gender in Descriptive Representation." *Political Research Quarterly* 48(3): 599–612.

Rosenthal, Robert. 1979. "The File Drawer Problem and Tolerance for Null Results." *Psychological Bulletin* 86(3): 638–41.

Rosenwasser, Shirley M. and Norma G. Dean. 1989. "Gender Roles and Political Office: Effects of Perceived Masculinity/Femininity of Candidate and Political Office." *Psychology of Women Quarterly* 13(1): 77–85.

Rule, Wilma. 1981. "Why Women Don't Run: The Critical Contextual Factors in Women's Legislative Recruitment." *Western Political Quarterly* 34(1): 60–77.

Sanbonmatsu, Kira and Kathleen Dolan. 2009. "Do Gender Stereotypes Transcend Party?" *Political Research Quarterly* 62(3): 485–94.

Sanchez, Gabriel R. 2006. "The Role of Group Consciousness in Political Participation among Latinos in the United States." *American Politics Research* 34(4): 427–50.

Sapiro, Virginia, Katherine Cramer Walsh, Patricia Strach, and Valerie Hennings. 2011. "Gender, Context, and Television Advertising: A Comprehensive Analysis of 2000 and 2002 House Races." *Political Research Quarterly* 64(1): 107–19.

Schaffner, Brian F. 2006. "Local News Coverage and the Incumbency Advantage in the U.S. House." *Legislative Studies Quarterly* 31(4): 491–511.

Schneider, Monica C. 2014. "Gender-Based Strategies on Candidate Websites." *Journal of Political Marketing* 13(4): 264–90.

Schneider, Monica C. and Angela L. Bos. 2014. "Measuring Stereotypes of Female Politicians." *Political Psychology* 35(2): 245–66.

Schudson, Michael. 1996. *The Power of News*. Cambridge, MA: Harvard University Press.

Schwindt-Bayer, Leslie A. and Renato Corbetta. 2004. "Gender Turnover and Roll-Call Voting in the U.S. House of Representatives." *Legislative Studies Quarterly* 29(2): 215–29.

Seltzer, Richard A., Jody Newman, and Melissa Voorhees Leighton. 1997. *Sex as a Political Variable: Women as Candidates and Voters in U.S. Elections.* Boulder, CO: Lynne Rienner.

Shor, Erian, Arnout van de Rijt, Charles Ward, Saoussan Askar, and Steven Skiena. 2014. "Is There a Political Bias? A Computational Analysis of Female Subjects' Coverage in Liberal and Conservative Newspapers." *Social Science Quarterly* 95(5): 1213–29.

Sides, John. 2006. "The Origins of Campaign Agendas." *British Journal of Political Science* 36(3): 407–36.

Sides, John and Lynn Vavreck. 2013. *The Gamble: Choice and Chance in the 2012 Presidential Election.* Princeton University Press.

Sigelman, Lee and Emmett H. Buell, Jr. 2004. "Avoidance or Engagement? Issue Convergence in U.S. Presidential Campaigns, 1960–2000." *American Journal of Political Science* 48(4): 650–61.

Smith, Eric R. A. N. 1989. *The Unchanging American Voter*. Berkeley: University of California Press.

Smith, Eric R. A. N. and Richard L. Fox. 2001. "A Research Note: The Electoral Fortunes of Women Candidates for Congress." *Political Research Quarterly* 54(1): 205–21.

Smith, Kevin B. 1997. "When All's Fair: Signs of Parity in Media Coverage of Female Candidates." *Political Communication* 14(1): 71–82.

Stalsburg, Brittany L. and Mona S. Kleinberg. 2015. "A Mom First and a Candidate Second: Gender Differences in Candidates' Self-Presentation of Family." *Journal of Political Marketing*. DOI: 10.1080/15377 857.2019.959684.

Stevens, Daniel, Dean Alger, Barbara Allen, and John L. Sullivan. 2006. "Local News Coverage in a Social Capital Capital: Election 2000 on Minnesota's Local News Stations." *Political Communication* 23(1): 61–83.

Stokes, Donald E. 1963. "Spatial Models of Party Competition." *American Political Science Review* 57(2): 368–77.

Swers, Michele L. 2002. *The Difference Women Make*. University of Chicago Press.

2013. *Women in the Club: Gender and Policy Making in the Senate*. University of Chicago Press.

Tajfel, Henri. 1981. *Human Groups and Social Categories: Studies in Social Psychology*. New York: Cambridge University Press.

Taylor, Shelly E. and Susan G. Fiske. 1978. "Salience, Attention, and Attribution: Top of the Head Phenomena." *Advances in Experimental Social Psychology* 11: 250–88.

Thomas, Sue. 2005. "Introduction: Women and Elective Office: Past, Present, and Future." In *Women and Elective Office*, 2nd edn, ed. Sue Thomas and Clyde Wilcox. New York: Oxford University Press.

Thurber, James A., Candice J. Nelson, and David A. Dulio. eds. 2001. *Crowded Airwaves: Campaign Advertising in Elections*. Washington, DC: Brookings Institution Press.

Tidmarch, Charles M. and Brad S. Karp. 1983. "The Missing Beat: Press Coverage of Congressional Elections in Eight Metropolitan Areas." *Congress & the Presidency* 10(1): 47–61.

Todorov, Alexander, Anesu N. Mandisodza, Amir Goren, and Crystal C. Hall. 2005. "Inferences of Competence from Faces Predict Election Outcomes." *Science* 308(5728): 1623–26.

Tolleson-Rinehart, Sue. 1991. "Do Women Leaders Make a Difference? Substance, Style, and Perceptions." In *Gender and Policymaking: Studies of Women in Office*, ed. Debra Dodson. New Brunswick, NJ: Rutgers University Press.

1992. *Gender Consciousness and Politics*. New York: Routledge.

Turner, John C. 1996. "Henri Tajfel: An Introduction." In *Social Groups and Identities: Developing the Legacy of Henri Tajfel*, ed. W. Peter Robinson. Oxford: Butterworth-Heinemann.

Vavreck, Lynn. 2009. *The Message Matters: The Economy and Presidential Campaigns*. Princeton University Press.

Vinson, Danielle C. 2003. *Local Media Coverage of Congress and its Members: Through Local Eyes*. Cresskill, NJ: Hampton Press.

Volden, Craig, Alan E. Wiseman, and Dana E. Wittmer. 2013. "When Are Women More Effective Lawmakers than Men?" *American Journal of Political Science* 57(2): 326–41.

Wadsworth, Anne Johnston, Philip Patterson, Lynda Lee Kaid, Ginger Cullers, Drew Malcomb, and Linda Lamirand. 1987. "'Masculine' vs. 'Feminine' Strategies in Political Ads: Implications for Female Candidates." *Journal of Applied Communication Research* 15(1–2): 77–94.

Weaver, David H. 1996. "What Voters Learn from Media." *Annals of the American Academy of Political and Social Science* 546(1): 34–47.

Weaver, David H., Randal A. Beam, Bonnie J. Brownlee, Paul S. Voakes, and Cleveland Wilhoit. 2006. *The American Journalist in the 21st Century: U.S. News People at the Dawn of a New Millennium*. New York: Routledge.

Weikart, Lynne A., Greg Chen, Daniel W. Williams, and Haris Hromic. 2007. "The Democratic Sex: Gender Differences and the Exercise of Power." *Journal of Women, Politics & Policy* 28(1): 119–40.

Weir, Sara J. 1996. "Women as Governors: State Executive Leadership with a Feminist Face?" In *Women in Politics: Outsiders or Insiders*, 2nd edn, ed. Lois Lovelace Duke. Upper Saddle River: Prentice Hall.

Welch, Susan. 1978. "Recruitment of Women to Office." *Western Political Quarterly* 31(2): 372–80.

West, Darrell M. 2013. *Air Wars: Television Advertising and Social Media in Election Campaigns, 1952–2012*, 6th edn. Los Angeles: SAGE/CQ Press.

Westlye, Mark C. 1991. *Senate Elections and Campaign Intensity*. Baltimore, MD: Johns Hopkins University Press.

Windett, Jason. 2014. "Gendered Campaign Strategies in U.S. Elections." *American Politics Research* 42(4): 628–55.

Winter, Nicholas J. G. 2010. "Masculine Republicans and Feminine Democrats: Gender and Americans' Explicit and Implicit Images of the Political Parties." *Political Behavior* 32(4): 587–618.

Witt, Linda, Karen Paget, and Glenna Matthews. 1994. *Running as a Woman*. New York: Free Press.

Wittmer, Dana. 2011. "Toward a Theory of Institutional Representation: The Link between Political Engagement and Gendered Institutions." Ph.D. dissertation, University of Ohio, Columbus.

Young, Lori and Stuart Soroka. 2012. "Affective News: The Automated Coding of Sentiment in Political Texts." *Political Communication* 29(2): 205–31.

Zaller, John R. 1992. *The Nature and Origins of Mass Opinion.* New York: Cambridge University Press.

Zaller, John and Stanley Feldman. 1992. "A Simple Theory of the Survey Response: Answering Questions or Revealing Preferences?" *American Journal of Political Science* 36(3): 579–616.

Index